POWER AND PRUDENCE

NUMBER SEVENTEEN
The Presidency and Leadership
James P. Pfiffner, General Editor

Power and Prudence

The Presidency of George H. W. Bush

Ryan J. Barilleaux

& Mark J. Rozell

Texas A&M University Press : College Station

First edition

The paper used in this book
meets the minimum requirements
of the American National Standard for Permanence
of Paper for Printed Library Materials, Z39.48-1984.
Binding materials have been chosen for durability.

Library of Congress Cataloging-in-Publication Data

Barilleaux, Ryan J.
Power and prudence : the presidency of George H. W. Bush / Ryan J. Barilleaux and Mark J. Rozell.—1st ed.
p. cm.—(The presidency and leadership ; no. 17)
ISBN 1-58544-291-7 (alk. paper)
1. United States—Politics and government—1989–1993. 2. Bush, George, 1924– 3. Political leadership—United States—Case studies. 4. Prudence—Political aspects—United States—Case studies. I. Rozell, Mark J. II. Title. III. Series.
E881.R686 2004
973.931—dc22 2003015131

To Mary Wasick (R. B.) and Debbie Rozell (M. R.)

Contents

Acknowledgments

We are grateful for the contributions of a number of individuals who made this book possible. First, there are the Bush White House staff members who agreed to be interviewed for this study: Phil Brady, Andrew Card, Mary Kate Carey, David Demarest, Marlin Fitzwater, Andrew Furgeson, C. Boyden Gray, Ronald Kaufman, Bobbie Kilberg, Dan McGroarty, Tony Snow, Curt Smith, and Roscoe Starek. Second, the staff of the George Bush Presidential Library in College Station, Texas, who assisted with the research during a visit by one of the authors (M. R.). Third, the former Center for Presidential Studies at Texas A&M University, then directed by our colleague George C. Edwards, provided financial support for the Bush Library visit and also the opportunity to participate in one of the Center's presidential studies conferences. Fourth, Dilchoda Berdieva and Joseph Moser of Miami University of Ohio provided research assistance. Fifth, Melissa Cidade and Dale E. Wilson thoroughly proofread and copyedited the manuscript. Sixth, we appreciate the very helpful and detailed manuscript comments by two anonymous reviewers for the press. Finally, we thank series editor James Pfiffner and Texas A&M University Press for their support for this project and enormous patience in awaiting its completion.

Power and Prudence

CHAPTER 1

Incrementalism in Theory and Practice

GEORGE H. W. BUSH took the presidential oath of office on January 20, 1989, perhaps with the most impressive background of any man entering the presidency in the modern era. Bush was a former member of Congress, national party leader, Central Intelligence Agency (CIA) director, ambassador to China, and two-term vice president. In addition, at the time he enlisted in 1943 he was the navy's youngest pilot. After the war he graduated from Yale and became a successful businessperson. In short, if job credentials and life experiences are a proper guide, Bush had all the makings for being a successful president.

In 1992, in the midst of a mild recession, the American public resoundingly determined that Bush's presidency had been a failure. The public's judgment was unusually harsh: only 38 percent voted to reelect the incumbent president. Exit polls evidenced a widespread public judgment that the president had done a poor job of leading the nation and managing the economy.

Public decisions in the voting booth are the ultimate acts of presidential evaluation. Citizens have varying bases for their political judgments. Some are fairly sophisticated (for example, the president's record on issues that the voters care about) whereas others are quite impressionistic (for example, the president just does not seem like a strong leader). These collective judgments determine whether presidents seeking reelection are given second terms and ultimately the opportunity to make a major mark on U.S. history.

Citizens evaluate the president's performance while in office and throughout most of the Bush years the collective judgment of his leadership was quite different from that rendered on Election Day, 1992. George Bush had enjoyed impressive public support throughout much of his term in office.[1] At one point in 1991 the president's approval ratings were the highest recorded in modern presidential polling at the time. When a recession hit the country later that year, his approval rating began to dive. It failed to recover even to respectable levels before the election.

How could a president with an unprecedented approval rating in one year lose his reelection bid with just 38 percent of the vote against two weak opponents the next year? Certainly a good president simply did not become an incompetent one unworthy of the office practically overnight. In fact, circumstances had changed and the public's bases for evaluation had shifted to reflect such change. The afterglow of a military victory had worn off and a strong economy became a weak one. It was as though the public had said, "Nice work, but what have you done for me lately?"

V. O. Key once called voters "rational Gods of vengeance and reward."[2] Some analysts decry the fickle nature of public opinion and argue that such dramatic shifts reflect an unsophisticated view of leadership. However, Key and others have noted that there is a certain degree of sophistication in retrospective public judgments of a leader's successes and failures. Voters might not conform to the rational model of understanding all the issues, the candidates' positions and records, and then voting accordingly. Yet they are quite good at understanding their own circumstances and they have a sense that incumbent public leaders bear some responsibility.

Public opinion nonetheless is not a satisfying basis for evaluating a presidency. Presidents who were popular in their time (for example, Eisenhower, Kennedy, and Reagan) do not always fare so well at the hands of scholars over the long term, whereas some who suffered from low public opinion ratings while in office (for example, Truman) are later judged to have been fine leaders.

For scholars, the act of presidential evaluation involves much more than judging current circumstances and the incumbent's role. Evaluation requires establishing standards of success and failure that are not wedded to the politics or the economy of the moment. Standards are inherently subjective, although social science strives to achieve some level of consistency. Yet uniform criteria are impossible to achieve given varied expectations and beliefs about the president's role in governing. Different governing contexts experienced by presidents make the use of standard criteria highly suspect. Comparisons between and among presidents often make little sense for that reason. Many historians and political scientists contribute their assessments to presidential rankings lists, an exercise that is much more fun than it is revealing of anything important about our chief executives. The most fruitful exercises in presidential evaluation are thorough analyses of single administrations.

This book is such a study in presidential evaluation. Its focus is the George H. W. Bush presidency. Although leading analysts during the Bush years said the president did not lead—specifically charging that he lacked leadership "vision"—the argument presented here is that Bush had a leadership method that largely suited his own goals and the nature of the times.

None of this is intended to suggest that presidents should be judged merely against the backdrop of their own standards for success.[3] It is, however, a necessary first step in evaluation to understand a president's leadership approach and goals for what they are rather than to immediately stand the president against the backdrop of some widely used standards that may or may not make sense in any particular context. Evaluating a president's leadership against a set of standards that he openly rejects also makes little sense.

Observers said that Bush lacked leadership vision largely because his style and goals did not conform to the reigning model of success: one in which the president identifies a broad-based policy agenda and tries to bulldoze his policies through Congress by using both popular-opinion leadership and legislative arm-twisting.[4] That model of success may suit certain presidents. In particular, it would suit a president who ran an issues-based campaign, won election by a landslide, and carried strong partisan majorities in Congress with him to Washington. As Charles O. Jones reminds us, however, there are few cases in which all of these circumstances coexisted. Nonetheless, Jones observes that a single dominant evaluation model prevails.[5]

The model of the activist-visionary president is one largely derived from idealized recollections of the accomplishments of past "great" presidents. Franklin D. Roosevelt's presidency did the most to establish the standards of presidential success that persist to this day, even though much of what is remembered about FDR is more myth than reality. As one fine study put it, all presidents since have been "in the shadow of FDR."[6] Yet none of them has held office during a period that in any sense resembled FDR's time. A president's first one hundred days in office has nonetheless become a standard benchmark period for evaluating presidential performance.

At best, FDR's leadership suited his own unique situation and the particular background and skills that he brought to the office. To judge his successors against this backdrop is to consign most of them automatically to the status of failures. No other president has experienced leading the nation during times of economic calamity and world war. The president who guides a peacetime and relatively prosperous country effectively might look less impressive in contrast, but that does not mean that he is a failure. Different presidents have different leadership skills and styles; and different times call for different leadership approaches.

Bush saw his mission as being to guide the country effectively during a period of transition, rather than precipitating large-scale changes. He managed events competently, he protected the powers and prerogatives of his office, and he effectively minimized the influence of his opponents. None of these accomplishments sounds particularly stirring or likely to inspire future references in studies of presidential "greatness." But some times call for boldness, whereas others require quiet leadership and perhaps defensive action. There simply is no imaginable way to compare the circumstances faced by FDR in 1933 and Bush in 1989.

Although his more modest leadership approach suited his own style and goals and the nature of the times, Bush undermined his policy objectives by ignoring the need to establish a governing identity of some kind and by placing insufficient importance on communicating his priorities. A modest agenda and low-key leadership approach do not indicate a lack of a guiding philosophy or relative inattention to the public presidency. Bush's goals and priorities were defensible in the context of the times during which he led, yet somehow his White House conveyed an image of lacking any agenda and being indifferent to the domestic needs of the nation. Bush had a record to rebut such images, but he was never effectively able to do so.

The Incrementalist

George H. W. Bush did not come to the presidency promising to transform American politics or even to lead the charge for dramatic new policy initiatives. In his inaugural speech, the president emphasized the policy limits imposed by a large budget deficit and said that new programs and increased government spending were not the answers to the problems that ailed the country. He called on the nation to renew its commitment to private acts of charity and generosity. Rather than "high drama," he said that he saw leadership as a collection of small actions that one at a time add up to something significant in the nation's history.

Bush identified some national issues in his speech. He spoke most directly of the need to rid the nation of the "drug scourge," to encourage free markets around the world, and to deal with the budget deficit. However, he offered neither a long list of policy objectives nor identified solutions to any problems. Bush's inaugural speach struck many observers as a symbolic step toward establishing his own identity as president, distinct from that of his vice presidential days and most different from the image of his predecessor, Ronald Reagan.

Bush's style was to take one step at a time and guide the nation toward improvements. In his first formal speech to Congress three weeks into the administration, Bush sounded similar themes but with greater specificity. He called for "modest" increases in public spending where appropriate, but overall recommended a cautious approach on the domestic front. He expressed a preference for policy continuity rather than change. He spoke of "prudence" in dealing with international change and said that the nation must "review our policies carefully, and proceed with caution."

Although he did not espouse it as such, Bush's leadership approach very much followed what David Braybrooke and Charles Lindlom call "disjointed incrementalism."[7] Although on the surface that phrase appears to carry a negative connotation, the authors offer a strong defense of their theory's utility in the U.S. policy-making process. They perceive many social scientists as being too easily attracted to abstract ideals in policy making and evaluation. Social scientists are more comfortable with ideal standards than with the practical and the real. The leader must be guided instead by what is possible under the circumstances.[8] Standards of evaluation based on abstract ideals rarely suit the realities of the U.S. policy process, which is incremental by nature. The authors describe disjointed incrementalism as "moving away from known social ills rather than moving toward a known and relatively stable goal."[9]

The theory of disjointed incrementalism most often is applied to the domestic policy context. It can be applied equally as well to foreign policy making, although it is necessary to take into account the greater latitude presidents enjoy in formulating foreign rather than domestic policy. This study posits that Bush was an incrementalist both in domestic and foreign policy. An incrementalist may be more active abroad because he perceives it as being necessary to protect the status quo of institutions at home.

The argument here is contrary to the conventional view of Bush's contemporaries that he exerted one form of leadership at home and a substantially different one abroad.[10] Bush's incrementalist style did not suit the expectations of those who preferred activist government. His domestic agenda was modest and his response to dramatic changes internationally appeared subdued. This approach may indeed have suited the times, but Bush ultimately did little to teach the public about the utility of his leadership approach and why it was better than anything his opponents had to offer.

The dominant model of presidential evaluation calls on the chief executive to articulate broad policy goals and the means toward achieving them. Yet rarely do leaders have the opportunity to fulfill grandiose objectives given the diffuse and separated nature of the policy-making system.[11] The theory of incrementalism posits that "policy making is not simply a pursuit of objectives but is rather an expenditure of some values in order to achieve others."[12]

In examining the record of the Bush presidency, that statement is particularly apt. Given the lack of an issues-based campaign and therefore the absence of any strong electoral mandate, and given the situation of divided government, Bush was not in a solid position to articulate far-reaching policy objectives and to achieve them. He was better positioned to make policy tradeoffs and to defend against Democratic majorities in Congress intent on ultimately setting the agenda.

Still, it was not a given that Bush should run an almost issue-free presidential campaign. To be clear, in 1988 Bush ran one of the most relentlessly negative campaigns in modern presidential history and that had a substantial impact on his governance. Without a solid issues base, analysts widely viewed his forty-state electoral landslide as lacking any mandate at all. Having run a harshly negative campaign, many Democratic opponents came to Congress in 1989 with little desire to work with the president and thus do things that would bolster his record in office. Yet even with a minimalist policy agenda, it was not a given that the president would fail to link his modest goals with some governing philosophy.

For these reasons, it is a mistake to characterize Bush's leadership as simply a victim of circumstances. In numerous interviews with Bush White House officials, individuals reiterated the circumstances of divided government, hostile Democratic leadership in Congress, and budget deficits as having established an almost impossible leadership context. They blamed Congress for Bush's leadership problems. They blamed the Democratic Party. They blamed the media. And they blamed Reagan's budget deficit legacy.

Bush's leading White House staffers correctly identify divided government and the budget deficit in particular as keys to understanding why he should not be judged against a static model of presidential activism. But to be fair, it is also important to recognize that the president played an important role in creating aspects of the leadership context. He did not have to run the kind of campaign that he did in 1988 or steadfastly support a chief of staff and budget director who went out of their way to create friction with opposition party members in Congress, to cite just a few examples.[13]

In stark contrast to the theory of disjointed incrementalism is what Braybrooke and Lindlom call the "rational-deductive ideal." In the latter case, the policy maker engages in a thorough process of examining all of the available evidence, weighing options, and choosing the best solution to a problem. Policy goals in this model tend to be global in nature: What is the solution to poverty? How can we end inner-city crime? How can we eliminate all educational disparities? The authors argue that the process of identifying ultimate goals and examining all evidence and all possible solutions is a fruitless endeavor because it is inhospitable to our policy process. Rather, focusing on realistic short-term policies that hopefully move the nation toward improvements in its state is a more effective paradigm.[14]

Bush commented a number of times that he did not think in terms of grandiose objectives, that he did not have some large-scale blueprint for reforming society already organized in his mind. Most memorably, he once said that he had "trouble with the vision thing." Scholars have written about and extensively debated Ronald Reagan's governing philosophy, but few have ventured to identify a Bush philosophy. Bush himself has admitted not having one. The lack of a thought-through philosophical approach to leading did not disturb him; he simply did not think it important to have one.

Braybrooke and Lindblom appreciate the utility of the theory of disjointed incrementalism because it fits comfortably with the nature of the policy process. Yet the theory has many critics who perceive it as a justification for a radical lowering of expectations. The theory is ultimately unsatisfying to those who believe in the potential for government to solve problems expeditiously.

Such criticisms usually derive from liberal thinkers and policy activists who believe in activist government. Criticism of Bush from the more progressive-oriented quarters of American politics was often quite harsh. Bush did not accept their assumptions about government's proper role in society. There was little or nothing he could do to satisfy their expectations of him as president. But many of Bush's harshest critics were conservatives.

One legacy of the Reagan era was the growing emphasis on the Right of the use of active government to promote conservative policy agendas. A number of Reagan conservatives brought into the Bush administration relatively late offered strong criticisms of Bush in interviews for this study, largely focusing on the lack of an activist domestic policy agenda. Many were exasperated that the administration did not move quickly to capitalize on the president's high popularity after the Gulf War and wage an "operation domestic storm" as one White House aide put it.

Given conflicting values in the political system, broad-based consensus is hard to achieve, even when the president is very popular and aggressively promoting his goals. Consequently, policy typically moves in incremental steps reflecting compromises among competing actors. This feature is particularly appropriate given the divided governance that Bush confronted. Comprehensive analysis is fruitless because comprehensive policy usually cannot be achieved. Bush may have withstood criticism for lacking leadership vision, but there arguably was little point in expending effort to articulate large-scale objectives that would never pass under divided government and huge budget deficits. Even if Bush had been so inclined, it is hard to imagine that after the Gulf War he could have overcome the stalemate built into the system of separated powers and develop consensus on large-scale domestic initiatives because of a temporary upswing in his popularity.

There is perhaps no stronger validation of Bush's emphasis on incremental policy development than the experiences of the Republican Congress elected in 1994. The conservative wing of the GOP had its "revolution," replete with a large-scale agenda to change the nation's policy direction. However, as Richard Fenno argues, the Republicans ran into the predictable barriers of an incrementalist policy system. In rejecting the nature of the policy system and trying to work against it, they minimized their influence and ultimately found themselves on the political defensive and heavily divided.[15] Another example is former president Bill Clinton's attempt in 1993–94 to achieve massive health-care reform. His legislative package was clearly a nonincremental attempt at a major departure from existing policy. Despite having partisan majorities in both houses of Congress, the effort failed. Clinton's big gamble wound up costing his administration and his leadership repute dearly.

Even recognizing the limitations of the policy process, it is important nonetheless for a president to have some organizing scheme for governing. Incrementalists need to develop a sense of the direction in which they want to lead the nation. It may be slow going at first, but at least there will be some philosophical guide or road map that points the nation in a clear direction.

For some of Bush's critics it is not just that he rejected activist government but rather that he lacked any organizing scheme at all for governance. Historian Forrest McDonald offers perhaps the most devastating indictment of Bush's leadership: "He was, in the parlance of people inside the beltway, a pragmatist, meaning a person who had no guiding philosophy or ideology but who tried to manage the machinery of the government well. But, to shift the metaphor, merely being competent at steering the ship of state became meaningless, for the passengers felt that the skipper knew not his destination."[16]

There is surely much truth in this assessment. Bush had a good many successes in managing the government and he achieved many more of his objectives than his contemporaries recognized or acknowledged. Yet even during peaceful and relatively prosperous times, managing the government is not enough. A president must establish guideposts for the nation even if his ultimate goals are incremental in nature. Bush said he wanted to be known as "the education president" and "the environmental president," but no one knew exactly what he meant when he made those claims. To borrow from McDonald's metaphor, without such guidance from the ship of state, the passengers will ultimately choose a new skipper to lead them. There is indeed some irony in the fact that the man who won the presidency by blasting his opponent's claim that the election was "about competence, not ideology," offered leadership that hinged on competent management rather than any ideological or philosophical guidepost.

In sum, in evaluating Bush's presidency, it is necessary to know how the president himself perceived his governing role. Bush was an incrementalist. He rejected the expectations of others for activist and "visionary" leadership. Bush saw no need for a philosophical approach to governing. Although even incrementalists can have conceptions of leadership, Bush did not effectively organize his objectives according to some governing scheme. In failing to do so, he somewhat lessened his effectiveness in office and substantially undermined his chances for reelection in 1992.

Perhaps the ultimate question in evaluating Bush's presidency is this: Could he have been more successful with a different approach? If the standard of evaluation is the model of the activist president, it is hard to imagine Bush having much, if any, success at all. The activist president pursues both an outside the government strategy of opinion leadership and an inside government strategy of elite persuasion. Bush lacked his predecessor's rhetorical gifts and could not credibly have exercised Reaganesque public leadership. He had to work with an opposition-party-led Congress that was not inclined to support Republican presidential initiatives. Even Reagan had GOP control of one house of Congress for six of his eight years in office. If the Reagan model is inappropriate as the standard for Bush, the FDR-influenced model is most certainly not germane to the task here.

This evaluation of the Bush presidency follows from these questions: What was Bush's conception of leadership? What were his leadership objectives? How successful was he in achieving his goals? Were his leadership approach and goals appropriate given the nature of the times and the needs of the country? Could he have done better using a different leadership approach?

Chapter Plan

This volume is composed of four major chapters examining different aspects of the Bush presidency. The purpose is not to present a comprehensive review of the Bush presidency. Instead, we feature particular aspects of the Bush presidency that facilitate an understanding of Bush's leadership approach. Our major sources include personal interviews with numerous Bush White House officials, a variety of White House–legislative correspondence (provided to us by legislative staffers), archival materials from the Bush Presidential Library and other government documents, and secondary sources where appropriate.

The following chapter defines Bush's leadership approach and presents evidence of how that approach worked in practice. We begin by examining Bush's presidential leadership origins in the 1988 campaign and during his transition to power. The theme of Bush as an incrementalist is presented to explain the connection between his early actions and conception of leadership.

Bush's emphasis in the campaign on nonfederal wedge issues and on his opponent's shortcomings was consistent with the approach of an incrementalist with a modest policy agenda. Bush emphasized in the campaign that he opposed flag burning and state government furloughs for convicts. Neither was a prominent federal issue. He promised not to increase tax rates and to maintain continuity with Reagan's economic policies. He said that he would manage international affairs cautiously.

The incrementalist identifies issues that are electorally effective while limiting his or her commitments to active government. Opposing flag burning effectively draws a wedge between a conservative candidate and his civil libertarian opponent while not committing the candidate to doing anything in particular. Promising not to raise taxes does not commit the candidate to any proactive economic policy. Opposing a former state governor's furlough policy casts the opponent in a negative light but has nothing to do with presidential responsibilities.

The Bush transition also fits the incrementalist theme. The president-elect downplayed the importance of a one-hundred-days agenda. He downplayed expectations for large-scale government action. He said that he wanted the public to know that the government did not always have to be doing very much. The people Bush selected for his staff were mostly competent, experienced managers rather than ideological crusaders. He did not surround himself with "big ideas" people in the conservative movement who were attracted to Reagan.[17] The most important criterion for selection to a position in the Bush White House was previous experience working with the president-elect. Bush wanted people he knew were competent managers and loyal to him.

The Bush agenda best reflected the president's incremental approach. His early policy proposals evidenced a go-slow approach both in domestic and foreign policy. His proposals disappointed analysts who expected bigger ideas and larger initiatives from a new president, but Bush was not about to make his actions conform to those kinds of demands. Despite a modest agenda, Bush achieved some substantial policy successes at home and abroad during his presidency. These successes came about as a result of his competent managerial approach and incremental agenda.

The third chapter examines Bush's public presidency. An incrementalist with modest goals sees no reason to employ grandiose rhetoric. Bush's rhetoric reflected his minimalist agenda and he in fact used rhetoric to downplay expectations of his presidency. Despite these efforts, Bush suffered unflattering comparisons with his predecessor and from expectations that all presidents aggressively use the "bully pulpit" to promote their goals. These evaluations were not appropriate to Bush or his administration's goals. Nevertheless, he ultimately erred by downplaying too much the importance of the public presidency to promoting policy goals and reelection. Even an incrementalist needs to communicate effectively with the public.

In comparison to his predecessor, Bush's presidency was low on public relations stunts and high on cultivating personal relations with individual reporters. Bush minimized the size of his speechwriting staff and gave much less emphasis than his predecessor to presidential communications and managing the media. He respected the media's role as the proper conduit of information and he did not seek to undermine or minimize that role through manipulation. Bush respected the proper roles of other institutions and therefore did relatively little to promote his goals outside of Washington. These actions were in keeping with the strategy of an incrementalist who respected the proper role of other institutions and players in the system.

The fourth chapter examines information control in the Bush administration. This coverage provides the best portrait of Bush as the competent manager of government affairs. There is definitely an element of hidden-hand leadership in Bush, although we would not go so far as to equate that approach with Eisenhower's more consciously developed strategy. Because Bush understood the government so well—especially how to work the system to his benefit in a quiet, understated fashion—his successes were more substantial than credited by his contemporaries. As some interviewees put it, Bush was an astute bureaucrat who understood the machinery of government. He used that knowledge to his advantage, enhancing his influence and minimizing the power of the opposition-party-led Congress.

Bush was a president highly prone to secrecy. He understood how to enhance his power by controlling the flow of information. Employing a variety of secrecy devices, he shielded information from Congress and the public, which had the effect of limiting his opponents' ability to put forth policy alternatives. Among the devices Bush used to enhance his power were enacting tight press restrictions during military operations and wartime, concealing executive privilege, claiming a "secret opinions policy," and issuing numerous National Security Directives (NSDs). Bush also made occasional use of the little-known legislative signing statement to alter Congress's lawmaking intent and direct the implementation of policies.

The importance of Bush's secrecy policies and use of signing statements was that they enabled him to overcome many of the disadvantages he suffered from trying to lead a Democrat-dominated Congress. Bush did not fare particularly well by the standard bases of evaluating presidential effectiveness with Congress. His *Congressional Quarterly* support scores were poor and he achieved few significant domestic legislative successes. Yet he was, in many cases, highly successful in shaping laws and their implementation—not only through the use of secret actions, unilateral decisions such as NSDs, and signing statements, but also through effective veto threats.

The fifth and final chapter describes and analyzes Bush's leadership approaches in both foreign and domestic policy. The long-held conventional wisdom is that Bush was an activist in the former arena, and inactive to the point of indifference in the latter. A review of Bush's leadership on a number of specific foreign and domestic issues suggests that the conventional view provides an incomplete picture. The cases show just how effectively Bush employed his incrementalist approach in practice.

The concluding chapter also presents a review and analysis of the Bush presidency along with an interpretation of the meaning of our findings for the art of presidential evaluation. We argue that conventional interpretive models are inadequate for assessing a presidency such as Bush's and therefore a more flexible approach to judging presidents is needed. Our bottom-line interpretation may certainly seem much more kind to Bush than earlier reviews of his presidency. We are, nonetheless, clearly less than enamored of excessive presidential secrecy, strategies to govern that avoid Congress, and the lack of any philosophical underpinning to an administration. In large part, our somewhat kinder view of the Bush years reflects the fact that we reject the conventional model of presidential evaluation. It is our hope that this study both places Bush in a more appropriate context for presidential evaluation and highlights the need for scholars to more fully examine common leadership assumptions.

CHAPTER 2

Incremental Leadership in the Bush Presidency

IN AN INSIGHTFUL STUDY of George H. W. Bush's "guardianship presidency," British scholar David Mervin traces the roots of the president's leadership style. Although Bush grew up in a privileged environment, his early family experiences instilled in him beliefs that guided much of his political career. His father, Sen. Prescott Bush, taught the values of obligation to community, civility, and compassion. "The dominant ethos was clearly one of conservatism tempered with the norms of *noblesse oblige*."[1] George Bush was reared in an environment of respect for hierarchy and "largely content with things as they were." Mervin writes: "An emphasis on duty and service is consistent with the lack of vision that Bush was so often charged with. It involves no lust for change, but requires individuals to give something back in return for the advantages that have been bestowed upon them."[2]

The ideas that framed Bush carried with him through a distinguished career in public service. In his numerous public offices—Congress, national party leader, ambassador to China, UN ambassador, CIA director, and vice president—Bush evidenced respect for hierarchical authority and the order of things. He was distrustful of crusades for change and believed that positive reform proceeded cautiously and slowly. Throughout much of his career in public service, critics charged him with being overly deferential to authority and unwilling to lead the charge for needed change. His experiences taught him that it was more effective to accept the conventional norms of institutions and to work for gradual change if needed.

Bush had the unenviable task of leading the Republican National Committee during Watergate. Critics faulted him for too eagerly defending the president even when the evidence against the Nixon White House mounted. During confirmation hearings for his appointment as CIA director, Democrats demanded—and received—a pledge from Bush that he would not accept a vice presidential nomination in 1976. Bush was outraged at being required "to forswear his political birthright," but he agreed to the arrangement in order to get the position he wanted.[3] As CIA director, many credited Bush with having restored morale to the beleaguered agency and once again critics characterized him as the quintessential organization man.

Bush ran for the presidency in 1980 as the GOP candidate with the best résumé of public service. His campaign appeals boasted that he was the one candidate who would not need to be trained in office. Unlike opponent Ronald Reagan, Bush lacked a clear ideological or policy-oriented message. He was merely the best-trained candidate.

Although he impressively won the Iowa caucuses, Bush's campaign faltered in New Hampshire, the first primary state. Perhaps the key event of the campaign was a preprimary debate scheduled between frontrunners Bush and Reagan. The other GOP candidates excluded from the event showed up and demanded to participate. While Bush meekly appealed for the agreed-upon rules to be respected, Reagan invited the others to join the debate in a theatrical moment that seemed to define the difference between the two GOP front-runners: Bush quietly sitting, asking that the rules be abided by; Reagan seizing the political moment with perfect timing.

Although Bush lost the nomination, his strong showings impressed Reagan enough to choose him as the vice-presidential candidate. Once again, Bush appeared to define himself by the nature of his new position. As a presidential candidate, Bush had staked out moderate positions on many controversial issues, clearly in contrast to Reagan's ideological stands. In a widely quoted quip, Bush had earlier called Reagan's economic proposals "voodoo economics"—a mockery of the notion that the goals of federal deficit reduction, a massive tax cut, and a defense spending increase could all be achieved. As vice-presidential nominee and later as vice president, Bush more and more aligned his positions—not only on economic issues but social ones—with Reagan's.

Bush sustained regular criticism during his vice presidency once again for being too deferential, unwilling to assert an independent role or opinion. The vice president's press secretary, Marlin Fitzwater, said that reporters who interviewed Bush always tried to find some area of disagreement with the president. When Bush refused to play their game, Fitzwater added, the reporters criticized him harshly for lacking independent thought.[4] "Doonesbury" cartoonist Gary Trudeau portrayed Bush as an invisible character who had placed his manhood in a blind trust. Devastating critiques characterized Bush as a "wimp" and a "lapdog" of President Reagan.[5]

In fairness, vice presidents are easy targets for partisan and press criticism. On one hand, the vice president has a responsibility to be loyal to the chief executive; on the other, political observers demand that the vice president establish a separate identity.

Bush's temperament was well suited to the expectations of loyalty and subservience by vice presidents. Nonetheless, political observers believed that once he ran for the presidency in 1988, Bush would have to establish an identity independent of Reagan's and map out his own unique leadership vision. Many wondered whether this cautious and deferential person would make a strong and independent-minded leader.

The 1988 Campaign

The presidential campaign presented Bush with his best opportunity to establish an independent identity. By most accounts, he failed to do so.

Much already has been written about Bush's low-road campaign in 1988 in which he characterized his opponent as soft on crime, insufficiently patriotic, and an extreme civil libertarian. Little has been written about how the campaign strategy suited the man's overriding view of governing.

For the incrementalist, the emphasis on negative appeals keeps the focus away from future policy goals and governing philosophy. An incrementalist is unlikely to be successful in a campaign context by emphasizing the desire to accomplish little and articulating no long-term or future goals. The choice is either to overpromise or to change the campaign's focus. Bush chose the latter by making the campaign in many respects a referendum on his opponent's fitness to serve. To that end, Bush had the perfect opponent: Democrat Michael Dukakis did not effectively respond to the charges made by the Republican campaign.

Bush's appeals often avoided substantive issues altogether as the campaign focused on symbols and attacks on Dukakis. Rather than debate the complexities of First Amendment rights, Bush lambasted Dukakis as being unpatriotic for failing to support required reciting of the pledge of allegiance by school children. Bush dramatized the difference between himself and Dukakis by visiting American flag manufacturers.

To the extent that Bush discussed issues during the campaign, he did so by focusing on those over which presidents have little formal authority: crime fighting and education. The use of the crime issue worked well for a presidential candidate who favored an incrementalist approach to governing. It enabled Bush to make popular appeals regarding a problem about which voters expressed strong concern, while at the same time not committing his administration to an expansionist federal agenda. Similarly, Bush pledged to be the "education president" even though the establishment and implementation of education programs and goals are primarily handled at the state and local levels.

Bush's campaign, although successful, ultimately failed to provide a governing mandate to achieve certain goals. Charles O. Jones has written: "Given the lack of issues during the campaign, it was difficult to interpret Bush's substantial victory in policy terms."[6]

Press coverage of the campaign emphasized that Bush had taken the low road, had failed to articulate a governing vision, and had lost his best opportunity to achieve a meaningful mandate. To *Time*'s Walter Shapiro, Bush was a "political chameleon."[7] *Newsweek*'s Jonathon Alter and Mickey Kaus reported that "Bush's ideological amorphousness is still troubling to anyone trying to predict how he will govern."[8] Kenneth T. Walsh criticized Bush's "content-free campaign" and failure to define "a governing strategy."[9] Columnists Rowland Evans and Robert Novak criticized Bush's "ideological flabbiness" and lack of interest in issues.[10] George F. Will called Bush an "ominously empty" man, "a sailor without a compass."[11]

Critics said most often of Bush that he lacked a governing "vision." To be fair, to the extent that Bush articulated his overriding goal as president, he said that he wanted to continue his predecessor's policies. To that end, Bush was campaigning to consolidate the conservative gains of the Reagan years, not to embark on a dramatically new policy direction.

Bush also defined himself as more of a pragmatist than a visionary. At the outset of his 1988 campaign he told voters: "I am a practical man. I like what's real. I'm not much for the airy and the abstract. I like what works. I am not a mystic, and I do not yearn to lead a crusade."[12] Bush described his perception of the government's proper role: "The government's first duty is like that of the physician: Do no harm."[13] It was a clear commitment to a minimalist role for the federal government.

Bush's most memorable policy commitment in the campaign told voters that he would not raise taxes. Although Bush ultimately broke that pledge, his statement to the GOP convention evidenced his view that leadership entailed using the powers of the presidency to stop the initiatives of others. Bush made it clear—and this commitment he did mostly fulfill—that if the Democratic majority in Congress tried to direct the policy agenda from Capitol Hill and reverse the conservative gains of the Reagan years, he would use his powers when needed to negate their initiatives.

The negating role that Bush promised to employ also fit comfortably the leadership approach of an incrementalist who wanted to preserve the status quo. Bush perceived his role as one of continuing his predecessor's agenda. He promised voters in effect that he would protect the Reagan legacy from legislative encroachments.

Transition/Staffing

The transition period and staffing of the administration reflected Bush's preference for a low-key, status quo presidency. Bush downplayed expectations for an activist presidency by cautioning the public that he had no grand scheme for change or policy innovations. Bush candidly told reporters that he had trouble with "the vision thing" and did not believe that policy change was needed. When pressed about his plans for the administration's first one hundred days, Bush said that he had no timetable for achieving his goals. He quipped to reporters that the FDR standard for the first one hundred days did not suit him.[14]

A within-party transition in which the vice president moves up to the presidency ideally suits the incrementalist approach. It afforded Bush the opportunity to preserve the status quo by reappointing incumbents and working closely with the outgoing administration to plan for the change in government.

Yet Bush also faced the dilemma of wanting to establish his own unique administration while preserving the status quo. That required substantial personnel changes, which offended some Reagan staffers who wanted to continue working in the new Republican administration.

Roscoe Starek, the deputy director of the transition and later of personnel in the Bush White House, explained that the transition began during the campaign.[15] Quietly organized by Chase Untermeyer was a pretransition planning project to ensure a smooth transition in the event Bush won. The pretransition group worked closely with members of the Reagan administration in the summer of 1988 and continued to do so after being reformulated as the transition team after Bush's victory.

Starek explained that Bush had an "unofficial policy" when it came to staffing: that some of the most able on Reagan's staff would be reappointed, but that Bush ultimately wanted mostly his own people. A leading criterion for selection was whether Bush personally knew and felt comfortable with an individual.[16] Transition director Chase Untermeyer said that Bush "was acquainted with every member of his Cabinet before he named them to office. They were people he had known and with whom he had worked for many years."[17]

Bush's choices to fill key posts reflected his preference for experienced, competent individuals rather than ideological crusaders. He generally avoided Reagan-era ideologues intent on dramatic change or reform. Among his leading appointments were Secretary of State James Baker, National Security Adviser Brent Scowcroft, Office of Management and Budget director Richard Darman, Labor Secretary Elizabeth Dole, and Health and Human Services Secretary Louis W. Sullivan. Among the moderate Reagan appointees he retained were Treasury Secretary Nicholas Brady and Attorney General Richard Thornburgh.

An incrementalist will choose to surround himself primarily with competent, experienced managerial staffers rather than ideological crusaders. There were some exceptions to this rule: Housing and Urban Development Secretary Jack Kemp, Drug "Czar" William Bennett, and James Pinkerton, the deputy director of policy and planning. The conservative "ideas people" were clearly in the minority in the Bush administration. Bush's incrementalist approach did not suit their ideals of an activist, visionary conservatism. Disappointed with Bush's cautious approach, Kemp eventually became openly critical of White House inaction, fueling divisions between Bush loyalists and movement conservatives in the GOP. Some Bush loyalists interviewed for this study expressed contempt for Kemp's actions because he failed to suit the ethos of a White House that favored a more quiet low-key approach. One even called him "disloyal" and a "back stabber."[18]

One of the most often heard criticisms of Bush's transition was that the incoming administration was being staffed too slowly. An incrementalist is likely to proceed slowly and carefully in making appointments and that is just what Bush did. To critics, the slow-paced staffing of the administration evidenced poor leadership, when in fact the White House wanted only to scrutinize appointments carefully and was not in any hurry to promote change. Moreover, because he was making a within-party transition, Bush thought that the slow pace was not a problem because the posts for unfilled positions were being maintained by Reagan-Bush administration holdovers.[19]

As Starek commented, contrary to the conventional wisdom, staffing during a within-party transition may be the most difficult task of all. For a between-parties transition, the first step is to fire all of the previous administration's high-level appointees—something that is expected. A large number of posts are then available to be filled by loyalists of the incoming president. For a within-party transition—especially one in which the incumbent vice president succeeds to the Oval Office—many from the outgoing administration lobby to keep their posts or try to attain new positions. Party loyalists often are offended and become angry when they are replaced.[20]

As with any transition, despite cautious planning, there were the usual embarrassments for the president-elect. Several of his prominent appointees came under scrutiny and criticism for alleged conflicts of interest. Bush's initial choice for secretary of defense, John Tower, became a major humiliation when some of the former senator's foes made allegations of financial and personal improprieties.

Bush made his chief-of-staff appointment relatively late in the transition. Former New Hampshire governor John Sununu had the reputation of being a brilliant but arrogant manager. Although Bush's chief-of-staff appointment became mired in controversy and ultimately embarrassed the president, there was a credible rationale for giving Sununu that post: the former governor's skills and demeanor helped Bush promote his objectives and sustain support for a time.

As scholar Richard J. Ellis shows, Sununu was, for a substantial portion of Bush's term, an effective "lightning rod"—someone who "takes the heat" for the president in difficult situations.[21] Sununu's presence in the White House helped Bush placate movement conservatives somewhat while staking out a more modest and moderate agenda than they would have preferred. Sununu gave conservatives a powerful voice within the White House. On environmental issues, for example, Sununu's rhetoric pleased conservatives and angered the environmental movement. Yet the latter group perceived Bush as reasonably moderate on environmental issues and believed that the chief of staff was their real enemy.

This approach enabled Bush, for much of his term at least, to promote a cautious, moderate environmental agenda while keeping conservatives contented and not being personally blamed by environmentalists for his compromises.[22] As scholar James Pfiffner wrote: "[Sununu] provided a sharp contrast in personal style to the president. He was the president's 'pit bull' dog who would act mean and allow the president to take the 'kinder and gentler' stance."[23]

The problem was that Sununu overplayed the role of White House pit bull and alienated so many members of the Washington community that there was almost no one willing to defend him—and many delighted to see him falter—when he became mired in scandal in 1991. Sununu's abuse of the privileges of his office—including the use of military aircraft for personal travel—led to his downfall and the appointment of a replacement chief of staff: Sam Skinner, who was ethical but ineffective in the job. Several White House staff members interviewed for this study lamented that because Skinner lacked Sununu's managerial skills, the White House atmosphere was one of chaos during the crucial reelection campaign.

Bush's intense loyalty to people around him also reflected his generally cautious approach to governing. He was reluctant to replace staff members even when it appeared to be in his interest to do so. In part, he wanted to honor the commitments he had made, and in part he did not want to disrupt the order of things too much. By most accounts, he took too long to accept having to replace Sununu; and many thought that he should have replaced Vice President Dan Quayle on the 1992 GOP ticket.

The Policy Agenda

The clearest reflection of Bush's incremental approach was his policy agenda. Bush's leadership in both domestic and foreign affairs evidenced a cautious conservatism that may have suited the electorate in 1988 but by 1992 was seen as indifference to problems at home.

The dilemma that confronted Bush from the outset was that he favored an incremental approach whereas political observers defined presidential leadership as action-oriented. To be faithful to his own preferences while appearing to be promoting action from the White House required a careful selection of issues to emphasize.

As he had in the presidential campaign, Bush placed his emphasis domestically on areas in which the federal government plays a relatively minor role: education policy and crime prevention. This emphasis allowed Bush to maintain support by speaking out on those powerful issues while his administration took little substantive action.

For an incrementalist president intent on preserving the status quo, the veto power is a logical tool. A senior presidential adviser said that Bush's veto strategy allowed him to stop the Democratic majorities in Congress "from governing from the Hill."[24] For Bush, the veto was not merely an act of last resort to stop what he considered undesirable legislation; it was a tool that enabled him to shape the crafting of legislation more to his liking.

Bush made it clear from the outset that he would not hesitate to use the veto power. Consequently, that threat enabled him to influence the legislative process at various stages. White House lobbyist Nicholas Calio said that the Bush administration was able to impose its will on the legislature "by either vetoing bills it opposed or issuing veto threats that forced lawmakers to compromise."[25]

Bush's pragmatic approach led him either to use the veto or threaten its use under the appropriate circumstances. A former Republican House member, Rep. Lawrence DeNardis, drew the distinction between Reagan, who used the veto to take an ideological stand on an issue regardless of the possibility of having the veto sustained, and Bush, who chose his battles cautiously.[26] A report in *Congressional Quarterly* confirmed that legislators knew that Reagan's veto threats were not always credible, whereas Bush had "made few empty veto threats and . . . picked his fights with care."[27]

Bush had an active, and successful, veto record. Among all presidents from 1889–1993, Bush had the third highest annual average of public-bill vetoes (7.25), behind the record pace of Gerald Ford (15.30), and closely following Franklin D. Roosevelt (8.75). Congress overrode only one Bush veto: a bill to regulate the cable industry. Bush also was not reluctant to use the pocket veto, having done so seventeen times in four years.[28]

Further evidence of Bush's incremental approach was the policy agenda he chose to promote and his strategies for positive action. From the outset, he expressed a preference for a cautious, limited agenda.

BUSH'S POLICY APPROACH: THE FIRST YEAR

Bush's cautious approach was manifested early in the first term. Nearly three weeks after taking office the president addressed a joint session of Congress on the federal budget problem. He proposed incremental adjustments to federal spending on education, child care, and fighting the drug problem. Despite many cries for serious action to stem rising deficits, Bush told Congress: "I don't propose to change direction. We are headed the right way."[29] Columnist David S. Broder lamented that with such a "spare domestic agenda" Bush had already "squandered an opportunity to put his mark on the future."[30]

On education policy, many criticized Bush for proposing what a *Time* story called a "paltry" sum of federal dollars. Reporter Walter Shapiro lamented that rather than clear priorities and a serious commitment of public funding, Bush had offered "marginal adjustments in the status quo."[31] George F. Will calculated that Bush's education initiative was 1/800th of the cost of a manned flight to Mars that the president endorsed.[32] Bush's major education commitment was largely symbolic, as evidenced by an education summit with the nation's governors held in Virginia.

Regarding the war on drugs, Bush also emphasized symbolic measures. He devoted his first nationally televised address to the drug problem. Bush proposed to Congress a modest program of enhanced law enforcement, prison building, drug-abuse treatment, increased border patrols, and international aid. Despite these actions, critics denounced the initiatives as too incremental, "underfinanced," and even "cheap."[33] The *New York Times* lamented that the president's initiatives "would bring progress measured in inches."[34]

Bush's major legislative achievement his first year in office was renewal of the 1970 Clean Air Act. Congress had failed to renew the act since 1981 and had kept it in effect through continuing resolutions. Bush's leadership in bringing environmental advocates and business groups together broke the legislative logjam. Nonetheless, critics suggested that the compromise plan once again showed that Bush would be satisfied with incrementalism when bolder action was needed.[35]

Because Bush's domestic policy approach favored incrementalism over large-scale change, he ran afoul of certain standard leadership expectations of journalists and pundits. Press secretary Marlin Fitzwater lambasted those who constantly criticized the president for a lack of bold initiatives and a lack of leadership "vision." "You Liberal writers are just like the Democrats in Congress," he complained. "You think government isn't doing anything unless it's taxing and spending and creating new bureaucracies."[36]

Bush received the highest plaudits for his foreign policy leadership. Nonetheless, during his first year in office, many criticized what R. W. Apple Jr. called Bush's "plodding, almost timid foreign policy style" and "aversion to initiative."[37]

This criticism had some merit, as the president described his foreign policy as "status quo–plus." That is, he favored no dramatic change from the Reagan years plus cautious alterations in policy to accommodate new circumstances. Bush's favorite word to describe his approach was "prudence." For Bush, prudence required a go-slow, cautious, wait-and-see response to changes abroad rather than bold, dramatic action. It also meant avoiding Reagan-style ideological crusades in directing foreign policy. Bush's approach contrasted immediately with his predecessor's when he decided to break the executive-legislative feuding over Central American policy and drop the futile insistence on large-scale aid to the Nicaraguan Contra movement.

What many found objectionable was Bush's status quo approach during a time of profound change abroad. As in the domestic sphere, his critics charged, Bush showed a lack of vision to lead U.S. foreign policy through a series of profound international transformations.

During the early months of the Bush presidency, this status quo leadership appeared in marked contrast to the dramatic steps taken by Soviet leader Mikhail Gorbachev. In 1989, Gorbachev embarked upon a series of important domestic and foreign policy reforms. Under his leadership, the Soviet Union held elections, withdrew its forces from Afghanistan, withdrew some troops from Eastern Europe, and made cuts in its short-range nuclear forces (SNF).

The Soviet leader's popularity grew in Western Europe, putting the U.S. president under pressure to accept Gorbachev as a new kind of Soviet leader and negotiate with him for further weapons reductions. As Gorbachev and his foreign minister Eduard Shevardnadze traveled throughout Europe promising perestroika and an end to East-West ideological conflict, the Bush administration expressed skepticism about the Soviet leadership's motives and urged caution.

Bush's critics blasted his response to Gorbachev as overly cautious, timid, and inadequate. They accused him of being reactive to events abroad, of "indecision," "do-nothing leadership," "absence of a strategic design," "no vision," and of conducting a "small-minded foreign policy."[38]

Bush appeared to change course in mid-1989 just prior to the June North Atlantic Treaty Organization (NATO) summit in Brussels. Prior to that meeting he announced a major disarmament plan, including the reduction of U.S. forces in Europe by thirty thousand men. At the summit, Bush offered a plan to reduce short-range nuclear forces. For a change, the president was on the receiving end of some praise for bold and innovative leadership, although many analysts suggested that he was merely reacting to the earlier criticisms.[39]

Bush's "prudence" in foreign affairs meant a preference for quiet diplomatic maneuvering over grandstanding. Prior to the NATO summit, the administration had engaged in a series of low-key negotiations, as well as a lengthy analysis of the issues, leading up to the U.S. proposals. Bush's approach was effective, although it did mean short-term criticism for appearing to do nothing in response to changes abroad.

Bush's cautious and unemotional response to the crumbling of the Berlin Wall in November, 1989, perhaps best encapsulated what many found exasperating about his leadership: No fanfare, no stirring rhetoric to capture the drama and the historical significance of the event. By contrast, many political observers said, imagine the response that President Reagan would have had to the collapse of the world's most visible symbol of communist oppression. Bush simply refused to respond as others would have preferred. He believed that it was undiplomatic and even unseemly to appear to being boastful under the circumstances. He preferred a wait-and-see approach in response to dramatic events abroad. He preferred to manage international change quietly and carefully.

The most important meeting of international leaders in 1989 occurred on December 2 and 3 in Malta, as Bush and Gorbachev held their first summit. The superpower leaders discussed troop cuts in Europe and the futures of Eastern European nations.

In keeping with Bush's low-key approach, the administration went to great lengths to downplay the significance of the summit, to lower expectations. Analysts once again expressed disappointment with what David Broder called the president's "cautious, plodding" and "unimaginative" leadership.[40]

In part, the administration's strategy was to lower expectations and then surprise Bush's critics with significant summit proposals. The tack worked, as Bush proposed that the superpowers conclude the Strategic Arms Reduction Treaty (START) talks and sign an agreement to reduce conventional forces in Europe. He also offered to help the Soviet economy by lifting trade barriers and granting most-favored-nation status to the Soviet Union in return for an easing of Soviet emigration laws. Bush and Gorbachev also discussed their nations' future roles in Europe and the conditions for a reunited Germany.

Although many of Bush's critics praised his unusually bold summit leadership, they saw little else in his first-year foreign policy to merit similar accolades.[41] His lack of any strong initiative against Chinese human rights abuses best evidenced Bush's commitment to a cautious leadership approach. In 1974–75, Bush served as the U.S. envoy to China, and he clearly did not want to do anything that would undermine long-term U.S.-China relations.

Nonetheless, the severity of the Chinese government action against prodemocracy demonstrators could not be ignored. On June 3–4, 1989, the Chinese military killed hundreds of prodemocracy demonstrators at Tiananmen Square. News coverage of protesters erecting U.S. symbols of liberty and peaceably standing down tanks provided compelling and moving images.

During the early stages of the demonstrations, Bush did not offer any stirring rhetoric in defense of the prodemocracy movement. After the massacre at Tiananmen Square, Bush condemned the action, suspended high-level diplomatic and military contacts with China, extended visas for Chinese students in the United States, and provided sanctuary for a dissident couple.

Yet, in keeping with this approach, Bush did not take harshly punitive actions against the Chinese government. For that, critics again said he was failing to demonstrate strong leadership. Congress believed that Bush had not extended Chinese student visas for a long enough period and voted for an additional four-year extension. Bush vetoed the legislation—a decision widely lambasted as a "presidential *kowtow*."[42]

Bush believed that it was in the long-term interest of the United States not to take strongly punitive action against China. He wanted to work for positive change through quiet, diplomatic channels and did so by sending National Security Adviser Brent Scowcroft as an emissary to meet with China's leaders. Although this action generated substantial criticism, Bush stuck with his approach hoping that a constructive dialogue would ultimately be more effective over the long run than public posturing and punitive measures.

The brutal Panamanian regime of Gen. Manuel Antonio Noriega posed a different challenge for Bush's foreign policy leadership. In May, 1989, Bush expressed his desire to see the Panamanian dictator removed from power. Noriega's many human rights abuses and international drug dealing had created an atmosphere in the United States in favor of intervention in Panama. Overthrowing the dictator would not be easy, however.

Bush initiated action to encourage Noriega's ouster from power by advocating that Panama's defense forces stage a coup d'etat. He also negotiated with leaders of Latin American countries to obtain their support for possible U.S. intervention in Panama and dispatched eighteen hundred troops to Panama to protect U.S. citizens and symbolize his resolve.

In October, a government opposition group in the Panamanian military attempted a coup. The attempt failed, causing a setback for Bush, who had established the expectation of U.S. backing for a coup and then tendered weak support to the anti-Noriega forces. Once again, Bush's critics blasted his "timidity," "innate caution," and lack of policy follow-through.[43] William Safire wrote that Bush had failed to "separate prudence in policy from hesitancy in execution."[44]

A president who prefers incremental, cautious leadership will make decisions according to his own preferred time frame and not that of those who demand bold action. Bush resisted action in October that may have gratified his critics but failed to achieve the necessary ends. In late December, Bush ordered a military invasion of Panama. The army captured Noriega and brought him to the United States on charges of international drug trafficking. Bush's action temporarily blunted criticism and showed that he was surely capable of decisive action under what he considered the proper circumstances.

Despite some foreign policy achievements, journalists and political analysts gave Bush's first-year leadership low marks. According to David Broder, the trouble with Bush was that he was merely "a good manager" and "a status quo man," not a leader.[45] An analysis in *U.S. News* referred to Bush's first-year leadership as "the year of living timorously." Bush allegedly deserved low marks because he "refused to get off to a running start, rejected the notion of a first hundred-days agenda" and did not propose bold domestic initiatives.[46] The *New York Times* called Bush "a capable shepherd of the status quo." The *Times* wanted bold presidential leadership and found Bush lacking: "The education summit was all wind. The housing plan, ditto. The famous War on Drugs, mostly ditto. There's little new money, and no will to find any. . . . Mr. Bush doesn't shout charge! He whispers it."[47]

THE TWO GEORGE BUSHES

Perhaps in response to criticism for inaction, Bush's January 31, 1990, State of the Union Address emphasized the need for government action on education, health care, the economy, the environment, and housing. Although symbolically Bush wanted to show that he cared about domestic problems, substantively he remained an incrementalist. Bush submitted a budget plan that reflected his preference for marginal adjustments to the federal government's spending on programs. He also tried to use rhetoric emphasizing his commitment to domestic programs to rebut criticism that he was a "do-nothing" president. Yet critics looked for programs, not talk.

Perhaps no Bush program was more frequently derided as a symbol of his do-nothing approach than the Points of Light Initiative. The purpose of the program was to encourage community service throughout the country.[48] Critics, however, refused to take seriously the notion that the president's solution to domestic ills was to encourage volunteerism.

To many of Bush's critics, the president appeared too preoccupied with events abroad to show any leadership at home. Columnist Jim Hoagland suggested that perhaps what Bush really needed was a prime minister: someone to handle the messy affairs of domestic politics while the president was "out building the new international order."[49]

Perhaps the most memorable news magazine cover during the Bush years was *Time*'s 1991 "Man of the Year" issue. It featured "Men of the Year: The Two George Bushes." The point was to convey that Bush appeared strong and resolute abroad but weak and vacillating at home: "One finds vision on the global stage; the other displays none at home."[50]

Bush had demonstrated foreign policy leadership in a May-June, 1990, summit meeting with Gorbachev. The Soviet leader appeared vulnerable during a period of unrest in the Baltic region and Bush's cautious approach appeared to pay off with better relations between the superpowers. Although some criticized the president's unwillingness to pressure Gorbachev into supporting independence movements in the Baltic nations, most depicted Bush's leadership as effective under difficult circumstances.[51] In December, as the Soviet Union suffered from food and provisions shortages due to an unusually harsh winter, Bush lifted trade restrictions and offered $1 billion worth of food on official credit to the Kremlin.

Bush earned his highest accolades for his leadership during the 1990–91 Persian Gulf crisis. After Iraq invaded Kuwait on August 2, 1990, Bush effectively forged an international coalition against the Iraqi government of Saddam Hussein. Bush then secured economic sanctions against Iraq, followed by UN resolutions authorizing the use of military force to restore Kuwait's freedom. The Soviet Union joined the coalition after Bush convinced Saudi Arabia to give $1 billion in aid to the Kremlin. His earlier cautious response to the events at Tiananmen Square appeared vindicated when he convinced China to join the international coalition.

As the crisis continued, Bush had to be concerned not only about the need to hold together the international coalition but also to maintain domestic support. On September 11, 1990, he addressed a joint session of Congress to announce his resolve to drive Iraq out of Kuwait. It was, according to many, the best speech of his presidency. The *New York Times* responded with an editorial praising Bush for his "clear-eyed purpose" in pursuing an end to the crisis.[52]

Yet Bush's leadership success in the Persian Gulf crisis inspired stories of what columnist Paul A. Gigot called his "split personality." As Gigot put it, "on foreign and domestic policy, Mr. Bush can seem like two different men."[53]

Bush's early diplomatic efforts and international economic sanctions did not force Iraq out of Kuwait. Consequently, the president had to make a convincing case for a continued and ultimately expanded U.S. military presence in the Persian Gulf. As the crisis dragged on, Bush's trouble with "the vision thing" again became evident. He presented numerous and often incompatible objectives in U.S. policy: restoring Kuwait's sovereignty, protecting U.S. national interests, preserving U.S. economic interests, defeating a Hitler-like dictator, stopping international aggression. The *New York Times,* which had earlier praised Bush's purposefulness, now said that he had "vacillated in declaring his objectives."[54]

Bush insisted that his goals remained clear. To alleviate any doubt, he issued an ultimatum to the Iraqi government in December: leave Kuwait by January 15, 1991, or be forced to do so.

From the initiation of U.S. missile attacks on Baghdad on January 16, 1991, until the cease-fire on February 28, the nation rallied behind coalition forces and the president. Bush's popularity soared. It reached 86 percent—the highest level of any president in thirty years—the day after the war against Iraq began.[55] After the cease-fire, Bush's approval rating soared to 91 percent.[56] With such high approval ratings, many political observers asserted that Bush would be impossible to defeat for reelection in 1992. The Democrats had become so marginalized, Andrew M. Rosenthal observed, that "maybe they can get George McGovern to run again" for president.[57]

Yet the disastrous postwar situation in the Middle East surely soiled Bush's finest moment. The president's failure to order a serious response to the Iraqi slaughter of Kurdish and Shiite rebels invited renewed criticism of his leadership. To be sure, Bush had said from the outset that he wanted only to remove the Iraqi military from Kuwait and that he did not seek to settle a protracted civil war. His immediate goal did not require coalition forces to destroy the Iraqi military or remove Saddam from power. Despite advice from some military leaders to the contrary, Bush stuck to his stated objective and did not pursue the destruction of the Iraqi military or ending Saddam's rule.

Scholars Cecil Crabb and Kevin Mulcahy observed that Bush's incremental leadership was well suited to dealing with a short-term crisis such as the one in the Persian Gulf. Bush understood the immediate problem at hand and had no difficulty taking resolute action. His "elitist model of leadership" also served him well as he worked closely with a small circle of advisers and dealt directly with international leaders. He was less comfortable dealing with the plurality of interests and players on the domestic front. He also had difficulty thinking about long-term U.S. strategies and objectives, Crabb and Holt noted. In that regard, although Bush's effective leadership during the Persian Gulf crisis earned him well-deserved plaudits, he was less able to "[envision] the future role for the U.S. in a quickly changing world."[58] He was not clear on how to respond to the postwar Middle East situation.

Bush's rhetoric and actions in the postwar environment evidenced his confusion over the emerging role of the United States internationally. He spoke of creating a "New World Order," yet he did little to infuse that concept with a clear meaning. By the end of his term, the phrase had become a matter of derision and few could agree on exactly what it meant beyond some vague notion of post–Cold War international stability led by the United States.

Bush's cautious approach also served him well in responding to a crisis in the Soviet Union in 1991 that threatened the process of democratization. The July summit in Moscow had produced the Strategic Arms Reduction Treaty, the hallmark of which was an agreement to limit superpower nuclear arsenals. Less than a month later, a coup attempt against the Soviet government tested Bush's international leadership again.

Bush's initial response was to take some measure of the events in Moscow before deciding on a course of action. He initially refused to condemn the coup attempt as illegal because he wanted to protect future U.S. interests depending on the outcome. Although some believed that he had been too reluctant to endorse Russian Republic president Boris Yeltsin's gestures against the coup plotters, Bush's flexible response appeared vindicated when the plot failed.

Bush followed with an arms-reduction initiative in October to which Soviet leader Gorbachev responded positively. The initiative offered to eliminate ground-launched short-range nuclear warheads. Gorbachev not only agreed; he offered to cut Soviet long-range warheads well below the START requirements. For initiating and then facilitating these agreements, observers credited Bush with the kind of "visionary" and "bold" leadership that they so often had said he lacked.[59]

Nevertheless, the dissolution of the Soviet Union in late 1991 failed to inspire Bush to issue bold pronouncements and policy initiatives. Once again, the president's critics were stunned by his innate caution in response to such a dramatic event. Some likened it to his tepid rhetoric in response to the fall of the Berlin Wall.[60] Many criticized Bush for not immediately offering substantial new aid to the former Soviet republics to encourage a more stable democratic transition.[61] Columnist Charles Krauthammer summarized the views of many when he criticized the president's "silence" in response to the dramatic event: "Ronald Reagan ran for president on ideas and promises. George Bush did not. Bush had no agenda. He promised only to be an adequate steward for the country. . . . George Bush does not believe in very much. He never pretended to. . . . Take away George Bush's belief in internationalism and free trade, and what's left?"[62]

This criticism appeared particularly apt to Bush's domestic policy leadership. Some of his actions appeared calculated to maintain popular support while he proposed little change in policies. In 1990, the president spoke out in favor of a constitutional amendment to outlaw flag burning. He expressed contempt for a Supreme Court decision that gave First Amendment protection to a form of protest that he considered deplorable. Although Bush had widespread public support for his position, it was undeniable that flag burning was not one of the leading domestic problems of the time. The more Bush spoke out on the subject, the more he appeared to be trying to divert attention from more pressing problems at home. It was a tack that had worked for him in his nearly issue-free 1988 campaign and he was no less reluctant to use the same appeal during his presidency.

Bush did make one unequivocal commitment in his 1988 presidential campaign: "Read my lips. No new taxes." A number of Bush White House staffers interviewed for this study said that the president was uncomfortable with making that pledge but became convinced that it was necessary to win the election.[63]

The president's break with the tax pledge occurred during the lengthy 1990 budget negotiations. It became clear that the government had to send a signal of seriousness about deficit reduction to the financial markets. Democrats in Congress insisted that the budget discussions include some consideration of new taxes. Bush felt that to negotiate in good faith meant that various options—whether ultimately adopted or not—had to be considered. In June he signed a pledge to consider "tax revenue increases" in the deficit reduction plan. The *New York Post*'s screaming bold-print headline best summarized the public reaction: "READ MY LIPS—I LIED."[64]

In part, Bush's difficult position in the budget negotiations arose out of his own conciliatory approach to congressional Democrats. The president was conciliatory during negotiations with Democratic leaders, while he largely shut congressional Republicans out of the process. In early October, GOP members revolted and enough Democrats joined the opposition to the initial budget proposal, which did not include tax increases. That left Bush with the option of allowing drastic across-the-board budget cuts to take place when a budget agreement was reached, or to work out an alternative agreement with congressional Democrats. He chose the latter course of action, which resulted later that month in a package that included tax increases largely on wealthier citizens. The agreement included few real budget cuts. Congressional Democrats had succeeded in getting Bush to accept their spending priorities.

Bush knew that the budget agreement would cause him some trouble. He tried to mitigate it by referring to the budget agreement as having included "revenue enhancements" rather than tax increases. Press Secretary Marlin Fitzwater later wrote: "we deluded ourselves into thinking that calling a tax increase by another name . . . would fool the world." He called the agreement the single biggest mistake of the administration.[65]

The budget agreement proved to be a political disaster for Bush. Ed Rollins, the cochair of the GOP congressional campaign committee, advised party nominees to openly oppose the president's deal in the midterm elections. Many did. Of the roughly one hundred nominees who had filmed campaign commercials with the president, only a few actually used the spots. Many canceled scheduled campaign appearances with the president. One member from Vermont, Rep. Peter Smith, actually used the occasion of a joint appearance with Bush to blast the president publicly for the budget deal. Another member, Rep. Alfred McCandless, requested from the White House a picture of the president to use in campaign literature. In addition to printed materials, McCandless used the picture as a prop in a TV commercial to make the point that he had stood up to the president on the tax issue. Bush's polling numbers declined and the GOP lost nine congressional seats in the midterm elections. The president thus had lost party seats in Congress in both his own election year and in the midterm elections.

For a president who prefers incremental leadership, the budget agreement made sense. It enabled Bush to solve the short-term problem of a lack of an agreement and the immediate need to calm financial markets. For Bush, taking a politically pleasing stand and allowing automatic spending cuts without a budget agreement would have been irresponsible leadership. For an incrementalist, the lack of core ideological tenets and the desire to solve problems as they arise means that it is acceptable to alter a policy in response to changing circumstances. For nearly two years, a policy of no tax increases had suited Bush fine. However, when economic circumstances changed and deficit reduction was immediately needed, his advisers said agreeing to a tax increase made sense to Bush.

The president did not help his own case. He failed to communicate effectively to the public that circumstances had changed since 1988, that he could no longer act unilaterally on budgetary policy but instead had to achieve the politically feasible while working with an opposition-led Congress. Under the circumstances, he could plausibly have argued that the tax increase was a necessity. Yet Bush never appeared to make the case for his actions. Then, during his daily jog on October 11, the president responded to a query about the budget deal by pointing to his backside and yelling, "Read my hips!" The embarrassing photograph, along with a caption explaining Bush's dismissive retort, appeared on newspaper front pages across the country and reminded people again of his unpopular breaking of the tax pledge. The Gallup poll showed that only 29 percent of the public approved of Bush's handling of the economy.[66]

With victory in the Gulf War, Bush had won renewed political capital, despite negative perceptions of the domestic economy. Many of his aides urged him to use his enormous popularity to launch a "domestic desert storm"—an aggressive conservative agenda at home. Bush, however, did not perceive the need for such action. His preference was to respond to immediate needs and not embark on a series of domestic policy reforms. The president and many of his advisers were convinced that he needed to do little at home to sustain his political support.

Yet there were signs of potential trouble on the horizon. The declining state of the economy throughout 1991 precipitated a steady drop in Bush's public support as more and more people became disgruntled with the lack of economic policy initiatives from the White House. Although the president believed that a go-slow approach to the economy was best, the public perceived Bush as indifferent to the suffering caused by the recession. Many felt that he was more interested in international affairs than in taking care of troubles at home.

Bush lost credibility with much of the public over his handling of the proposed revisions to the Civil Rights Act. Congressional Democrats, with the support of moderate Republicans, pushed for the civil rights legislation despite the president's objections that their proposal was a "quota bill." Bush was referring to provisions that would have allowed the use of statistical data to prove discrimination in employment—a practice that would, he argued, force employers to hire on the basis of racial quotas.

The use of the heated term "quota" created a divisive atmosphere and led many critics to suggest that the president was exploiting racial tensions for political gain.[67] After two years of objecting to congressional proposals, Bush finally signed a revised bill in October, 1991. What perplexed everyone was the fact that the legislation the president signed still contained the provisions to which he had expressed such strong opposition. His response to critics was that the revised legislation was no longer a "quota bill" because it had overcome his earlier objections. As the *New York Times* accurately put it: "after insisting for two years that the measure was a 'quota bill,' Mr. Bush suddenly discovered that a new draft, barely distinguishable from the old ones, was not a quota bill. His instant revision of history fooled nobody."[68]

In some respects, Bush's response to the civil rights issue was similar to that of the budget deal: He tried to promote his own goals, yet he preferred the adoption of an imperfect bill over no legislation at all. In both cases, he found that the opposition party in Congress—as well as some defecting Republicans—held sway and he decided to compromise after it became clear that he could not get what he wanted.

For Bush, such a pragmatic approach served his interests and those of the country far better than embarking on a losing ideological crusade. The downside was that Bush's pragmatism made it appear that he lacked core convictions and emboldened the opposition-party-led Congress to challenge him at every turn.

Events in 1991 may have been what tipped Bush's hand in favor of compromise on civil rights legislation. The Louisiana GOP had nominated an ex-Klansman for governor, fueling enormous negative coverage of the national state of race relations. In this more heated climate, Bush may have wanted to rise above the tensions by adopting a conciliatory position on civil rights.

Furthermore, Bush had taken a beating when he nominated Clarence Thomas for the U.S. Supreme Court. What especially bothered many was that the president had chosen Thomas, a forty-three-year-old ideological conservative who lacked a distinguished judicial or scholarly background, to replace the retiring Justice Thurgood Marshall, the man who stood as the strongest symbol of American judicial commitment to civil rights. Some suggested that Bush's selection of Thomas was cynical because liberals allegedly would have enormous political difficulties making the case against a black appointee to replace Marshall. No one thought Bush's claim credible when he said that he chose Thomas because the young jurist was the most qualified candidate for the Supreme Court. David Broder called the Thomas selection Bush's "new front in the 'quota' war."[69]

When Prof. Anita Hill, a former subordinate of Thomas's at the Equal Employment Opportunity Commission, stepped forward during the nomination hearings to accuse him of sexual harassment, the nomination process turned into an ugly political battle. Without specific facts about what had transpired between Thomas and Hill in the past, ideological conservatives and liberals took opposing stands, using the nominee and accuser as vehicles to promote political agendas.

The White House adopted a confirmation strategy that called attention to Thomas's personal triumphs against poverty and racism. That strategy turned public opinion in Thomas's favor and probably saved his confirmation by the Senate. Civil rights leaders who already had opposed Thomas's confirmation became especially angry at what they perceived as Bush's crass use of a racial appeal to save the nomination.

Some observers suggested that Bush was responsible for the increasingly disturbing racial climate that attended Thomas's selection and controversial confirmation.[70] That Bush reversed his course on the Civil Rights Act soon after the Thomas confirmation did not appear to be strictly coincidental.

Bush's political fortunes also suffered in November, 1991, when his former attorney general, Richard Thornburgh, lost a special election for a Pennsylvania Senate seat to a political neophyte, Democrat Harrison Wofford. During the campaign, Thornburgh stressed his Washington experience and close relationship with the president. Bush, meanwhile, actively campaigned for his former attorney general. Underdog candidate Wofford also emphasized Thornburgh's Washington experience and close relationship with the president and made domestic issues—especially health care—the centerpiece of his campaign.

Time magazine called Wofford's election a "wake-up call" to Bush to start moving aggressively on domestic policy.[71] The *Wall Street Journal* implored the president to start taking action on the domestic economy. "Bush can't stand above this debate without becoming another Dick Thornburgh," the *Journal* presciently editorialized.[72]

CAMPAIGN POLITICS AND INCREMENTAL LEADERSHIP

Bush's enormous popularity in early to mid-1991 persuaded many leading Democrats not to challenge him in 1992. Such major figures as Mario Cuomo, Bill Bradley, Jay Rockefeller, Sam Nunn, Albert Gore Jr., and Richard Gephardt declined to run. Six months before the opening of the Democratic nomination contest, only former senator Paul Tsongas had officially declared his candidacy. The other candidates who were late to enter the fray were Virginia governor L. Douglas Wilder, Arkansas governor Bill Clinton, former California governor Jerry Brown, and Sens. Bob Kerrey and Tom Harkin. At the time they announced their candidacies, none of these challengers was considered to be a man of sufficient national stature capable of seriously threatening Bush's reelection. However, by the end of 1991, polls showed that Bush had become electorally vulnerable. His popularity drop was the largest ever recorded, from nearly 90 percent in March, 1991, to only 47 percent in December of that year.[73]

The dramatic drop in the polls reflected the public's discontent with Bush's handling of the domestic economy. People had grown anxious about the nation's economic condition and demanded presidential action. Many remained convinced that the president cared more about foreign policy than problems at home.

For Bush, this public sentiment posed an immediate dilemma in 1992, an election year. He had earlier scheduled a January trip to Australia and the Far East and some of his advisers were imploring him to cancel his travel plans in light of public sentiments. The president refused to back out of a commitment and then, in response to public concerns, said that the trip abroad was really about "jobs, jobs, jobs." To make matters worse politically, he invited eighteen corporate CEOs—whose previous year's salaries averaged $3.1 million—to travel with him at taxpayer expense. Press accounts portrayed that aspect of the trip as a symbol of the weakening U.S. economy: the country's leading businesspeople allegedly groveling for jobs from the Japanese.[74]

The president's trip became an even worse public relations fiasco when he vomited and then fainted during a state dinner with the Japanese prime minister in Tokyo. Although film footage of the president becoming suddenly ill—repeatedly shown on network television for several days—

looked disturbing enough, he had merely contracted gastroenteritis. *Time* referred to the scene of the Japanese prime minister cradling Bush as "an obvious metaphor for the American economy: flat on its back, seeking succor from a resurgent Japan." Bush's illness "reminded voters that Dan Quayle remains only a heartbeat away from the Oval Office." The bottom line was, "he should have stayed home."[75] *Newsweek* compared the imagery of the event to that of former president Jimmy Carter nearly passing out while jogging at Camp David in 1979: "That grisly picture became a metaphor for a failed presidency."[76] Yet, buried in the *Newsweek* account—replete with a photo sequence of the president fainting—was this statement: "the president actually accomplished more than the American press gave him credit for."[77]

In an effort to create the image of a president ready to concentrate on domestic concerns, White House strategists said that the January 28 State of the Union Address would be the "defining moment" of the Bush presidency. They established high expectations that the president would finally propose a bold domestic agenda and quash the charge that he lacked vision at home.

What the president proposed remained consistent with his incrementalist approach to domestic issues: some budget cuts, several tax incentives, a reduction in the capital gains tax rate, among others. The conservative *Wall Street Journal* characterized Bush's economic initiatives as "too timid for our tastes." The *Journal* demanded more "dramatic" action from Bush "to liberate the American economy."[78] The *New York Times* observed that despite promises of bold action, Bush's proposals showed that he remained a "tinkerer."[79] The *Washington Post* agreed that Bush had "outlined a dressed-up, standstill program of more of the same."[80] Many others agreed, opining that Bush was a "one-step-at-a-time man," "a man who is eminently comfortable with the status quo," in short, a man who lacked an economic policy.[81]

More devastating than the criticism that he was a status quo president was the characterization of Bush as a man out of touch with the lives of ordinary Americans. An erroneous news report in February, 1992, bolstered this negative image. The *New York Times* published a pool report account of Bush marveling at the technology of a supermarket electronic price scanner during a National Grocers Association convention.[82] A typical reaction came from columnist Jonathan Yardley: "The man who runs the United States of America . . . [is] so out of touch with the daily lives of his constituents, he doesn't even know how they go about buying the food that they put on their tables."[83] The trouble was, the report was inaccurate, yet it comported so well with the presidential image that the national media continued to feature it, oftentimes in mocking fashion. To this day, analyses of the Bush presidency report the story as evidence of the man having lost touch with the people.[84]

Bush's appearance highlighted another problem that he would face in the 1992 campaign. Just thirteen months after the Persian Gulf War victory, Bush's appearance before the group was preceded by a slick video portrayal of the triumph. Nobody applauded. The presidential afterglow from the triumph had worn off and opinion polls confirmed that Bush's leadership in the Persian Gulf War would not reap electoral rewards. High-profile congressional hearings raised the question of whether Bush's prewar policies toward Iraq had actually contributed to the onset of the conflict, further diminishing public esteem for the president's leadership.

An internal GOP challenge for the presidential nomination also precipitated Bush's declining political fortunes. Conservative commentator Patrick Buchanan launched a long-shot campaign to deny an incumbent president renomination and no one gave him any chance to win. But grassroots conservative support for Buchanan's candidacy showed that Bush was no longer strong even among much of the base GOP vote.

Because of his pragmatism and past moderation on environmental, social, and civil rights issues, Bush always had a difficult relationship with the conservative wing of his party, much of which never considered him a "true conservative." Grassroots conservatives were disgruntled with his breaking of the no-new-taxes pledge; the Americans With Disabilities Act, which they viewed as intrusive government; and a number of smaller presidential decisions, such as the one to allow representatives of two gay-rights organizations to attend the White House ceremonial signing of the Hate Crimes Act. Bush fired Doug Wead, the White House liaison to the conservative community, when Wead openly complained of the White House invitations to gay-rights advocates. As James Ceaser and Andrew Busch wrote: "To liberals it was the 'Reagan-Bush administration'; to conservatives it was the Reagan and *then* the Bush administration."[85]

But Buchanan's candidacy represented more than just a vehicle for disgruntled conservatives to express their disapproval of Bush's actions as president. His candidacy also provided an outlet for voters who wanted to "send a message" to the president that he was not paying enough attention to the economy and other domestic concerns.

To many observers, Bush's initial response to Buchanan's candidacy was perplexing. Bush appeared merely to go about the business of the presidency without paying the commentator much attention. It was not until Buchanan fared "better than expected" in the first primary held in New Hampshire that the Bush campaign began to take the challenge seriously.

In part due to low expectations and in part due to poor reporting and analysis, Buchanan came out of the New Hampshire primary as a force to be reckoned with. Initial reports of the primary results suggested that Buchanan would break 40 percent of the vote against Bush, and possibly come close to winning the contest. Postprimary headlines and news stories marveled at the commentator's "impressive" showing. Many portrayed the New Hampshire result as a thorough repudiation of Bush's economic leadership and said that voters had sent the president a "message."[86]

The trouble was, Buchanan did not fare so well in the primary. When the official results were tallied, he had achieved only 37 percent of the vote—a trouncing by any reasonable standard. Nonetheless, the primary gave his candidacy considerable media momentum and Bush could not afford to ignore the challenge.

Bush responded to the challenge by drawing attention through campaign ads to some of Buchanan's controversial issue positions, such as opposition to the Persian Gulf War, and past statements, and by trying to mend fences with movement conservatives. The former strategy made perfect sense given Buchanan's many colorful statements and often-extreme positions on issues.

The latter strategy made less sense because it made the president appear to be letting a media commentator define his message. By adopting more stridently conservative rhetoric, Bush may somewhat have repaired his standing with the base conservative vote but he ultimately harmed his stature with the broader electorate. He began to focus more openly on conservative social themes and, in direct response to the Buchanan challenge, fired National Endowment for the Arts director John Frohnmayer, a social moderate who had drawn the ire of movement conservatives for refusing to back censorship of "obscene" art. For his sudden moves to the right, Bush earned the *New York Times*'s label "President Noodle." *Newsweek* reported that "it isn't true, as the critics claim, that George Bush stands for nothing: he seems to stand for whatever Patrick Buchanan wants him to."[87]

As expected, Bush prevailed over his opponent in a sequence of primaries and by mid-March it was clear that the Democrats would nominate Clinton. Neither major party nominee excited the electorate and *U.S. News* characterized the match up this way: "Which represents the greater danger—Bush's directionless status quo or Clinton's suspect character and amorphous agenda?"[88]

Bush conducted what undoubtedly will be remembered as one of the most lackluster, if not *the* most lackluster, presidential campaign in modern history. He delayed seriously campaigning until after Labor Day, allowing the Clinton camp to establish the issues and themes for the election. His lackluster campaign was reinforced by a noninterventionist response to what appeared to be a worsening economy.

Bush's natural inclination as an incrementalist was to take a go-slow, wait-and-see response to the economy rather than to propose bold government action. Economic advisers who assured him he needed to do nothing because the recession would be short-lived bolstered this inclination. There was considerable debate within the Bush White House over whether the incremental approach was best, particularly in an election year in which the country had been growing increasingly anxious about the economy. At root, the public wanted the president to "do something."

Democrats successfully characterized Bush's inaction as crass indifference to the suffering of others. In retrospect, it is clearly debatable whether some stimulating fiscal policy would have improved the economy. A tax cut or an increase in government spending to prime the economy would have further bloated the federal deficit and most likely have caused more long-term damage. Economic reports soon after the 1992 elections and in early 1993 seemed to bolster the validity of Bush's cautious approach, but they were too late to help his campaign.

Many critics thought the president also responded too slowly to racial tensions and riots in Los Angeles in May. Such criticism reflected a preference for a more activist federal role than Bush was willing to support. He eventually backed federal assistance to riot-torn regions of the city, but many believed that his response was inadequate. That he waited until a week after the riots to visit the city and to address the nation on urban unrest fueled further criticism of his leadership.[89] Vice President Quayle wrote in his memoirs that the greater problem was the "confused" message coming from the White House: suggesting at one point that Democratic Great Society programs had created the conditions for the riots, suggesting the need for less government action; at another point defensively responding to critics that the administration had increased spending on social and economic programs designed to help the poor.[90]

By the end of June, the president's stature was so low that *Time* magazine featured a report titled "The Incredible Shrinking President." It pictured a serious-looking Vice President Quayle speaking behind a podium with a miniaturized Bush sitting on the vice president's shoulder and grinning. The news story suggested that Bush's stature was so low that "world peace and a cure for the common cold might not revive him."[91]

Bush tried a number of tacks to revive his campaign. He appointed his highly regarded secretary of state, James A. Baker III, to serve as campaign director, only to be criticized for putting election politics above foreign affairs.[92] The Bush campaign then tried to recast the president as an agent of fundamental change—a tack that completely lacked credibility given his incremental leadership approach.[93]

The GOP convention that convened in Houston on August 17 provided the president with possibly the best opportunity to revive his faltering campaign. It was not to be, as the Bush camp failed to sufficiently control the proceedings and the message of the convention was one of extreme conservatism not in keeping with Bush's moderate-conservatism.

The first evening of the convention was supposed to highlight former president Ronald Reagan's address. Yet the controversial decision to allow defeated candidate Buchanan to address the convention ruined chances for a positive display of the party. Although the Bush camp allowed the former candidate to speak only in return for an endorsement, it made the costly mistake of not clearing Buchanan's speech in advance.

Because of some longer than anticipated speeches, Buchanan's address was delivered during prime time; Reagan's came later. Buchanan declared that the country was in the throes of a cultural war, and the excessive tone of his rhetoric clearly offended many more moderate and independent voters than it mobilized disgruntled far-right voters for Bush.

A number of commentaries panned the convention as a "family values fest" characterized by attacks on the GOP opponents' allegedly less than wholesome lifestyles. Speeches by Rev. Pat Robertson, Marilyn Quayle, Dan Quayle, and Barbara Bush were singled out as being divisive and even mean-spirited.[94] George F. Will compared watching the proceedings to being stuck in slow traffic behind a smoke-belching bus with a bumper sticker screaming, "HAVE YOU HUGGED YOUR KIDS TODAY?"[95] Most commentaries also criticized the president's nomination acceptance speech as too negative, even shrill.[96]

Bush indeed was susceptible to the charge of running a negative campaign, as he had in 1988. He had a positive record of foreign policy accomplishment to tout, but campaign polls showed that voters did not care. Because of his minimalist domestic agenda, the president's promise to conduct an activist second term did not convince voters, for he did not articulate many specific policy goals.

In September, Bush tried once again to bolster his campaign with an address to the Economic Club of Detroit. Billed as an effort to clarify the president's economic vision for a second term, Bush offered to expand free-trade agreements to open markets for U.S. goods and to support health care and educational reform among other ideas. Yet the speech failed to satisfy expectations for an activist program for a second term. The *Washington Post* panned it as "just the same old stuff," while *U.S. News* concluded that the speech was nothing more than a political ploy to unsay the charge that Bush lacked a domestic agenda.[97]

The Bush camp ultimately seized upon Clinton's character flaws as its focal point for the campaign. Bush criticized his opponent's efforts as a young man to avoid military service during the Vietnam War and alleged that Clinton had organized anti-American demonstrations in London and Moscow in 1969. At several points in the campaign Bush resorted to name-calling. He characterized Albert Gore as "ozone man" and Clinton and Gore as "bozos." Bush also openly expressed disdain for independent presidential candidate H. Ross Perot.

As he had in the 1988 campaign, Bush chose to go negative rather than emphasize his minimalist domestic agenda. As noted earlier, such a strategy suits an incremental leader who must campaign in the face of expectations for activist, visionary leadership. For example, rather than respond substantively to criticism for choosing not to attend an international environmental conference, Bush turned his attention to Democratic vice-presidential nominee Albert Gore's allegedly extreme views on environmental issues and mocked Gore as a man who favored protecting spotted owls over promoting jobs.

In addition to continuing his go-slow approach to the domestic economy, Bush hurt his reelection chances by conducting a traditional-style campaign that failed to take advantage of new communications technologies. His preference for the status quo led him in part to reject advice that he make use of the emerging forms of communications that the Clinton camp used so effectively. While Bush ran an old-style campaign with whistle stops and speeches at airports and to large sympathetic crowds, the Clinton campaign effectively communicated with larger segments of the electorate through such devices as television talk shows, alternative television networks geared toward special audiences such as MTV, and use of the Internet.

After the Elections

Clinton handily won the election with 370 electoral votes (and 43 percent of the popular vote) to Bush's 168 electors (and 38 percent of the vote). Perot pulled 19 percent of the vote, but no electors. Bush's 38 percent showing was the poorest for any incumbent president since William Howard Taft.

The major factors in Bush's defeat were perceptions about the state of the economy, a terribly run and lackluster Bush campaign in contrast with a smoothly run Clinton campaign, the lack of a clear campaign theme in contrast to Clinton's clearly focused economic message, media coverage that tilted heavily toward Clinton, comments critical of Bush by the Iran-Contra special prosecutor the weekend before the election, and the presence of Perot, whose attacks on Bush bolstered Democratic charges.

New York Times exit polling data showed that Bush lost 30 percent of his 1988 base vote and that 27 percent of GOP voters deserted their presidential nominee. The largest defections were among moderate Republicans, undoubtedly due to the heavy emphasis by Bush and Quayle on socially conservative issues, dismay over the Houston convention "family values fest," and Clinton's claim to be a "new Democrat" who rejected liberal ideological responses to problems.

Postelection analyses suggested that Bush's legacy would be strong in foreign affairs but weak domestically. Many revisited the "two George Bushes" theme and pointed out the disconnect between the president's foreign affairs activism and domestic passivity.[98]

For an incrementalist, this alleged disconnect was not unusual. Presidential scholar Richard Rose has pointed out that "a guardian president wants to be more influential abroad than at home."[99] It is not inconsistent for a president with an incremental agenda at home to take an active role in protecting domestic interests abroad. A president who wishes to protect the domestic status quo will act forthrightly against threats from abroad and try to promote U.S. interests in an interdependent global economy. Domestic politics and budgetary shortfalls limited the president's choices at home, whereas he had much greater discretion to act internationally.

In the last weeks of the Bush administration after the election, the president engaged in a flurry of foreign policy activism. He committed U.S.

troops to Somalia, demonstrated greater commitment to combat Serbian aggression against Bosnians, signed off on START with Russia, and concluded negotiations on the North American Free Trade Agreement (NAFTA) with Canada and Mexico.

Bush's leadership approach both at home and abroad made sense for an incrementalist, but it fostered the perception that he cared more about international than domestic affairs. That perception was devastating to his quest for reelection. The following chapter examines the difficulties that Bush experienced with the public relations presidency and how his leadership approach undermined his media and public evaluations over time.

CHAPTER 3

THE PUBLIC PRESIDENCY OF GEORGE H. W. BUSH

GEORGE BUSH BECAME PRESIDENT after the conclusion of perhaps the most public relations driven presidency in U.S. history. Bush suffered the dual problem of having to establish his own identity while others contrasted his public presidency to that of his predecessor.

Although many expected Bush to follow the Reagan model of public leadership, it is clear that the Bush White House developed its own distinct strategies. Bush's approach was compatible with that of the incrementalist leader. Because he lacked a bold agenda, he saw no reason to employ grandiose rhetoric. In comparison to his predecessor, his rhetoric was spare and his use of public relations ploys limited. Because he preferred a limited, status quo agenda, he believed that it was necessary to use rhetoric to downplay expectations of what he could accomplish as president.

To understand the Bush approach, we conducted a number of interviews with White House staff members who worked on Bush's press relations, communications strategy, speech writing, and public liaison.[1] This chapter describes and analyzes the Bush presidency's press relations and public outreach strategy, including the effort to distinguish the president from his predecessor.

This chapter features two main sections. The first examines the different White House entities that communicated the president's activities and goals: the press office, the communications office, the speech-writing division, and the public liaison office. The second assesses the key factors to understanding the president's failures in communications and press relations: the leadership context, Bush's rhetorical style and approach, and the administration's agenda and legislative strategy.

The following makes it clear that although Bush suffered unfairly from the inevitable comparisons to his predecessor, his administration erred by downplaying the importance of the public presidency to achieving its policy objectives. Bush was correct to emphasize that he was not like

Reagan and that he should not have been compared so frequently to his predecessor. The Bush White House continually pushed the theme that its president was more "hands on" or better informed than Reagan and therefore did not need public relations promotion. Of course, this theme itself was a self-serving effort to make Bush look better in some ways than his predecessor. But Bush nonetheless dismissed many of the positive lessons from the Reagan years about presidential press relations, communications, and public outreach that could have helped to advance his policy goals.

In that respect, the Bush approach of claiming to focus on substance rather than style more resembled the Carter than the Reagan presidency. Like Carter, Bush believed that appearing well informed about issues and the policy process would serve his administration's ends far better than any public relations gimmickry.

Although there is merit to that belief, what would have best served the president was a political strategy that better linked public and press relations with the administration's policy agenda. A telling illustration of the problem is a White House memorandum from Press Secretary Marlin Fitzwater in August, 1991, urging that the Bush White House adopt some unifying slogan that could be linked with the administration's substantive policy agenda.[2] That should have been done at the outset of the Bush presidency rather than being debated over two and one-half years into the president's term. The suggestion never was adopted, but even if it had been the effort would have appeared contrived given that it would have commenced on the heels of a reelection campaign.

Bush was too eager to reject his predecessor's approach to the public presidency. In so doing, he rejected those aspects of the Reagan approach that could have served the Bush administration's own goals. Even an incrementalist needs to use the public presidency to achieve his limited objectives, to maintain public support, and, in Bush's case, to promote his prospects for reelection.

The White House Press Office

The focal point of White House outreach to the public is the press office. Its major responsibility is to respond to news media inquiries. Other responsibilities include holding daily press briefings, holding special briefings to announce new programs, preparing press releases on the president's activities, and making arrangements for members of the news media who cover and travel with the president.

Modern presidents have handled these duties differently. In the Nixon White House, the press office was tightly controlled and the press secretary, Ronald Ziegler, was not always fully informed of presidential activities and strategies. A great deal of distrust existed between the news media and the press office because the latter often appeared uninformed and therefore unable to facilitate the work of the reporters. The press secretary had limited access to the president and oftentimes was left out of deliberations over White House activities. During the Watergate scandal, Ziegler lost the press' confidence and the deputy press secretary, Gerald Warren, took over the briefings.

The Ford White House adopted a different approach so as to avoid the contentious press relations of the Nixon years. Ford's first appointment as press secretary was well-respected journalist Jerald F. ter Horst. It was a symbolic gesture to convey a more media-friendly White House. Ford emphasized his openness to the press and ensured that the press secretary had direct access to the Oval Office and was fully informed on policy decisions (although Ford violated that approach when he pardoned Nixon). When ter Horst resigned in protest of the Nixon pardon, Ford again appointed a journalist, Ron Nessen, to fill the slot.[3] As Ford's media coverage deteriorated, Nessen's relationship with reporters became contentious. Years later, Nessen admitted that he had been "overly defensive" of Ford and had unduly angered many reporters, but he still believed the media had treated his boss much too critically.[4]

President Carter also emphasized his openness to the press. There was little effort to control the media or dictate the terms of coverage.[5] Although Carter had a troubled relationship with the White House press corps, his press secretary, Jody Powell, was a fully informed presidential adviser who did an excellent job of responding to media inquiries and facilitating reporters' jobs. Yet journalists did not reward these efforts with favorable coverage. Indeed, their coverage of Carter was relentlessly harsh for nearly his entire term.

The Reagan White House reverted to the earlier approach of controlling the media and restricting the information flow. The press office worked closely with the Office of Communications and the Legislative Strategy Group to manage the flow of information from the White House and ensure that all officials spoke with a "single voice." Access to the president was limited and many reporters complained of being "spoon fed" the White House "spin" while being shut off from the real action. Nonetheless, the approach appeared to work for Reagan because many in the media uncritically reported his activities as presented by the White House. A formal study of Reagan's press relations blasted leading reporters for a nearly sycophantic coverage of the White House and claimed that the usually cynical modern press corps had been thoroughly manipulated by the president and his media-savvy advisers.[6]

Bush wanted to move away from the Reagan-era approach and open up the press office, provide access to reporters, and facilitate their work. In November, 1988, Bush asked Marlin Fitzwater to serve as presidential press secretary. Fitzwater accepted and wrote a memorandum to the president-elect suggesting the elements of a White House press strategy. As Fitzwater explained, "the idea was to grant maximum exposure to the press" and to approach press relations very differently from the Reagan presidency.

Many conservatives perceived any attempt to differentiate Bush from Reagan as an attempt to denigrate the Reagan legacy. Fitzwater responded that Bush never tried to denigrate Reagan by adopting a different press-relations strategy. The purpose instead was to develop a strategy that best suited George Bush's own style, strengths, and preferences. The press and public also had to accept that after eight years as vice president, despite all the criticism to the contrary, Bush was his own man.

Fitzwater had a good deal of experience learning the approach that would best suit Bush. He had served as Vice President Bush's press secretary during most of the Reagan years before becoming the presidential spokesperson in 1987. In 1985, Fitzwater and Bush agreed on an arrangement under which the vice president would grant a number of one-on-one interviews to leading reporters and columnists. Based on the assumption that Bush would run for president in 1988 and win, this strategy would enable him to establish a good rapport with journalists that would pay off when he became president. Bush participated in about seventy-five such interviews in 1985 and 1986. Fitzwater recalled that most of the stories characterized Bush as a weak vice president who was loyal to a fault to President Reagan. Yet he told Bush to keep doing the interviews because the long-term relationships with reporters eventually would pay off.

In his November, 1988, memorandum, Fitzwater recommended that the president-elect make use of his relationships with journalists by granting the press a great deal of access. "I knew that Bush was good at it one-on-one," he recalled. "He knew the media and he tended to practice a personal brand of leadership anyway."

The press secretary also recommended giving up the elaborate White House East Room press conferences in favor of less formal afternoon conversations with reporters in the White House briefing room. This approach had three advantages: (1) more effective communications with reporters that would give the president better quality feedback; (2) it provided an opportunity to showcase Bush's command of process and policies; (3) it contrasted Bush from Reagan both stylistically and substantively.

Fitzwater felt that this strategy worked well for Bush—at least for the first three years of the term. Bush maintained a good rapport with the journalists and, although "they were critical of him, there was never really a bitter edge to it at all."

Bush gave 280 press conferences during his four years in office, far more than Reagan had given during either of his terms. That once again showcased Bush's policy of openness with the press in contrast to the Reagan White House.

In part because of reporters' sensitivity to media manipulation after the eight years of Reagan's presidency, Bush gave less emphasis than his predecessor did to public relations stunts. There were events such as the president declaring his dislike of broccoli followed by the Broccoli Manufacturers of America dumping a semitruck full of their product on the lawn at the south end of the White House.[7] For the most part, however, Bush's strategy was to show that he was open to reporters' questions, knowledgeable of issues, and not enamored of public relations gimmickry.

Several of Bush's communications advisers said that the president's openness toward the press and friendly relations with reporters had failed to earn him any positive coverage—a conclusion bolstered by academic research.[8] Although, as Fitzwater said, there was not a "bitter edge" to Bush's relationship with the press, reporters were critical of the president's leadership nonetheless. Speechwriter Curt Smith noted that it disturbed Bush greatly that White House efforts to do what the press wanted did not help much to improve press coverage. Smith stated that Bush operated with a "code of honor": treat people decently and they will behave the same in return. Smith pointed out that, unfortunately for Bush, reporters have a different "code." That is, they are not supposed to be guided in their work by their personal feelings toward politicians. Many others iterated Smith's point, leaving the strong impression that despite his enormous experience in public life, Bush harbored a remarkably naïve view of the craft of journalism.

Fitzwater later recalled the difficulty that Bush sometimes had accepting how journalists did their jobs:

> Politicians oftentimes have trouble understanding that reporters are different. They're not politicians. The rules for them are different. The rules for journalists are completely their own. Nothing else applies.
>
> For example, if you do a favor for a congressman, you expect a favor in return. If you do a favor for a reporter, don't ever expect a favor in return. President Bush had that difficulty because he saw reporters in a personal light. . . . He put a lot of emphasis on personal relationships.
>
> I remember one case where a reporter wrote a very negative story about the president. Bush was surprised. "Why did he do that?" he said. "We had him over to the house, we had such a nice conversation, he came out for the hot dog fry."
>
> Dealing with reporters is like giving gifts to relatives. You do it because it's the right thing to do, not because you think you'll get something out of it.

Interviewees agreed that Bush both lacked his predecessor's media savvy and was more conscious of that lack than anyone. Bush naïvely believed that if he showed himself to be an informed, policy-minded president and treated reporters with professionalism, that he would earn their gratitude and good coverage in return. The interviewees told a number of stories of Bush becoming exasperated toward the end of his term at how reporters covered his administration and ultimately he became very bitter about the experience.

Although Bush himself expressed a clear preference for downplaying the public presidency, the White House press office was actively engaged in seeking positive coverage. Of course, the president certainly was not indifferent to his coverage, as evidenced by his open anger at the press by the end of his term.

The press office actively tracked Bush's coverage and developed strategies for promoting the president's message and his image. Some of the efforts were rather large-scale for a White House led by a president who at least publicly professed an almost indifference to how journalists covered him. In one such case, the press office developed a thirty-five-page booklet detailing Bush's first-year accomplishments and distributed some twenty thousand copies to various media.[9] Along with the report's release there were a number of public events at which leading members of the administration and even the president appeared to promote the first-year record.[10] The effort was elaborate but ultimately disappointing: journalists are not easily duped by such self-serving reports. Indeed, many of the sources the White House specifically reached out to were among the most critical of his first-year leadership.[11]

The Bush White House continued to produce end-of-year "accomplishments" reports. At one point, Bush personally urged Press Secretary Fitzwater to make an extra effort to get a favorable report into the hands of "some key political pundits (Broder et al)" and the president had the press office arrange "exclusive" interviews with various leading media people to discuss the administration's record.[12]

The White House Office of Communications

The Nixon White House established the White House Office of Communications (WHOC) to help the administration control the flow of information. Nixon perceived the office's role to be conveying the White House "spin" on events so as to work around what he perceived to be a hostile White House press corps.

While the press office existed to tend to the needs of White House reporters, the WHOC's purpose was to feed information about the administration to local media throughout the country. It provided editors and broadcasters outside the Washington community with copies of speeches, press releases, and other information; acted as the White House contact for radio stations, television networks, and independent stations; supervised public affairs activities in various federal agencies; and set up interviews between correspondents and federal officials.

Presumably the local media would be less critical of White House spin and thus more likely to convey the news in a way the president preferred. The WHOC orchestrated a "line of the day" so that White House officials would not contradict each other in public.

Under Director Kenneth Clawson's leadership, Nixon's WHOC took on a number of highly partisan activities and became a central resource in the White House's public relations response to the Watergate scandal. Among the partisan activities was a campaign orchestrating letters to the editor to make it appear that news consumers did not approve of negative editorial opinions. Administration officials using false names wrote some of the letters. Eventually, the WHOC became identified with the White House effort to cover up the Watergate scandal.

In keeping with his promise to conduct an "open presidency" and move away from Nixon-era practices, President Ford initially disbanded the WHOC and assigned its functions to the press office, which had many fewer employees and a smaller budget than in the Nixon White House.

The office's downscaled responsibilities included mailing White House information to newspapers, arranging speeches before groups by administration officials, and compiling a daily news summary for the president, as well as his briefing book for encounters with the media. The WHOC was eventually restored in the Ford White House and it played a crucial role in communicating the president's message to local media throughout the country.

Carter placed the Office of Communications under the press office. For about the first half of his term, there was little effort to communicate a "line of the day" or to enforce discipline among various administration officials not to contradict one another's statements in public. The public image consequently was one of confusion. Carter did, however, try to change course and pay more attention to communications by appointing political consultant Gerald Rafshoon to head the operation. Rafshoon attempted to help the administration better orchestrate its message and convey a more clear sense of policy direction. Unfortunately for Carter, the news media saw the ploy as superficial and labeled the various public relations techniques to present Carter in a more favorable light as "Rafshoonery." Carter disbanded the Office of Communications in August, 1979.

Reagan's Office of Communications in many ways resembled Nixon's in that it existed primarily to promote the White House spin on events and devoted enormous effort to orchestrating a "line of the day" and "theme of the week." Under David Gergen's leadership, many credited the WHOC with successfully controlling the content of the message coming out of the White House, ensuring that the administration spoke with "one voice," and consequently protected Reagan's reputation from the kind of media portrayals of internal chaos and confusion that were so damaging to the Carter presidency.

The effort must indeed have been successful, as the reality of the Reagan White House was one of almost unprecedented levels of infighting, turf battles, and endless conflict. Yet the message conveyed to the public was one of single-minded purposefulness and a high degree of coordination of goals and activities.

David Demarest served as Bush's WHOC director from January, 1989, until August, 1992. In the Bush administration, the WHOC's functions included speech writing, media relations, interest group outreach, and intergovernmental communications, whereas under Reagan it engaged primarily in long-term strategies to promote the White House spin on events.[13] According to Demarest, the Bush WHOC operated very differently from the Reagan administration's: "The Reagan White House worked at establishing a 'line of the day' and all operations were held hostage to the phrase of the day that the White House wanted that evening on the news. . . . Generally, the press resented that, considered it manipulative."

Demarest said that he wanted the WHOC to operate differently because many journalists had become tired of the Reagan-era practices and in part because he believed that such heavy-handed tactics were degrading to both the White House and the press corps. He added that it did not mean the Bush White House ignored the need "to emphasize certain themes . . . to advance our goals." Rather, "We felt that having a more open, two-way relationship with the press made better sense. We tried to normalize that relationship, make it more business-like and to place the onus on the press to decide what it was going to cover as the most important message or theme of the day."

The WHOC would advertise key events or presidential actions, but it did not limit media contact and visibility to those activities. Each day, the White House compiled a list of "news events" broken down into the categories of "major" events and "issues of the day." The daily lists indeed illustrate the lack of any effort to focus the message or limit the media to a single event in order to control coverage. Typical lists included four to six "major" daily news events and an equal number of issues, with no attempt to prioritize any of them.[14]

The bizarre result of such strategies was that journalists criticized the Bush White House for not being as skillful as Reagan's at controlling the message and manipulating journalists. *Washington Post* editor David Ignatius weighed in with an essay entitled "Press Corps to Bush: Manipulate Us."[15] Reporters actually complained about Bush's practices of openness, accessibility, minimizing public relations gimmickry, and avoiding what Reagan's people called "manipulation by inundation."

Demarest acknowledged that there was "a good deal of tension in the White House over this strategy." Some in the White House argued that the administration needed to do a better job of getting "the message out." Demarest disagreed:

> To me, there was always more than one issue that warranted presidential participation. And I wasn't willing to determine, if two important issues were being dealt with at a particular time, that we had to close the press off from one meeting so it could only cover another. That probably cost the president some of the appearance of focus because most of the media want things to be simplified. We were reluctant to do that.
>
> We were not afraid of access or criticism. We decided to have an open relationship with the press. . . . David Gergen spent half of his day spinning the networks. I never did that . . . I was much more comfortable having the president's words taken at face value. For me, or anyone else, to presume to tell people what the president *really* meant, struck me as arrogant.

Much of the impetus for this approach, of course, came from the president who, according to Demarest, "did not like to be stage-managed." The president did not worry a great deal about press coverage or improving his public relations because he was popular for most of the first three years of his term. Once the president's popularity began to slide in late 1991, panic set in at the White House. Many blamed the lack of focus and failure to communicate a message.

In a scathing book on the failures of the Bush presidency, Charles Kolb, assistant to the president for domestic policy, argued that the WHOC never linked presidential communications with the administration's policy agenda. By downplaying rhetoric and communications strategy, Kolb maintained, the White House undermined its own goals.[16]

Several of the speechwriters assessed that the Bush White House had gone so far to prove that it was not at all like Reagan's that Bush had failed to do such fundamental things as simplify a message to build public support for policies. Andrew Furgeson and Tony Snow, for example, said that the White House failed to give sufficient attention to the process of writing and editing speeches, much to the detriment of Bush's image. "And in all candor," Furgeson added, "I don't think that the president did." Snow described Bush's relations with the speech-writing division as "distant."

The Speech-Writing Division

President Nixon maintained a diverse speech-writing staff led by the moderate Ray Price and conservatives William Safire and Patrick

Buchanan. As Robert Denton and Gary Woodward note, this staffing allowed the president to rely upon the appropriate writer for a targeted message. For example, a speech that called for a tone of reconciliation and compassion best suited Price. A speech that required the president to offer sharp partisan prose suited either Safire or Buchanan. Some of the most memorable prose from the Nixon White House actually came from Vice Pres. Spiro Agnew's attacks on the news media, largely written by Safire, who later became a prominent journalist himself.[17]

President Ford placed considerable emphasis on speech writing. The writers had substantial access to the president, having met with him twice each week for one-hour sessions. He provided direct feedback on speech topics and made clear what he expected from the writers. He also gave a "door knock privilege" to the director of the division, meaning that the director was one of a limited number of persons who could meet the president in the Oval Office without a prior appointment. There were six full-time writers in the Ford White House and staffers from some of the other divisions also occasionally helped to write speeches.

Two major problems emerged nonetheless: first, because the speech-writing department was a nexus of considerable power in the White House, turf battles ensued and many staffers outside the division clamored for influence over the president's pronouncements. Second, Ford was not a very good speaker. All of the organizational support and talent within the speech-writing division could not overcome that overriding problem.

Carter's speech-writing division suffered a dual problem: the president placed little emphasis on the speech-writing process and he was a generally uninspiring speaker. Most of Carter's speechwriters complained they had little or no contact with the man whose words they were supposed to convey. They felt they had little direction from the president and inadequate feedback.

The head of the division, James Fallows, on many occasions has recounted how he and the other writers almost never saw the president, lacked any sense of Carter's sense of himself philosophically, and had almost no contact with the policy people in the White House. Consequently, the writers could not blend a presidential message with a clear set of policy goals to which the public could respond.[18]

The Reagan White House placed enormous emphasis on presidential speeches, with nine full-time writers and a large support staff. This approach suited Reagan's strength drawn from his earlier experience as an actor. The White House went to great lengths to coordinate speech-writing efforts with those of staff members responsible for devising and promoting policy. On many occasions, Reagan attempted to create direct public support—and hence support in Congress—for his initiatives through national addresses and frequent speeches. Although not always successful, the president's addresses were crucial to the favorable outcome in Congress of a number of high-priority proposals such as the votes on the economic recovery package in 1981. During that year, the president made eight major televised addresses to the nation, the most of any president in a single year.

A number of Bush's speechwriters commented that their operation, unlike Reagan's, did not have sufficient staffing and support. They cited a telling contrast: President Reagan gave about 180 speeches per year and had nine speechwriters, each with his or her own researcher. President Bush delivered from 360 to 400 speeches per year usually written by five speechwriters.

In addition to the smaller-sized staff, the Bush White House gave the speech-writing office a relatively small budget and the writers a mediocre salary. One speechwriter said that—unlike the Reagan White House—the Bush White House, under John Sununu's leadership, revoked dining privileges for the writers and did not always hire the best people for the speech-writing office. Some aides outside the speech-writing division confirmed this assessment. Boyden Gray lamented that Bush had stronger speechwriters when he was vice president in the Reagan White House. The weaker caliber of writers in the Bush White House harmed "his ability to communicate" his goals. Andrew Furgeson said that all of these slights—which another speechwriter, John Podhoretz, bitterly detailed in a book[19]—had sent "a strong signal": "This wasn't going to be like Reagan. We weren't going to be trying to sell the big speeches, we weren't going to be having the prime time speeches or going on TV all of the time. This president doesn't need to sell himself that way. He's more hands-on. We don't have to coddle him. We can let him out in front of the press on his own."

Many people in the White House vetted speech drafts. A typical Bush speech draft was distributed for comment among a large number of policy people, communications staff, the White House counsel's office, and ultimately the president himself. If many of Bush's speeches had the markings of having been crafted by committee, it is because they often were. Many of the speechwriters felt powerless as they longed for a process with less input from others so that the president's speeches could better flow and have the intended emotional effect.[20]

Although several of the speechwriters said that they felt the White House had somewhat denigrated their operation, for the most part they had little else critical to say of Sununu's leadership. They leveled their strongest criticisms at White House staffers who openly denigrated Reagan's legacy and bragged that someday historians would judge the Reagan years as merely having set the stage for "the Bush era." Many criticized the leadership of Sununu's replacement, Sam Skinner, and attributed to him much of the negative image of the Bush White House in 1992 as disorganized and lacking a coherent strategy to move forward an agenda. According to Demarest, "we suffered chaotic paralysis the six months that he was chief of staff. Nothing got done." Although many of Bush's aides lamented an overly harsh election-year media, several said that the chaotic and disorganized image of the White House under Skinner's leadership dovetailed with reality.

The speechwriters maintained that there was little coordination of White House activities with the speech-writing operation during the 1992 campaign. A part of the difficulty was the fact that Bush generally gave the same speech everywhere he went on the campaign trail. The White House consequently paid little heed to the speech-writing office.

The Office of Public Liaison

The Ford White House created the Office of Public Liaison (OPL). William Baroody was its first director and his mandate was to use the office to reach out to various interest groups and form a communications link between those groups and the administration. The OPL staff arranged town meetings throughout the country to solicit ideas from various constituencies and develop a sense of what people thought about the administration's actions. Ford spoke at many of the regional meetings. The staff also organized meetings with interest groups in the Old Executive Office Building. Unlike Charles Colson's operation (under a different title) in the Nixon White House, the goal was to foster positive communications rather than build grassroots support for the president's programs and reelection quest.

Carter's OPL operated differently in that it emphasized creating coalitions in support of the president's programs. Director Midge Costanza and her successor, Anne Wexler, were responsible for bringing groups to the White House to hear briefings on the president's agenda and then use those meetings to build grassroots support. In that sense, the operation was somewhat similar in function to Colson's operation, except it did not exist as an arm of the president's reelection apparatus. Carter appointed a number of senior aides with the title of special assistant to the president, each responsible for focusing on a particular constituency (for example, blacks, women, Hispanics, the elderly, Jews, labor, consumer advocates, and so forth).

The Reagan OPL also took on an overtly political cast as it built support for the president's programs by encouraging grassroots coalitions. The office not only brought groups into the executive branch for meetings and organized regional meetings throughout the country, it also pressured groups to lobby for important administration programs as a price for the president's support for other initiatives. On several occasions, the OPL successfully organized mass mailing and telephone campaigns to pressure members of Congress to support the president's initiatives. At its height, the Reagan OPL had fifty-six staffers and ten commissioned officers, or senior staff members. Under Reagan, the office focused its efforts on conservative groups that shared the president's philosophy and were willing to build grassroots support for his programs.

President Bush's deputy assistant for Public Liaison, Bobbie Kilberg, said that Reagan's approach offered "a very legitimate and valid view of what the Office of Public Liaison should do. It was not George Bush's view." The Bush operation was closer in philosophy to the Ford approach in that the president did not use the office so overtly to serve the administration's political ends. Bush insisted that a wide variety of interest groups should be invited to the White House to express their views and participate in influencing policy development. This approach reflected his conviction that the divisive approach of the Reagan era should be ended and that groups perceive the White House as inclusive and open to different points of view.

This approach also had a political motivation: once a variety of groups had been given an opportunity to openly express themselves and participate in a meaningful way in the formulation of policy, they would then be more likely to support the administration's initiatives. Or, even if opposition groups did not become sympathetic to the president's initiatives, perhaps they would be less fervent in their opposition if they were listened to, somewhat accommodated, and treated respectfully. Whereas the Reagan approach encouraged ideological groups to stridently oppose one another—a tactic that was effective at mobilizing grassroots conservative support—Bush wanted to try to accommodate different sides.

Bush's low interest in using the OPL to mobilize groups was reflected in the way he staffed it. The full-time staff went from fifty-six under Reagan to thirteen under Bush (including two detailed from other offices). The Bush OPL had, in Kilberg's words, "virtually no support staff." She noted that the office was forced to rely heavily on college interns to get its work done.

Because of a White House regulation that subjected any staffer hired for more than three months to a full background investigation—at a cost of $8,000—about eight interns were rotated through the OPL every quarter. The chronic understaffing meant college interns often were responsible for organizing and scheduling events, as well as escorting interest-group representatives to the Oval Office. Staffers and interns worked unreasonably long hours to complete the necessary tasks.

Regular staff members received poor salaries, which also reflected the president's priorities. Consequently, the average age of staff members was twenty-five. Kilberg commented, "I had twenty-five-year-olds dealing with Roger Smith from GM [General Motors] and every other CEO in the world, and the head of the National Women's Political Caucus, and the head of Concerned Women of America, and Phyllis Schlafly, and Ralph Nader on the left, and religious conservatives on the right."

Like the speechwriters, OPL staffers also were denied access to the White House dining room and given poor office space. Although seemingly trivial, Kilberg said such decisions mattered:

> The White House mess is the best place to eat in town, in the sense of prestige. And if you have somebody that is dealing with CEOs and he says, "Come on, let's go out to McDonald's," it makes a very different image than if you can take him into the White House mess and talk to him about issues of importance to the president. We had very small office space. And again, when you have the head of a major women's organization or the head of the NAACP sitting in an office with a [low-level] staff member . . . [who] has an office about the size of two leaves of this table, that makes an impact, too.

Kilberg served in OPL from the beginning of Bush's term until April 4, 1992. She noted that during that period the OPL sponsored 605 events with the president and additionally held from sixty to a hundred briefings and meetings without the president each month. The office was not geared up to exploit new communications technology. The telephones were from the Ford era and could not even handle conference calls. The office had two small fax machines with limited sending ability and the staffers' computers could not "talk" to one another. The White House did not begin to update the communications technology until 1992—too late for the administration to use it for exploiting the news media during the election.

Bush's treatment of the OPL reflected his more general desire to downsize the White House. Much like in the Carter White House, many staffers believed that their own entities had to bear too much of the brunt of downsizing and that their effectiveness was therefore hampered. However, compared to the sophisticated communications technology used in the White House today, the Bush operation truly appears to be from another era altogether.

By placing the OPL under the Office of Communications, Bush signaled his intention that it be both a part of the White House communications apparatus and a part of the policy-making process, "feeding information in from the outside groups, and helping sell the communication process back out when a decision was made," Kilberg explained. Bush believed that this open communication process with the interest groups improved policy making. Unlike Reagan, however, "Bush prided himself on hearing from people who disagreed with him because he thought he could learn something from that process. It was a very active interchange." She cited the Clean Air Act's reauthorization in 1989 as an example. The president invited representatives from various business, consumer, and environmental groups to voice their concerns, resulting in an administration approach that reflected some of the preferences of the different interests. She noted that in response to issues raised by environmentalists, the president directed the staff to make changes in the administration proposal. This reflected his very different approach from Reagan, who rarely would take so seriously the views of those who disagreed with the administration.

To avoid the common pitfall of staffers being "captured" by the groups they dealt with, Bush organized the OPL staff around functions instead of specific interest groups. What Bush tried to achieve did not work in practice. As Kilberg described it, she worked with the Jewish organizations, the Hispanic staffer dealt with issues of concern to the Hispanic community, the African-American staffer handled issues affecting the African-American community, women's groups insisted on dealing with the female staffer they considered most sympathetic to their cause, and so forth.

Bush's use of the OPL initially reflected his intention that the administration work with members of Congress rather than try to pressure them to support his programs through grassroots lobbying. During the first year, Bush insisted that staffers not use the office to put pressure on members of Congress, believing that he could instead persuade individual members. What Bush eventually found out was similar to the difficult lesson he learned about the press corps: he could deal directly and openly with members rather than combatively, and they would still criticize him or oppose his policies. Bush changed his approach after the first year and allowed the OPL to do some direct lobbying of interest groups in order to generate support for programs.

Bush's policy of openness backfired in another way: By opening the White House to groups critical of the administration, he gave them greater credibility and visibility. Kilberg lamented that representatives of groups often would meet with the president, then turn around and meet with the news media outside the West Wing and criticize the administration. White House meetings consequently become a vehicle through which groups could communicate more broadly their grievances with administration policy.

Communicating through the Press, Bush Style

It is always difficult to try to isolate a single cause of a president's difficulties communicating through the media. According to Bush's communications advisers, several factors were key to understanding the difficulties the president experienced with his press relations. They included (1) the leadership context, (2) Bush's approach to the rhetorical presidency, and (3) the administration's agenda and legislative strategy.

CONTEXT

George Bush's rise to the presidency as the heir to the Reagan legacy profoundly shaped his press relations and strategy. Indeed, Bush ran for president in 1988 pledging continuity with his predecessor's policies. However, those who evaluated Bush's performance as president also expected him to demonstrate that he was his own man and not a Reagan carbon copy. At the same time, they constantly compared Bush to Reagan. According to David Demarest: "We were in a kind of conundrum early on, because whatever we did was compared to Reagan. The press wouldn't just let us be ourselves. And by just trying to be ourselves, the media portrayed that as our making an implicit criticism of Reagan."

Several press officers and speechwriters recalled the frustrations of that dilemma. As vice president, Bush could not escape the press' portrayal of him as loyal to a fault to President Reagan. When Bush tried to define himself as president, many said that he had chosen to denigrate Reagan.

Some of the speechwriters said that certain Bush White House staffers thought that they could best help their president by denigrating Reagan. Such efforts fueled news stories accusing Bush of trying to establish himself by implicitly criticizing Reagan. Even former president Richard Nixon temporarily abandoned his public isolation to weigh in and criticize the Bush White House for treating Reagan's legacy with disrespect.

To be sure, journalists perhaps had good reason to suspect that Bush would follow stylistically in Reagan's footsteps, at least initially. Not only had Bush loyally followed the Reagan game plan for eight years, his 1988 campaign was carefully scripted and packaged, Reagan-style. Bush's approach did not change until after the election, when he went out of his way to open the White House to former political foes and to speak graciously of Democratic leaders. Journalists interpreted many of these efforts to heal the wounds of a hard-fought campaign as conscious attempts to show that Bush would not emulate the partisanship that characterized the Reagan years. They subsequently portrayed Bush as being implicitly critical of his predecessor's leadership.

Conservative Reaganites in the Bush White House agreed that the president had gone too far to differentiate himself from his predecessor. Tony Snow joined the Bush White House in March, 1991, to direct the speechwriting operation. A conservative editorial writer for the *Washington Times*, Snow was convinced when he joined the White House that Bush had erred by misreading the mandate of 1988 and trying too hard not to be Reagan. "There was a deliberate decision right from the beginning to differentiate Bush politically from Reagan," Snow recalled. "The whole 'kinder, gentler' rhetoric was in part a response to the press portrayal of the 1980s as the 'decade of greed.' Bush did not want to appear greedy, cold-hearted, or, whatever."

Much of the impetus for the criticism of Bush was his inaugural address, which many took as being directly critical of Reagan's policies and the so-called decade of greed. In it, Bush asked, "are we enthralled with material things, less appreciative of the nobility of work and sacrifice?" Many thought that Bush's two-sentence inaugural tribute to Reagan was conspicuously brief and inadequate. Conservatives protested when Reagan's portrait was removed from the Bush White House while the portraits of Gerald Ford and Jimmy Carter remained. Some suggested that it was evidence Bush had gone too far in his attempt to show that he was not Reagan.

Former Reagan and Bush speechwriter Peggy Noonan, who crafted the "kinder, gentler" language, wrote after the 1992 election that Bush had made the mistake of believing that "the American people voted for *him* in 1988. They didn't. They voted for the continuation of basic Reaganesque policies." She attributed Bush's loss to the disconnect between what people expected him to be—Reaganlike—and who he actually was.[21]

Demarest maintained that the Bush White House communications strategy reflected the fact that the 1988 election was a referendum for continuity over change. Reagan's administration established elaborate procedures for getting its own message out to the public, such as generating a "line of the day" and constantly feeding it to the media. Because Reagan's 1980 election was about change, his administration needed to adopt such procedures to alter the dialogue coming out of Washington. For Bush, Demarest argued, there was no need for such "media manipulation" because the context had changed; the president was seeking to achieve continuity—with marginal revisions—with the Reagan years.

During the Bush years, critics often charged that the president purposefully escaped complex domestic issues to focus on his real priority: foreign policy. Many in the Bush White House acknowledged this criticism and retorted that the nature of the times had the most to do with Bush's emphasis on world affairs. Dan McGroarty, the deputy director of speech writing, said that "the circumstances of the times" dictated Bush's priorities. "Put yourself back to the events of 1989. With everything going on in the world, we put our emphasis where it belonged."

By the time of the 1992 election, much of the political context had changed significantly. The 1988 election may have been about continuity, but in 1992, "change" was the leading theme in election discourse. What many people found incredible was that Bush, in response to this context, tried to position himself as the "agent of change." As Snow and others pointed out, however, by 1992 "the White House simply had not responded to the changing mood of the electorate" in any substantive way.

Snow went so far as to suggest that the Bush White House, in response to the public's preference for change, put forth a number of domestic policy initiatives in 1992 merely to politically rebut the charge that Bush lacked an agenda. "In part," Snow observed, "the Bush White House was insincere. They went through the motions in 1992 to make it appear that they had an agenda. They put forth a health care plan that they had no intention of promoting. They talked some about Congress, but they never really took on Congress. People saw that Bush could not offer a distinct agenda that they could watch and evaluate over time. As a result, the public said, 'forget it. If you don't know what you want to do, we'll take our chances on someone who does. We'll take this Clinton guy. We may not completely trust him, but at least he has given us an idea of what he wants to do.'"

Others, including James Pinkerton, the special assistant to the president for domestic policy, confirmed this assessment. Pinkerton also questioned the genuineness of those in the White House who claimed that they were promoting an activist domestic agenda. He wrote that whenever Bush initiated a new domestic proposal, aides would tell reporters that the purpose was merely to rebut the charge of doing nothing. The original idea of the Bush presidency, he added, was the notion that it could succeed without any new ideas.[22]

The most common assessment was that while the context may have changed by 1992, Bush remained the same. What he had to offer, according to polling data, did not fit the electoral mood of 1992.

Almost every person interviewed for this study said that the various news media in 1992 were "a part of the agenda for change," as Demarest put it. He speculated that reporters "had become bored covering the Republican White House for twelve years. They wanted a new story, new personalities." The Bush White House staff agreed that media coverage of the 1992 campaign tilted heavily to Clinton and made Bush's task of conveying a positive leadership image exceedingly difficult. Yet White House counsel C. Boyden Gray, although very critical of the media's performance, said that it was a failure of White House communications that allowed the negative portrayals of the administration to go unchallenged. He concluded that it was therefore reasonable for some to suggest that the 1992 Bush campaign did not deserve to win.[23]

In sum, the interviewees assessed that evaluations of Bush's actions must account for the leadership context. The Reagan legacy, dramatic world events, an economic downturn, and a reelection campaign were the central factors that established the context for the evaluations of the Bush presidency.

SYMBOLISM/RHETORIC

In February, 1989, President Bush held a luncheon meeting with the White House speechwriters to explain his rhetorical approach.[24] What he told the speechwriters is very revealing of how he perceived himself and of how he wanted others to understand him.

The president asked the writers to avoid "rhetorical overkill." Bush said that he did not want to sound like he was promising too much; he did not like lofty language ("Churchill's o.k., but not the really lofty stuff"); he wanted to avoid broad thematic addresses and preferred to detail the administration's accomplishments; furthermore, he said that he did not want to sound too "Rambo-like" or "macho."

Bush emphasized that speeches and quotations used in speeches "must fit me comfortably." That meant avoiding the use of "I" in favor of "we"; using self-deprecating humor and not humor at someone else's expense; keeping speeches short; and using sports and historical analogies that people would understand. He asked the writers not to dwell on his wartime experiences in speeches.

Foreshadowing the leadership approach that he would adopt as president, Bush told the writers to emphasize that foreign policy was "where the action is" whereas domestic programs "are constrained by resources." Regarding Congress, he said that he did not want to publicly attack the institution and the Democratic leadership, but preferred instead to emphasize that the administration "must approach them and work with them." Bush said that he would "take [his] shots at Congress" when necessary through the use of the veto or when he thought the legislature was "encroaching" on presidential power.

Bush's rhetorical style and modest use of the bully pulpit reflected these preferences. According to his speechwriters, Bush understood himself well and consequently knew that he could never live up to the Reagan standard when it came to public speaking. "[Bush] knew that he wasn't that good with the public speeches, that he wasn't Reagan," observed Mary Kate Cary. She recalled that Bush had once told the speechwriters: "You're all good writers and are all capable of giving me a speech that's a ten. But don't give me a ten because I can't give a ten speech. Give me an eight and maybe I'll make it come out a five."

Cary also recalled how Bush conveyed his limitations to the speechwriters. Bush, she said, told them about a trip he made with Reagan in 1988 to a campaign event. When an aide handed Reagan a speech that the president had not yet seen, Reagan leafed through the text once in the car and then later delivered the speech as though he had done so ten times before. Bush told his writers: "don't ever think that I can do that. I am not Ronald Reagan." Bush established a rule requiring that his speeches be submitted forty-eight hours in advance of an event so he would have sufficient time to make changes, practice, and commit passages to memory.

Bush's speeches not only were uninspiring, he frequently spoke in incomplete sentences and occasionally committed a memorable gaffe. Some of Bush's phrases became fodder for comedians who also enjoyed mocking his awkward gestures. One of his better-known phrases was to describe trouble as "deep doo-doo." He named the spotted owl "that little furry feathery guy" and in a tribute to the Nitty Gritty Dirt Band called it the "Nitty Ditty–Nitty Gritty Great Bird."[25] When asked if he planned to replace Vice President Quayle on the 1992 GOP ticket, he responded, "do you want that by hand or do you want that by word?" In 1992 he taunted Democratic vice-presidential nominee Al Gore with the label "ozone man" and said: "this guy's crazy. He's way out, far out. Far out, man."[26]

Several speechwriters recalled the trouble that Bush had with syntax and his misuse of pronouns. Those habits also made the usually colorless president fodder for comedic imitators. Peggy Noonan explained how she dealt with Bush's speaking style: "I became adept at pronoun-less sentences. Instead of, 'I moved to Texas and soon we joined the Republican Party.' it was, "Moved to Texas, joined the Republican Party, raised a family.'"[27]

What perplexed many close to the president was the fact that he had such a strong command of the substance of policies. No one could accuse him—as many did Reagan—of having a disengaged mind. If the president could speak in great detail about policy issues, why could he not master the political rhetoric necessary to promote his agenda?

Curt Smith explained that Bush cared much more about other, more substantive presidential tasks than rhetoric and presentational style:

> I think that he saw the rhetorical aspect of the presidency as just one investment of his job. . . . He did not consider it as ubiquitous and all-encompassing as Reagan did. . . . [Bush] did not feel as comfortable as Reagan at giving the tour-de-force, stem-winding speech. But then again, who could compare to Reagan?
>
> Bush once said, "I'm not Ronald Reagan. I couldn't be if I wanted to." So he understood himself very well.

Tony Snow agreed: "Bush didn't try to be Reagan. Bush was not a naturally gifted speaker." The president would agree to speech coaching from Roger Ailes maybe once or twice a year. The president "would be on 'good behavior' for a while and then he inevitably would lapse into 'Bush-speak.'"

"Bush was very conscious that he was following Reagan," Andy Furgeson added. "He would say, 'now Reagan would do that, but I can't.'" Bush simply did not have Reagan's flair for telling good stories that illustrated broad themes with attention-grabbing anecdotes. "[Bush] was very suspect of any kind of sentimentality, high-flown rhetoric, big words, any kind of ideologically florid expressions. He was very uncomfortable with any kind of rhetorical extravagance."

None of this suggests that Bush was incapable of giving a good speech. Rather, Bush suffered from the inevitable comparison with his predecessor and had trouble downplaying expectations that better suited Reagan.

Bush nonetheless gave some strong speeches. His speechwriters identified those pertaining to the Persian Gulf War and a December 7, 1991, fiftieth anniversary remembrance at Pearl Harbor as particularly noteworthy.

Smith made the convincing point that the president delivered good speeches on subjects about which he felt strongly. In the case of the Persian Gulf War, for example, Bush had a keen sense of purpose about the use of the military and his convictions were clear. "The essence and moral fiber of George Bush really came out at that time." He did not need "high-flown" rhetoric and speech coaching to make those speeches work. The president wrote a good many of the speeches on subjects about which he felt most strongly. Several interviewees said that Bush was commanding and engaged when discussing foreign policy, but detached and uninspiring when discussing domestic issues.

Reagan had the gift of the actor. He understood role-playing. He therefore could make a convincing, emotional presentation on a topic about which he did not feel strongly, if he needed to do so. Bush lacked that ability. Nonetheless, Bush's speechwriters maintained that when he did feel real emotion about an issue, he could give a strong presentation, even, if not Reaganesque. Bush's Operation Desert Storm press briefings were "just spectacular. Everybody came away very impressed," according to Fitzwater. "During the war, his press briefings were incredible. They showed his ability to educate the people as to the purpose of the war and his knowledge of military issues at hand."

Bush's clarity of speech and firmness in presentation during the war reflected a quality that he had failed to showcase at other times: the ability to be clear and firm in his convictions. Indeed, the entire administration public relations apparatus geared up to control public discourse and promote the president's goals. Bush even displayed an astute ability to frame political language during the war to ensure that his objectives were communicated and the public accepted his definition of the stakes of U.S. military action.

Nonetheless, Bush's performance during the Gulf War was the exception. In general, he was uncomfortable with having image "handlers" and preferred to lead cautiously rather than offer stirring rhetoric. His spare rhetoric reflected his incremental agenda during normal times; his more grandiose rhetoric reflected his firm convictions and resolve during wartime.

Although many suggested that Bush could have had greater success by adopting a Reaganlike, image-conscious presidency, Fitzwater said, "Bush wanted to do it his way." Critics charged that Bush denigrated Reagan by trying to be different. Fitzwater replied: "drawing a distinction is not to denigrate. He was never trying to denigrate Reagan. The fact is, he knew he wasn't as good as Reagan at prime-time news conferences and major addresses." In four years, Bush gave only a few prime-time press conferences and those generally were poor performances.

Bush developed a press relationship that suited his own style. Whereas Reagan kept reporters at a distance and reached out directly to the public, Bush preferred being accessible to the press. Bush also liked informal, usually small gatherings with reporters better than the prime-time events. This approach reflected Bush's own view of his strengths. He perceived himself as an experienced, "hands-on" leader who understood issues and how the government works. Consequently, he saw no need to keep reporters at a distance.

> *Demarest:* He was very comfortable meeting with reporters. It was one of his best forums. He had no problems with access. . . . Whereas one of Reagan's weak suits was the press conference, that was one of Bush's strong suits.

> *Cary:* Bush didn't care for the big, high stakes speech. He was turned off the idea after the speech in 1989 in which he waved a bag of crack. He concluded that those events were overly scrutinized and just caused him problems. He much preferred short remarks and press conferences.

> *McGroarty:* President Reagan was carefully scripted. He was comfortable with doing that and he was good at it. Some who had come from the Reagan White House wanted to do that with Bush. . . . The Bush White House preferred instead the press conference strategy.

Bush did not warm up to television well, but he liked the "town meeting" format in which he could field questions from citizens. Fitzwater thought that this means of communication displayed Bush's strength as a knowledgeable statesman. "He was terrific at it. It also bred the impression—which was true—that he knew his stuff." Fitzwater added that if the event were staged for television, the president "would tense up and not do well." Fitzwater said that Bush "felt guilty about" doing contrived, stage-managed events of any type.

Indeed, everyone interviewed for this study pointed out that Bush, unlike his predecessor, did not enjoy the public relations presidency and many of its requirements. According to Fitzwater: "he did not like it or come to it naturally. He resisted the public relations [presidency]. . . . It represented a kind of phoniness to him, or fakery, that repelled them. There was the basic old-New England, Yankee honesty of spirit about George Bush that made him distrustful of anything that was staged. He used to say to me, 'don't tell me what to do Marlin, I'm not a piece of meat.'"

Curt Smith made a similar point: "Bush really didn't like the grandstanding, the glad-handing, the flesh-pressing, the phony-baloney rituals of politics. He doesn't like it. Doesn't think he's good at it. It's a stunning contrast with Clinton, who likes nothing better."

Vice President Dan Quayle wrote in his memoirs that Bush, unlike Reagan, "didn't enjoy giving speeches." Bush would not prepare adequately for speeches; he just wanted to "get them over with." Consequently, "the White House lost the chance to define itself through clear, focused rhetoric."[28]

That is not to suggest that Bush ignored public relations. As Demarest noted, the president understood, for example, the need to schedule events to meet media deadlines, and the importance of cultivating positive relations with reporters. "What Bush didn't like was anything that appeared to go overboard in trying to manage the news." Several of his speechwriters explained that when they would reach for some grandiose rhetoric or catchphrase, Bush would edit that portion out of the speech and send back a note stating "that's not me."

Charles Kolb argued that by downplaying public relations, Bush undermined his own effectiveness. "He inexplicably downplayed and virtually ignored two factors that had contributed mightily to Reagan's success: the importance of presidential rhetoric and the creation of a well-oiled propaganda machine for swaying public opinion."[29]

A good many of the speechwriters also believed that downplaying public relations hurt the Bush presidency. Smith said that he admired Bush for emphasizing substance over image. But he lamented that—because of the deemphasizing of public relations by 1992—too few Americans gained an appreciation for Bush's admirable qualities. People around the president saw "the fidelity to country, the decency, the honor, the integrity—the embodiment of the kind of person you want to have as your commander in chief," but the White House did not do enough to project those qualities. According to Smith:

> [Bush] was reticent to put himself forward. Bush believes that deeds—not words—speak for themselves. But unfortunately, in politics that's not always the case. In retrospect, we should have done more to try to push him to show the country who he was and what he had accomplished.
>
> He gave extraordinarily little attention to the public relations presidency. George Bush, to his credit as president but to his detriment politically, tried to divorce politics from policy.

Speechwriter Andrew Furgeson made a similar point when he argued that the Bush White House gave insufficient attention to presidential speeches as substantive occasions to communicate the president's worldview or policy priorities. This failure harmed the president's image and ability to lead. Yet it also reflected Bush's own sense of priorities. Bush "didn't like giving speeches," said Furgeson. "He didn't think he was very good at it. . . . Generally, [Bush] was a very pragmatic and practical man who was of the opinion, 'watch what we do, not what we say.' He thought of speeches as superficial P.R. events. . . . Bush was not a verbal man. His approach to politics was pragmatic, not rhetorical."

Tony Snow agreed when he stated, "Bush did not spend too much time worrying about how to polish his public image." The president also "did not spend a lot of time worrying about how to best schmooze with the media." Snow believed—and some of the other speechwriters agreed—that Bush would have helped himself had he done more to focus on the public relations presidency:

> The Bush administration did not do enough to develop its message or, like Reagan, a theme of the day. . . . Bush might deliver several messages in various speeches . . . and the press could choose whatever it wanted to focus on.

> Reagan understood the importance of having a central message of the day and he was not afraid to deliver the same message day-after-day, week-after-week, until it became fixed in the public's mind.
>
> Bush's people were sometimes so smug about how smart they were they figured, "we'll get five or six messages a day." Well what they did was create chaos.

Dan Quayle recalled that the administration "never had . . . a credible communication strategy." Bush was a competent problem solver but he lacked an overriding theme to convey "the big picture." The White House rarely held strategy sessions to map out a long-term strategy of how to communicate Bush's goals.[30] Quayle's observation is clearly confirmed by an examination of White House documents in the press office files. There are memoranda discussing efforts to influence editorial opinion,[31] detailing presidential media interview plans,[32] identifying which media appearances to accept and which ones to avoid,[33] assessing polling data,[34] and ways to rebut negative images.[35] What is lacking is a fully developed strategy for building positive media and communications. Discussions about themes and strategies are more along the lines of "why aren't we doing this?" rather than "here's the message of the week and the plan for communicating it."

Several White House staffers pointed out that this failure to focus the message was especially troublesome during the 1992 campaign because it reinforced the image of Bush as lacking a "vision" for directing the country for another four years.[36] Moreover, because the White House lacked a central message, the campaign floundered from one theme to another. Quayle wrote that this failure allowed the media, not the White House, to set the agenda for the campaign.[37] Snow argued that Bush's "old style" campaign—one that preferred political rallies over talk shows—"never geared up to give the quick response and control the message the way the Clinton campaign did. And that just strengthened the public's perception that Bush was out of touch and did not care."

Indeed, by 1992, opinion polls confirmed this perception of the president. A *Washington Post*/ABC-TV poll revealed that a majority of Americans did not believe that the president had "a vision for the future of the country." A majority also described Bush as an uninspiring leader. Despite his efforts in 1992 to show his concern for the nation's economic plight, 48 percent of the respondents said he was not compassionate.[38]

Fitzwater acknowledged that the Clinton campaign benefited from making better use of "the new communications technology," whereas Bush was reluctant to embrace some of the new campaign formats. "It caused the president to resist MTV, to resist the talk shows that are entertainment," Fitzwater recalled. "He saw them as a denigration of the presidency. If you suggested Donahue, Arsenio Hall, or even Larry King, the president saw their programs as entertainment, not something that a president should be involved with. It wasn't beneath his dignity. It was beneath the dignity of the office. We suffered for that."[39]

Although Bush was reluctant "to put himself forward," to develop a theme of the day, and to embrace new communications technologies, several interviewees said that he was cognizant of the impact of a presidential statement and disciplined about what he said. According to Fitzwater, "unlike President Clinton, [Bush] did not say things about foreign policy that he didn't mean or that he had to take back later." During Operation Desert Storm, for example, "Bush was always aware that the twenty-six member coalition was listening." The result was that the president crafted his statements carefully, fully aware that his words reverberated both domestically and abroad. Nonetheless, almost all agreed with Kolb's assessment that the Bush presidency "was an antirhetorical operation."[40]

POLICY DEVELOPMENT/AGENDA

According to the speechwriters, Bush's pragmatic nature influenced how he chose to identify policy priorities and build support for them. Several pointed out that Bush preferred bipartisanship over battling his political opponents. Bush accepted the reality of Democratic control of Congress and tried to work around that situation. The great problem, they said, was that the Democratic Congress had a different view. According to Smith, the president

> oftentimes said that his model for the presidency was Dwight Eisenhower. He tried to govern as Ike had—to be above the fray, to be bipartisan and nonpartisan, both abroad and at home.
>
> George Bush would have loved to govern like Eisenhower and could have done it if the 1990s were like the 1950s—they're not. The other side was not like Sam Rayburn and Lyndon Johnson, who, like Ike wished to be nonpartisan. The other side wished for Bush's surrender. They wanted the destruction of the Bush presidency.

Dan McGroarty contrasted Bush's relationship with Congress to that of Reagan's. For six of eight years in office, Reagan's party controlled the Senate. Reagan also had temporary working majorities in the House on certain issues. Bush lacked those advantages. Consequently, Bush found that many of his domestic policy initiatives stood no chance of passing the Democratic Congress. McGroarty maintained that in contrast to the press portrayals, Bush cared about domestic issues, "but everything we did was DOA in Congress." Opined McGroarty:

> How long do you think that an operation will continue doing that over and over and over and over again when everything is declared DOA? As opposed to going to the constitutional side of the equation—the latitude the president has in foreign policy, the interest and expertise George Bush has in foreign policy, the events of the world in 1989? Given all of those factors, where do you spend your time? This is not rocket science.
>
> Structurally speaking, if you knew you were going to get nowhere on the Hill, then why would you run up a string of DOA's? People in the White House were acutely aware of that reality. Once you get the two-by-four in the head enough times, you get the picture.

Some observers nonetheless suggested that if the president had better used the bully pulpit he could have had more success at setting the agenda. "Bush didn't seem to have an agenda," said Snow. By 1992, "There was no sense of what Bush was going to do. No sense of the two or three basic issues that would enable people to grasp the essence of the man and also his future administration. . . . I remember people from the campaign complaining, 'they didn't cover our message; they didn't cover our message.' Well, I was in the White House and *I* didn't know what the message was."

Fitzwater offered a similar assessment: "The president used to complain, 'we're not getting our message out.' Well the fact was, there wasn't a strong message on the economy to get out. A president can get out any message he wants. There is no such thing as a president not getting his message out. Everything that he does is covered. The fact is, he may be getting the wrong message out. Or, he may not have a message. But something is being communicated. In our case, it was that President Bush was out of touch with the economy."

Indeed, Boyden Gray vigorously disputed the widely reported notion in 1992 that the economy was in the doldrums. Nonetheless, the problem ultimately was the White House's failure to communicate an alternative message, he said. "We didn't do a good job of dispelling the negative and false perceptions about the economy."

Several of the speechwriters maintained that Bush paid relatively little heed to the political impact of his policy priorities. They claimed that he genuinely cared most about what was "best for the country." Smith said that the president's desire to be bipartisan and do what was right, not just what was in the administration's political interest, "governed the Bush agenda at home."

> It's evident in the Americans with Disabilities Act, the Clean Air Act, the Budget Agreement of 1990, [and] the Civil Rights Act of 1991.
>
> One could argue whether those policies were good or bad for the country. You cannot say that they were good for him politically.
>
> Mistakes that were made resulted from good impulses. George Bush wanted what was good for the country. He did try to sever politics from policy. The contrast with Clinton could not be more severe.

"What undid the Bush presidency ultimately, was policy," said Demarest. "It was throwing away the tax pledge in 1990 and it was not launching some kind of domestic desert storm after the troops came home from the Persian Gulf." Indeed, Demarest and others agreed with the press' criticism of Bush for not moving aggressively on the domestic front, for not being an "activist" or "visionary" president with a bold agenda.[41] For example, Yeutter said that Bush "lacked a well-defined agenda" on the domestic front. Moreover, he added, "Some of us often sought to persuade President Bush to better define his agenda and demonstrate his vision for the country, but he just couldn't do it. . . . Bush had incremental portions of a vision . . . but he could not pull it together into a cohesive whole and explain it to the American public."

White House correspondent Kenneth T. Walsh reported that during the Reagan-Bush transition, the president-elect told Fitzwater he did not want to convey to the country that the federal government or the president had an answer to every problem. Bush felt that the public wanted less government action and was satisfied with the status quo. He, too, favored an incrementalist approach. However, in meetings with leading transition advisers, Bush revealed that he had no specific action agenda.[42]

At midterm, Chief of Staff John Sununu said Congress could go home for the rest of the term because the administration did not have any initiatives that needed immediate action. This comment solidified the impression of Bush as having no agenda and fueled negative coverage of a presidency out of touch with the public.

Two months into the administration, Fitzwater told the National Press Club that Washington journalists were too preoccupied with the White House as the seat of action in the federal government. He implored them to branch out and cover the agencies and federal departments where the real work of the government was being done. "There are not enough stories out of the White House to keep one honest person doing an honest day's work," he said.[43]

Bush ultimately ran afoul of the common expectation that modern presidents lead by defining national priorities and acting aggressively to promote an agenda. Bush's incrementalist approach, combined with a lack of emphasis on presidential imagery, made him appear indifferent to the need to define a leadership vision.

Conclusion

According to Bush's communications advisers, the president suffered a number of disadvantages in press relations. First, there were the inevitable comparisons to Reagan. Bush could not live up to Reagan's public relations presidency and he did not aspire to be like the "great communicator." Second, the partisan composition of Congress made it almost impossible for Bush to become a successful activist domestic-policy president. Third, the White House downplayed public and press relations, placing its priorities elsewhere.

Nevertheless, they acknowledged that Bush hurt his image and the administration's ability to promote policies by downplaying public and press relations. The president did not ignore those areas altogether, but his White House rejected the use of Reagan-era tactics to focus the message, generate a line of the day, and control, to the extent possible, the outflow of news from the administration. Although some of his communications advisers defended Bush's approach as praiseworthy, others said that it ultimately caused the president to be rejected by a public that had no idea of the administration's goals, priorities, or "vision" for the future.

It is not surprising that Bush's communications advisers offered a critical retrospective of the administration's poor use of public and press relations. It was, after all, their job to make Bush look good to the press and the public. They understandably elevated the importance of their own areas of responsibility and lamented what they considered to be Bush's indifference to the public presidency. Although his communications advisers speak with understandable bias on this subject, their near unanimity of opinion regarding what went wrong at the Bush White House lends credibility to their conclusions.

Those most critical of Bush within the White House were Reagan Republicans (for example, Snow and Furgeson) who perceived it to be their duty to rescue Bush from his lack of Reaganesque qualities. They were disillusioned with Bush's moderate-conservatism, lack of emphasis on public relations gimmickry, refusal to adopt an activist conservative agenda, and perceived him as never having shown proper respect for Reagan's accomplishments. Chase Untermeyer, the transition and personnel director, recalled that some in the White House now portray Bush as having denigrated Reagan "to drive a wedge between the [two] administrations."

Bush indeed tried to separate himself from the Reagan years and offered a different leadership approach. Some of his advisers and staff felt that he erred by not only toning down confrontational rhetoric, but by being overly accommodating to his adversaries. During the debate over the Tower nomination, for example, opponents attacked the nominee's personal life and fitness for office, yet Bush maintained a conciliatory tone. It became clear from the outset, some suggested, that the costs associated with so openly challenging the president's interests were very low. Furthermore, Bush's conciliatory tone lowered his public profile because the news media are more attuned to conflict, controversy, and partisan attack.

It is worth speculating as to why Bush chose a low-key media strategy after the successes of the Reagan years. First, that strategy suited the man. Several people interviewed for this study said that Bush had learned from a young age that it is unseemly to engage in self-promotion, to brag. This lesson, they said, carried through to his presidency. He found campaigning for the presidency—which required self-promotion—to be an ugly necessity that he had to endure in order to serve. Bush lacked eloquence, a flair for the dramatic, and he knew that he did not look credible trying to imitate Reagan. Bush preferred the low-key approach because it best suited him.

Second, Bush's understated approach was compatible with his minimalist agenda. Bold initiatives and fundamental departures from the status quo merit bold gestures and grandiose rhetoric. Incrementalism merely requires cautious words and deeds.

A third explanation is tempered by the scholarly analysis of Kerry Mullins and Aaron Wildavsky. They perceived Bush as a "procedural president"; that is, one who respects the order and legitimacy of formal institutions and plays by the rules of the game as he understands them.[44] For such a president, going public with policy initiatives is disrespectful toward Congress's role in the policy process. Hence, Bush was reluctant to promote many of his initiatives outside of Washington. Media manipulation tactics are disrespectful of journalists' rightful role as conduits of information about the presidency. Hence, Bush gave them a great deal of access when he thought it appropriate. Yet he was reluctant to use public relations gimmickry most of the time because it would challenge the media's legitimate role as purveyor of information.[45]

During the Bush years, a number of studies evidenced the president's low public profile in comparison to that of his predecessor.[46] He made news far less often, even though he gave more speeches and held more press conferences. He reached out to accommodate reporters who wanted access, but when he granted it, he did not have much that was newsworthy to offer. In domestic affairs, his incrementalist approach assured his low profile. In foreign affairs, he offered no stirring rhetoric in response to the dramatic changes taking place in the world.

Some in the Bush White House reject the thesis that the president failed to communicate a vision because he lacked an agenda. They suggest that Bush cared about domestic politics, but was realistic enough to understand the limits of his agenda leadership with a Democratic-controlled Congress. Roger Porter has most strongly made the case that Bush had an active domestic agenda. Porter goes so far as to describe Bush as the "father" of the GOP Congress's "Contract with America." Porter identified various Contract provisions that he believes had their roots in Bush's domestic agenda.[47]

Porter's claim of an activist Bush merely limited by circumstances was unique. Most in the Bush White House said that Bush was less than enthusiastically committed to promoting a domestic policy agenda. He ran for the presidency in 1988 to preserve the Reagan-era status quo. But unlike Reagan, to the extent that he offered initiatives, his administration failed to link them to some broad governing philosophy that could be clearly understood by the electorate.

Because understanding the presidency is a mediated experience for most Americans, it is imperative for an administration to try to link its policy-agenda strategy with a workable public relations plan. For a president such as George Bush, that plan need not conform exactly to the Reagan White House model. Bush undoubtedly was correct to assume that he could not profit from many aspects of Ronald Reagan's approach because the two men possessed vastly different skills. But to reject the Reagan model as not appropriate to Bush is not to downplay public and press relations altogether. By refusing to offer a focused message, failing to properly link policy and image making, and lowering his public profile, Bush ultimately harmed the administration's ability to achieve its goals and be rewarded with a second term.

CHAPTER 4

INFORMATION CONTROL IN THE BUSH ADMINISTRATION

IN JANUARY, 1993, a U.S. district judge ruled that White House computer tapes of internal E-mail discussions were no different than other government records covered by the Presidential Records Act of 1978. This decision was a rebuke of the outgoing Bush administration position that the tapes were not a part of the public record and should not be subject to the same requirements as, for example, White House memoranda preserved on paper. The Bush White House reaction to the ruling was remarkable.

On inauguration eve, the White House ordered employees of the National Archives and Records Administration to collect all of the 4,852 computer tapes in boxes to be taken with the president to Texas. The effort was conducted in such a hurried, crisis atmosphere that some tapes were stuffed into boxes together without protective packaging material. Then, just several hours before he was to leave the presidency on January 20, 1993, President Bush entered into a secret agreement with Don Wilson, the archivist of the United States, to preclude all White House computer tapes and backup tapes from ever becoming public documents by giving Bush "exclusive legal control" over them.[1]

A nonprofit organization, the National Security Archive, challenged Bush's action. Had no one taken an opposing position, it would have established the precedent that presidents can enter into private deals to control this relatively new kind of White House record. In February, 1993, the U.S. district judge voided the agreement between Bush and Wilson, declaring that it violated the Presidential Records Act of 1978.

In what struck many as an implausible scenario, the Clinton Justice Department joined former president Bush in challenging the court's decision. In August, 1993, an appeals panel affirmed that White House E-mail communications were official White House records and had to be preserved. Several months later, the Justice Department changed course and decided not to challenge the ruling.[2] As government records, the White House E-mails were protected from Freedom of Information Act requests for at least five years after Bush left office.

It is not at all surprising that the Bush White House was concerned about the public release of E-mail correspondence. At the time it was a relatively new form of communication and the vast majority of E-mail users believed that messages disappeared forever when "deleted" from computer files. Many people probably still believe that is the case. Consequently, many in the White House who corresponded by E-mail fully expected that their messages were protected from disclosure. Public recognition of the ability to retrieve deleted E-mail messages is beginning to change in light of some highly publicized criminal investigations in which authorities in search of evidence gained access to such messages.

The Bush White House E-mail messages were ultimately retrievable from computer systems. Because Bush administration officials most likely believed that their electronic correspondence was completely safe from disclosure, they tended to be unusually candid in their interchanges. Such communications are exactly the kinds of correspondence that a White House does not want to be preserved for future examination.

Advocates of full disclosure, many of them academic researchers, have argued that administrations engage in tactics to protect their internal deliberations from disclosure in order to hide potentially embarrassing information. Although undoubtedly true, critics must acknowledge that political leaders have legitimate secrecy needs and that they may also have a well-founded fear of disclosure of materials that could harm the national interest. It is not clear that Bush, in trying to protect E-mail documents, had acted only out of a desire to spare him and his staff embarrassment.

Bush's final policy initiative as president nonetheless evidenced the enormous importance that he attached to government secrecy and information control. In any analysis of Bush's presidential leadership, it is necessary to recall that as a former national party leader, diplomat, director of central intelligence, and vice president, he had learned the value of secrecy and control of information to making policy decisions and protecting an organization's interests.

While Bush was president, many observers referred to his use of "rolodex diplomacy"—that is, his penchant for conducting foreign policy privately, by telephone, with international elites, rather than through bold policy pronouncements and public posturing. This approach earned him the scorn of domestic critics who said he had failed to articulate a "vision" for the post–Cold War world, as well as the admiration of many international leaders who appreciated the restraint he exercised in his public pronouncements.

Bush's approach to secrecy and information control was compatible with the leadership of an incrementalist who resists forces of change and seeks to protect the status quo. As one who respected the traditional arrangements of institutions, Bush exercised secrecy to protect the executive branch against what he perceived as harmful encroachments by outside forces, especially Congress and the media. Although Bush had a cautious and limited policy agenda, he was aggressive in promoting and protecting institutional prerogatives.

In what follows, we examine and analyze a number of the actions and policies that formed the basis of Bush's approach to governmental secrecy and information control. First, and most prominently, there were the administration's extraordinarily successful efforts at controlling and manipulating the dissemination of information about the Panama invasion and the Persian Gulf War. Although widely criticized by media organizations, the restrictions on journalists, including the Gulf War pool system and security review process, achieved the administration's aim of promoting positive news about the military's efforts. Second, the Bush White House adopted an effective strategy for handling executive-privilege controversies. Unlike his immediate predecessor, Bush successfully veiled executive privilege and was able to shield vast amounts of information from Congress and the public. Third, the Bush Justice Department's "secret opinions policy" contributed significantly to protecting the administration's internal deliberations. Fourth, the president issued seventy-nine secret National Security Directives, some of which are completely or partially declassified. The administration established specific procedures for responding to congressional requests for information about these directives.

The Panama Invasion and the Persian Gulf War

The Bush administration held firmly to the belief that normal press freedoms in a democracy during peacetime can be temporarily suspended when the nation goes to war. Although widely criticized by the press for so doing, the administration effectively restricted access to information about military actions and civilian casualties during the December, 1989, invasion of Panama.

The restrictions on media access to the invasion and accurate information about casualties had the intended effect of ensuring high levels of public support for the president's action. While official casualty reports were low, information uncovered months after the invasion found that there was substantial loss of civilian life.[3] During the invasion and subsequent military occupation, the public saw little of the cost of U.S. actions.

From the standpoint of promoting the administration's objectives, the media restrictions were enormously beneficial. Policy makers understood that pictures and film footage of many casualties would evoke strong public emotions and lead many to forget the strategic and security principles involved in the invasion. The Panama invasion case also made it clear that the media, if effectively restricted, can actually aid in the promotion of a sanitized version of military conflict. For the public, the most memorable pictures of U.S. military action were those of soldiers employing psychological terrorism by blaring rock music at the palace of Panamanian leader Manuel Noriega while he was holed up in the building.

The Panamanian case also showed the utility of evoking the right symbols to garner public support for military action. In the administration's language, the purpose of the invasion, code-named "Operation Just Cause," was to dislodge a leader who was a "thug," a "dictator," and a leading "drug trafficker."[4] Noriega had to be "brought to justice" for his acts. The demonization of Noriega conveyed a simple, yet powerful message about America's purpose and enabled the administration to sell its policy without having to debate complex issues of international and criminal law. The effective use of secrecy, press restrictions, and symbolism provided a powerful lesson for future military actions.[5]

It was during the Persian Gulf War that the Bush administration achieved its greatest success at information control and manipulating news coverage of events. As with any military operation, certain restrictions had to be placed on information about troop movements, campaign strategy, and weapons capabilities. The most controversial techniques for restricting military information were the journalist "pool" system and the "security review" process.

In brief, the pool system established specific rules governing how many journalists could cover combat operations, where journalists could travel, and whom they could interview. Specifically, the U.S. military allowed selected journalists to travel to the front lines in groups of six or more persons to cover the war. The journalists had to travel with military escorts who then supervised the reporters' conversations with soldiers. When the pool returned from what some journalists likened to a guided tour, all news stories and footage had to be submitted for a security review.[6] The U.S. military established this latter requirement to ensure that news reports did not disclose secret or sensitive information that could have damaged the coalition war effort. The approved pool reports then were shared among the press corps members stationed in Saudi Arabia.

Beyond the issue of security, the U.S. military had other concerns that led it to enforce the press restrictions that frustrated so many reporters. The most oft-cited concern was that it would be highly impractical for more than a thousand journalists to freely roam the war zone unsupervised. "There's a huge gaggle of reporters out there, and the press has absolutely no capacity to police itself," said Defense Secretary Richard Cheney. "There is no way we were ever going to put 100 percent of the reporters who wanted to go cover the war out with the troops."[7] Pete Williams, the Pentagon's chief spokesman, said that honoring press requests for more open, unsupervised coverage was "just not possible to do with all the reporters" stationed in Saudi Arabia.[8]

The military also expressed concern for the safety of reporters. Unsupervised journalists no doubt could have been subjected to hostile fire with no means of protecting themselves. In addition to not wanting to put soldiers at risk by sending them out to recover wounded and dead journalists from the battlefield, military leaders believed that such efforts would divert manpower from achieving the war's primary objectives.

Journalists widely denounced the restrictions. Many complained that the government was practicing censorship. Former CBS-TV news anchor Walter Cronkite succinctly stated their case: "With an arrogance foreign to the democratic system, the U.S. military in Saudi Arabia is trampling on the American people's right to know." Cronkite reasoned that the existence of the pool system proved that the military had something embarrassing or potentially unpopular to hide from the American people.[9]

Journalists also complained that when they were given access to information about the war, oftentimes they were brought into the process too late to be able to inform the public in a timely manner. They cited as particularly troublesome the security review system that frequently held up pool reports for hours, on some occasions even for days. Reporters who did not play by the Pentagon's rules risked having their press credentials revoked and being deported from Saudi Arabia.[10] Some reporters who tried to work outside of the pool system were detained by the military. Soldiers escorting pool reporters frequently prohibited interviews about subjects the military considered sensitive.

Press restrictions often seemed senseless, unrelated to any military or security objectives. After the war, a group of publishers and top executives from seventeen news organizations sent a report criticizing the press restrictions to Defense Secretary Cheney. The letter accompanying their report emphasized that the restrictions "made it impossible for reporters and photographers to tell the public the full story of the war in a timely fashion." The report detailed numerous objectionable examples of restrictions imposed on journalists. For example, the military censored a report about an EF-111 aircraft because of a breach of classified information and then released the information to the press the next day. The military refused to allow a reporter to cover a group of marines singing "Onward Christian Soldiers" due to concerns about offending "Saudi sensitivities."[11]

The security review process produced other absurdities. In one instance, a reporter's use of "fighter-bomber" to describe an F-117A had to be changed to "fighter." Another reporter's use of "giddy" to describe a fighter pilot was changed to "proud" (although in response to the reporter's complaints, the censors allowed him instead to use "pumped up").[12]

What reporters found especially objectionable was that they had been turned into what one called "mere conduits for official information."[13] *New York Times* reporter Malcolm W. Browne wrote: "Every pool member is an unpaid employee of the Department of Defense, on whose behalf he or she prepares the news of the war for the outer world."[14]

Retired army colonel Darryl Henderson told a gathering of the First Amendment Congress that he and other military personnel had undergone training in public relations techniques while in the military. He said that because of the widely held perception in the military that the news media had much to do with the erosion of public support during the Vietnam War, the armed services had become cognizant of the need for "marketing the military viewpoint."[15] For example, expecting favorable coverage from the local press, the Pentagon provided small-town news organizations free transportation to Saudi Arabia and even helped to set up interviews for the reporters with service people from their communities. Military aides read news reports and identified journalists inclined to write less-than-sympathetic accounts of events. Such journalists' requests for interviews often were denied.[16]

The press briefings by military officers were brilliant from a public relations standpoint. Journalists were wowed with video displays of the military's technological achievements. The press briefings provided the kind of awe-inspiring news footage that suits the media's need for exciting, interesting copy and visuals. The videos also sanitized the human costs of the bombing, as the footage mostly showed from some distance "smart bombs" successfully hitting buildings, but no human casualties. The selected footage showcased effective missions, leaving the erroneous impression that the bombs had almost always hit their intended targets. Former Reagan White House image-maker Michael Deaver commented: "The Department of Defense has done an excellent job of managing the news in an almost classic way. There's plenty of access to some things, and at least one visual a day. If you were going to hire a public relations firm to do the media relations for an international event, it couldn't be done any better than this."[17]

The media manipulation went well beyond control of information and slick public relations techniques. The military went so far as to dupe the media into becoming a tool for war strategy. Prior to the ground war, journalists ached for a chance to get close to where the action would soon begin. The military brought reporters along to cover rehearsals for a massive amphibious landing on Kuwait's coast. No landing ever occurred. The military had staged the entire event to fool the Iraqis. The diversion worked, in part thanks to the role played by the media in building up the nonevent. Early in the war, the CIA, hoping to encourage defections, planted a false story stating that sixty Iraqi tank crews had defected with their vehicles. The story was widely reported.[18]

The Pentagon also prohibited any filming or news coverage of war casualties arriving at the main military mortuary at Dover Air Force Base. Sydnet Schanberg protested that the policy represented "a concerted effort to try to edit out all reminders of Viet Nam."[19] The Pentagon feared that televised images of body bags and grieving families would convey too vividly the greatest cost of the war and eventually undermine public support for the coalition effort.

What became painfully aware to the media was that they could do little about military censorship, control, and manipulation. The pool system often set reporters against each other. Those privileged enough to be in the pool did not want to jeopardize their positions and did not lend much support to their colleagues left out of the system. Journalists often had to report what was fed to them or have nothing at all to report. For the first time since World War II, U.S. news accounts read: "Reports reviewed by military censors."[20] British reporter Robert Fiske noted the bitter irony of the media manipulation was that the United States claimed to be fighting a "war for freedom" while denying journalists the most fundamental right of press freedom.[21]

Furthermore, as top Bush administration officials recognized, the reporters did not have the support of public opinion. Margaret Tutwiler, the Bush administration's State Department spokesperson, put it bluntly: "I think Joe Six-Pack sitting out in his home in Sioux City—his first reaction is going to be, 'Screw the press.' If a military general stands up and says, 'This [live coverage] is an interference, it's putting young men's lives in harms way,' the networks are going to lose that battle."[22]

General Colin Powell, then chairman of the Joint Chiefs of Staff, said that if the United States had been losing the war while the media reported live events that emboldened the enemy, "I'd have locked all of you [journalists] up and you could have taken me to every court in the land. And guess who would have won that battle? I mean the American people would have stripped your skin off."[23]

Tutwiler and Powell were right. Opinion polls during the war showed high levels of support for censorship of the media.[24] A late-January, 1991, *Times-Mirror* survey found that 57 percent of the public wanted even tighter restrictions on war coverage than those already in place.[25] A *Washington Post*/ABC-TV poll offered a result that was most disturbing to the journalists. When asked hypothetically what the United States should do about plans to bomb an enemy communications center in Baghdad where reporters were working, 62 percent of respondents said the United States should issue a warning and then bomb the center even if the reporters remained there. Another 5 percent said the United States should issue no warning and just bomb the center with the reporters in it.[26]

The Bush administration's approach to controlling the information flow regarding the Persian Gulf crisis was enormously successful, especially during the crucial early stages. Numerous content analyses of the news coverage evidenced a strongly positive response to Bush's actions. Media analyst S. Robert Lichter surveyed major television network coverage of the war during the first two weeks and found that 76 percent of all references to the president were favorable. Network journalists even repeated in their own reports the strong language the president used to describe Saddam Hussein.[27] After one month, 86 percent of all references to the Iraqi leader were negative, while one in eight of the criticisms "went beyond the bounds of normal political discourse to portray Saddam as criminal or evil." In all, the networks presented the crisis as "a personal struggle between Saddam Hussein and George Bush," with the Iraqi leader portrayed as frighteningly evil and the U.S. president provided with adulatory coverage.[28]

Communications professor Patrick O'Heffernan concluded from his analysis of the coverage that the media had allowed the president to "set the terms of discourse" and that "American television crisis coverage often strayed into jingoism, with generous and unquestioning coverage of U.S. military operations and policy."[29] Walter Goodman wrote that the administration's media manipulation had "effectively shaped coverage from the beginning to the end of the Gulf War. That encouraged the natural wartime disposition to celebrate 'Our Brave Men and Women' and censure, or even censor, anyone who didn't pitch in heartily enough."[30] The major television news networks employed as on-air experts a number of former high-ranking military officials who, according to a study by Fairness and Accuracy in Reporting (FAIR), provided a nearly uniform pro-U.S. policy viewpoint, while critics of U.S. policy were given little chance to present their views.[31]

Bush's use of rhetoric was key to creating this favorable atmosphere. Similar to the Panama invasion, the president created emotional symbols designed to set the parameters of debate on his own terms. These included the analogy of Saddam to Hitler and rhetoric emphasizing the necessity of protecting freedom from invasion. In adopting this rhetorical approach, Bush was able to create favorable emotional responses to his policies and effectively silence opposition voices. As Mannheim has shown, the images that the administration created to sell its policies to the public were first tested on focus groups and then tracked through White House polling.[32] The use of emotional appeals once again made it difficult for a debate to emerge over the more complex issues of U.S. interests at stake in the Persian Gulf.

Gladys Engel Lang and Kurt Lang also noted as important the successful efforts by first the Reagan and then the Bush administrations to classify and withhold information that was crucial to an informed debate about the U.S. role in the Persian Gulf.[33] Would the media and public have been so receptive to Bush's actions had people been fully aware of the pre–Gulf War U.S. role in supporting Saddam's regime? Indeed, postwar investigations of the earlier U.S. actions revealed serious policy flaws. For a variety of reasons, investigators met substantial resistance to their efforts to learn more about prewar U.S. policies toward Iraq.

Bush's approach to these two foreign affairs crises reflected his conviction that in the international realm, the public did not possess a "right to know" all the details of presidential actions. Indeed, he did not want to foreclose policy options by making public statements and commitments. As White House correspondents Michael Duffy and Dan Goodgame reported, Bush used a prewar press conference to purposefully mislead the public about his intentions regarding the U.S role in the Persian Gulf and the extent of the anticipated military buildup.[34] He misled the public and withheld what he knew with the purpose of minimizing internal opposition to U.S. actions and allowing himself the freedom to pursue various policy options. To the extent that opposition to the U.S. military buildup in the Persian Gulf region was muted, Bush succeeded in his efforts.

He employed secrecy and deception about his actions on many other occasions as well. In early 1990, a spate of negative news stories emphasized that Bush had not been dealing forthrightly with the media and public on a number of issues. Reporters told Bush that they recognized the need for secrecy, but not deception, and that he should merely respond "no comment" rather than lie. Duffy and Goodgame reported that Bush nonetheless chose to say "no" untruthfully when "no comment" would have served his purpose when reporters asked him about some sensitive administration action.[35]

On some occasions, Bush promoted secret actions when he wanted to avoid any possible outpouring of public opposition. Because of the highly charged emotions surrounding the Chinese government's crackdown in 1989 on the prodemocracy movement, the Bush White House arranged secret negotiations with China's leaders. Brent Scowcroft and Lawrence Eagleburger made two secret trips to China at a time when the public would have preferred a strong public stand against the crackdown.[36]

For Bush, the low-key diplomatic approach better suited his own leadership style than any aggressive, public action. Critics blasted the president for his "*kowtow*" to the Chinese leadership, when in fact he perceived his approach as prudent rather than weak—a viewpoint perhaps bolstered by his successful efforts to include China among the community of nations that condemned Iraq's invasion of Kuwait.

Bush's exercise of secrecy was not limited to wartime and international diplomacy. He perceived secrecy to be a necessary, regular element of presidential decision making. Through such devices as executive privilege and the secret opinions policy, the administration succeeded at protecting its policy options by shielding executive branch information from congressional and ultimately public view.

Executive Privilege

Executive privilege is deeply mired in constitutional and political controversy. Under that doctrine, the president and important executive branch officials have the right to withhold information from the Congress, the courts, and, ultimately, the public. Executive privilege is always controversial in a liberal democracy because such a form of government presupposes citizen knowledge of public affairs. How, under such a system, some have inquired, can citizens possess the knowledge that they need to hold public officials accountable when secrecy is allowed? Advocates of executive privilege maintain that all forms of government, even liberal democracies, have legitimate secrecy needs.[37]

Despite the academic debate over executive privilege, the fact remains that all presidents have claimed the right to exercise that power and the judiciary has granted it legitimacy.[38] Every president has exercised some form of what is called executive privilege, although that term did not exist until the Eisenhower administration. Presidents have claimed the right to executive privilege to protect national security information, the privacy of internal executive branch deliberations, and the confidentiality of ongoing executive branch investigations.

Executive privilege became most controversial during the Nixon years, when the president tried to use that power as a shield to cover up wrongdoing. Nixon made insupportable claims of an unlimited executive privilege, privilege for all members of the executive branch, and that the coordinate branches had no right to challenge the president's exercise of such a power. The Supreme Court rejected Nixon's extraordinary claims while upholding the legitimacy of executive privilege.[39]

Although the Court upheld this presidential power, Nixon's actions gave executive privilege a bad name. Some administrations have shown great reluctance to exercise executive privilege for fear that any such claim will immediately be equated with a Nixonian abuse of power. Presidents Ford and Carter did not issue a formal policy on the use of executive privilege, choosing instead to resort to other justifications for withholding information.[40]

President Reagan issued a memorandum in 1982 detailing the administration's procedures for handling executive privilege matters and then attempted unsuccessfully on several occasions to use that power. In response to congressional pressure and media criticism for using executive privilege, Reagan backed down and released disputed documents to

Congress. Unlike his two predecessors, Reagan failed because he did not effectively shield executive privilege to avoid controversy. He instead tried to exercise that power by claiming the right to protect presidential prerogatives. This tack merely raised the level of controversy over his actions.[41]

In contrast, Bush never issued a formal policy on executive privilege, and he did not make a concerted effort to articulate constitutional principles as the basis for his actions. Bush's response to executive privilege controversies was never dogmatic. His response tended to be bureaucratic: find some way to work around the problem without raising the level of conflict. Bush consequently had more success at withholding information than did his predecessor. His approach was closer to those of Ford and Carter, although Bush was even more effective at withholding information and avoiding the kind of controversy that would have forced him to accede to congressional demands for full disclosure.

BUSH'S POLICY TOWARD EXECUTIVE PRIVILEGE

The Bush administration never adopted a formal policy regarding the use of executive privilege. Instead, the policies outlined in the 1982 Reagan memorandum remained in effect as the official Bush administration procedures on exercising that constitutional authority.

What is most important to recognize about the Bush approach to executive privilege is that his administration's policy toward and practice of that doctrine differed substantially. Whereas the Reagan administration on several occasions boldly proclaimed its constitutional prerogative to assert executive privilege, and then had to back down in the face of congressional and popular opposition, the Bush administration adopted a much more politically feasible strategy. Bush maintained in theory Reagan's policy of requiring the president personally to approve the use of executive privilege. His administration withheld information from Congress on many occasions without invoking executive privilege—in effect, without calling attention to the controversial doctrine. In brief, Bush's strategy was to further the cause of withholding information by *not* invoking executive privilege.

Perhaps there is no stronger indication of how far the doctrine of executive privilege has fallen into political disrepute than how the Bush administration sought to secure all of the benefits of governmental secrecy without making a case for this presidential power. Bush understood that to draw too much attention to executive privilege only would have the effect that his predecessor experienced—public confrontations with Congress, congressional contempt citations, and critical media coverage of executive branch secrecy.

On many occasions, rather than invoke executive privilege, the Bush administration used other names for justifying withholding information or cited some other source of authority for doing the same. Among the phrases and justifications often used to defend the withholding of information were "deliberative process privilege," "attorney-client privilege," "attorney work product," "internal departmental deliberations," "deliberations of another agency," "secret opinions policy," "sensitive law enforcement materials," "ongoing criminal investigations," and so forth.

These phrases and justifications are not all original to the Bush administration. Numerous administrations have, for example, withheld documents pertaining to "ongoing criminal investigations" in the Justice Department without specifically citing executive privilege. What is telling, though, is the extent to which the Bush administration went to cloak the use of executive privilege under different names. As Jim Lewin, the chief investigator to the House Judiciary Committee, explained: "Bush was more clever than Reagan when it came to executive privilege. You have to remember that Bush really was our first bureaucrat president. He knew how to work the system. He avoided formally claiming executive privilege and instead called it other things. In reality, executive privilege was in full force and effect during the Bush years, probably more so than under Reagan."[42]

The Bush administration further downplayed—and hence weakened—executive privilege by failing to articulate or defend any constitutional arguments for its exercise. Bush was content to effectively concede the constitutional issues over executive privilege to opponents and to ensure his short-term political need to avoid constitutional conflict while at the same time blocking congressional committees and the public from attaining certain information.

None of this is to suggest that Bush either did not believe in or never personally invoked executive privilege. On a few occasions Bush resorted to executive privilege when no other option was available to achieve the purpose of withholding information.

BUSH'S EXERCISE OF EXECUTIVE PRIVILEGE

Although President Bush never established his own formal procedures for using executive privilege, a number of controversies during his presidency bring to light how his administration exercised that power in a crafty, even hidden-hand, fashion.

The Kmiec Memo, 1989

The first executive privilege statement issued by the Bush administration never involved the president and did not result in any substantive policy decision. On March 24, 1989, the assistant attorney general in the Justice Department's Office of Legal Counsel (OLC), Douglas M. Kmiec, issued a memorandum proclaiming that, under the doctrine of executive privilege, inspectors general (IGs) are not obligated to provide to Congress "confidential information about an open criminal investigation."[43] Oddly enough, Kmiec did not issue the opinion memorandum in reaction to any specific controversy between the Bush administration and Congress. Nobody from the administration requested the opinion. In fact, Kmiec offered it as a response to a June 3, 1987, Reagan administration inquiry into how IGs should respond to congressional demands for information.[44] It remains unclear why Kmiec—who held his Justice Department position in both the Reagan and Bush administrations—waited almost two years to respond to the inquiry, after a change in administrations.

The Kmiec memo provided a brief historical justification for executive privilege. Furthermore, it stated: "Congress has a limited interest in the conduct of an ongoing criminal investigation and the executive branch has a strong interest in preserving the confidentiality of such investigations. Accordingly, in light of established executive branch policy and practice, and absent extraordinary circumstances, an IG should not provide Congress with confidential information concerning an open criminal investigation."[45]

In terms of influencing Bush administration use of executive privilege, the Kmiec memo amounted to nothing. Steven R. Ross, the general counsel to the House clerk, and Charles Tiefer, the deputy general counsel, responded that congressional committees did indeed have the "authority to obtain information on agency waste, fraud, and wrongdoing, from Inspectors General as from other agency officers. The Kmiec memo represents a gratuitous and unjustified break with a clear historic tradition and attempts to put aside explicit statutory language. It should [be] regarded as simply an error."[46] As Tiefer later explained, the Kmiec memo represented nothing more than an "abstract statement" that had no bearing on official policy or administration action. Indeed, during the Bush years, Congress met no resistance from IGs in its various requests for information.[47]

The Reagan Diaries, 1990

The Bush administration asserted executive privilege over the personal diaries of Ronald Reagan when the former national security adviser, John M. Poindexter, sought access to portions of those materials.[48] Poindexter sought access to the Reagan diaries for the purpose of substantiating the claim that Reagan had authorized certain activities in the Iran-Contra affair.

On January 30, 1990, a federal district court judge, Harold H. Greene, ordered Reagan to turn over to Poindexter excerpts from the former president's diaries. Reagan's attorneys had been attempting since November, 1989, to persuade Greene to cancel a subpoena for the diaries sought by the Poindexter defense. Greene instead ordered that the diary excerpts be released and gave Reagan's attorneys until February 5, 1990, to challenge that decision with an assertion of executive privilege. Greene had privately reviewed the Reagan diary excerpts and determined "that some but not all the diary entries produced in response to various subpoena categories are relevant to defendant's claim."[49]

On February 2, the Bush administration Justice Department moved in federal court to delay the order that Reagan's diary excerpts be produced for Poindexter's Iran-Contra trial. The maneuver was intended to avoid forcing Reagan's attorneys to assert executive privilege. The Justice Department maintained that the court order could become a "significant intrusion into what are probably a president's most personal records" and possibly result in a "serious constitutional confrontation."[50]

The tactic failed and on February 5, Reagan asserted executive privilege over the diaries. In the attorney's brief for Reagan, the former president's lawyer, Theodore B. Olson, wrote: "these materials are the private reflections of the former president prepared for his personal deliberations and touch the core of the presidency."[51] The former president's spokesman maintained that Reagan had decided to invoke executive privilege to protect the privacy of future presidents.[52] In his formal motion, Reagan maintained that he had no other choice because Judge Greene refused to disclose Poindexter's written statements of why the diary excerpts were important to the case, unless the former president claimed executive privilege.[53] Greene maintained that such a claim of executive privilege would require him to reexamine his earlier decision to compel release of the diary excerpts. In other words, Greene would have to determine whether the need for the excerpts in the trial must override any claim of executive privilege. The Bush administration countered by issuing its own claim of executive privilege over Reagan's diaries.

To further complicate the controversy, Judge Greene separately ordered Reagan to provide videotaped testimony in the Poindexter trial. Reagan consequently had to decide once again whether to assert executive privilege because Judge Greene gave the former president until February 9 to assert that authority and refuse to testify.

Reagan waited until the deadline before agreeing to provide the videotaped testimony. The Bush administration Justice Department that same day waived its claim of executive privilege over the order to testify to enable Reagan to present his testimony. Nonetheless, Judge Greene agreed to allow Reagan's attorneys and Bush administration lawyers to accompany the former president during the testimony to offer advice on when to refuse to answer questions on the grounds of executive privilege. Reagan's attorneys stated that the former president would defer to President Bush, "with respect to issues of executive privilege concerning national security or foreign affairs that may arise during the taking of the videotaped testimony."[54]

Reagan provided eight hours of videotaped testimony on February 16 and 17. He could not recall key events, information, and even some names in the Iran-Contra affair and consequently did not provide any significant new information about the controversy.

On March 21, Judge Greene ruled in favor of the Reagan and the Bush administration claims of executive privilege over the diary excerpts. Greene had again privately reviewed the disputed diary entries and determined that they offered "no new insights" into the Iran-Contra affair and, consequently, that the claims of executive privilege outweighed Poindexter's claim to need access to the diary entries. Greene determined that "the claims of executive privilege filed on behalf of the former president and of the incumbent president are sufficient under the facts presented here to defeat the defendant's demand." Furthermore, Poindexter's "showing of need for the diary excerpts and their indispensability for the achievement of justice in this case is meager." He explained that Poindexter's case might have been stronger if Reagan had earlier refused to provide videotaped testimony. Greene made clear that he had overturned his earlier decision to compel release of the diary entries because of the assertions of executive privilege. In doing so, he determined that "courts must exercise both deference and restraint when asked to issue coercive orders against a president's person or papers."[55]

Executive privilege prevailed in this controversy. Significantly, it was Judge Greene, not the Reagan attorneys or the Bush administration, who forced the issue of executive privilege in this case. Reagan's attorneys avoided the use of the phrase "executive privilege" in their formal response to Judge Greene's deadline for asserting such authority as the basis for withholding the diary entries. The Bush administration initially tried to get around the issue of executive privilege, but the tactic failed to produce that result. When compelled to do so, Reagan's attorneys and the Bush administration claimed executive privilege.

The Persian Gulf War, 1990–91

The Persian Gulf war raised many access to information controversies. The Bush administration did not use executive privilege as a basis for restricting press access to military information. Instead, the administration justified its many restrictions on the basis of national security concerns.

One executive privilege dispute did arise concerning congressional access to information regarding U.S.–Persian Gulf policy. On January 3, 1991, Rep. Barbara Boxer (D-California) introduced in Congress a privileged resolution of inquiry, House Resolution 19, seeking specific information on Operation Desert Shield. That resolution sought information about the following: the likelihood of a wider regional conflict in the Middle East; assessments of Iraqi military capabilities; projections of consequences of conflict on international oil supplies; assessments of U.S. vulnerabilities to terrorist attacks; information about U.S. efforts to seek support for Operation Desert Shield from other governments; memoranda of meetings between U.S. officials and foreign leaders; analyses of budgetary options for the military operation; and analyses of postwar options for Iraq. The resolution called for the administration to provide all of this information within ten days.[56]

On January 23, Counsel to the President C. Boyden Gray, responded as follows:

> The resolution requests extremely sensitive information that, if disclosed, could cause grave damage to the national security at this time of crisis in the Persian Gulf region.
>
> The requested information [concerns] some of our nation's most sensitive national security secrets, including war plans. Even indirect knowledge of those secrets, especially our war plans, would be of obvious use to Iraq in countering steps that the president has ordered, and may yet order, in accordance with H.J.

> Res. 77. It would be unconscionable to expose U.S. and coalition military personnel in the Persian Gulf region to the risks associated with disclosure of this kind of information.
>
> Because of the extraordinary sensitivity of such information, the courts have long recognized that the Constitution permits the president to protect such information from disclosure under the national security component of the executive privilege doctrine. This component of executive privilege also insulates from disclosure information relating to diplomatic discussions with foreign governments.

Moreover, insofar as documents requested by House Resolution 19 reflect predecisional discussions,

> advice, recommendations, and budgetary or other analyses, they are also protected from disclosure by the deliberative process component of executive privilege.
>
> In short, we believe that enactment of H.Res. 19 would be contrary to the national interest, and that it would be unconstitutional.[57]

On February 7, the chairman of the House Foreign Affairs Committee, Rep. Dante B. Fascell (D-Florida), and the chairman of the House Armed Services Committee, Rep. Les Aspin (D-Wisconsin), wrote to President Bush requesting "a more responsive answer than the initial reply by Mr. Gray." The letter further requested that the information be presented in a "timely fashion" so that Congress could fulfill its oversight responsibilities.[58]

Congress soon received much of the information requested from the Bush administration. The White House dropped the use of executive privilege and substantially accommodated Congress's need for information. On February 20, National Security Adviser Brent Scowcroft responded to the Fascell-Aspin letter by providing summary information from the White House, Defense Department, and State Department. He also explained that CIA information relevant to the areas of inquiry would be provided separately in classified form. The White House presented the information in less detailed form than requested, but nonetheless dropped the use of executive privilege in response to congressional protest. Congress received much of the desired information and did not dispute the administration's final response that some details could not be provided given time constraints.[59] Widespread public support for Bush's military action also made Congress's efforts to compel release of all of the detailed information about the coalition war effort politically difficult, to say the least. Consequently, the Bush administration was able to protect the information that it did not want to release without formally exercising executive privilege and without encouraging a constitutional conflict.

Department of Education and College Accreditation Standards, 1991

In 1991, the Bush administration Department of Education (DOE) received a good deal of criticism for challenging the use of cultural diversity standards in college accreditation decisions.[60] Specifically, on April 11, Education Secretary Lamar Alexander challenged the Middle States Association of Colleges and Schools' practice of considering the degree of faculty, staff, and student diversity in colleges in deciding whether to grant accreditation. The Subcommittee on Human Resources and Intergovernmental Relations of the House Government Operations Committee soon began an investigation into Alexander's controversial action. On April 17, the subcommittee, chaired by the late Rep. Ted Weiss (D-New York) requested DOE documents pertaining to Alexander's action.

Although the DOE furnished a good many of the requested documents, it also refused to supply some others. On May 7, Edward Stringer, the DOE's general counsel, wrote to Weiss that certain documents had to be withheld from Congress. Stringer claimed the "attorney-client privilege" and "deliberative process privilege" as reasons for withholding documents.[61]

The subcommittee rejected these claims of privilege. Staff members of the subcommittee and of the Education Department met on May 13 to try to resolve the dispute. No agreement could be reached and Stringer wrote another letter to Weiss informing the chairman that the OLC had advised the DOE to claim executive privilege over the documents.[62]

The next day, the subcommittee rejected this use of executive privilege and voted 6–3, along party lines, to issue a subpoena for the disputed documents. The DOE chose not to fight the subpoena, withdrew its claim of executive privilege, and turned over to Congress all of the disputed documents.

President Bush never personally got involved in this controversy. Despite administration policy—carried over from the Reagan administration—that executive privilege could only be invoked either by the president or with his personal approval, the OLC advised the DOE in this case to claim executive privilege. As the general counsel and the deputy general counsel to the House clerk wrote to Representative Weiss: "What was novel about this claim of privilege was the frankness with which the Office of Legal Counsel admitted that it was claiming executive privilege. The Justice Department's willingness to apply the term 'executive privilege' to the decisional documents of a department, and to documents for which attorney-client privilege was attempted to be asserted, contrasts with other occasions when, for tactical reason, the Justice Department has [devised] attempts at the withholding of similar records without admitting that it is really invoking executive privilege."[63]

The DOE initially tried to devise strategies other than executive privilege for withholding the documents before eventually claiming the constitutional doctrine. The trouble was, without presidential approval, the DOE had no legitimate grounds on which to assert executive privilege. President Bush obviously did not believe that the disputed documents were so important to protect from scrutiny that he was willing to risk a constitutional conflict over executive privilege. Congress proved its ability to compel production of disputed documents through vigorous use of its authority to investigate and to subpoena evidence.

McDonnell Douglas A-12 Navy Aircraft Program Investigation, August–September, 1991

In this controversy, President Bush asserted executive privilege and his action went unchallenged by Congress.[64] On August 1, 1991, the Subcommittee on Legislation and National Security of the House Government Operations Committee unanimously voted to subpoena Defense Secretary Richard Cheney for a document regarding cost overruns on the McDonnell Douglas A-12 Navy Aircraft Program terminated in January, 1991. The subcommittee, chaired by Rep. John G. Conyers Jr. (D-Michigan), gave Cheney until August 9 either to turn over the requested information or to respond to the subpoena.

On August 8, President Bush signed a memorandum to Cheney instructing the defense secretary to claim executive privilege and therefore not comply with the subpoena. The president instructed Cheney as follows:

> It is my decision that you should not release this document. Compelled release to Congress of documents containing confidential communications among senior Department officials

> would inhibit the candor necessary to the effectiveness of the deliberative process by which the Department makes decisions and recommendations concerning national defense, including recommendations to me as Commander-in-Chief. In my judgment, the release of the memorandum would be contrary to the national interest because it would discourage the candor that is essential to the Department's decision-making process. Therefore, I am compelled to assert executive privilege with respect to this memorandum and to instruct you not to release it to the subcommittee.[65]

What is interesting about this particular case is that, although governmental appropriations—not national security concerns—were at issue, the Conyers committee chose not to challenge Bush's claim of executive privilege. Bush prevailed for a number of reasons. First, the White House successfully lobbied the minority party members of the Conyers committee to back the president after the assertion of executive privilege. Second, Conyers determined that a committee divided along partisan lines was not likely to support a contempt citation against Cheney. Third, there would likely have been very little sentiment on Capitol Hill anyway in favor of a contempt citation against Cheney, who happened to be a former House member and remained very popular in Congress.

Congress could claim only one small achievement in this battle over executive branch information. That is, as a consequence of the Conyers committee's action, the president personally claimed executive privilege and further established a precedent for the view that executive privilege can only be claimed or approved by the president himself, and not by any other member of the executive branch of government.

The Quayle Council and the FDA, 1991–92

In September, 1991, the Human Resources and Intergovernmental Relations Subcommittee of the House Government Operations Committee began an investigation into Food and Drug Administration (FDA) dealings with the Quayle Council on Competitiveness.[66] In brief, the Quayle Council had recommended a series of reforms of the FDA's drug approval process. The FDA accepted the recommendations, some of which were controversial.

The investigating subcommittee ran into difficulty receiving documents pertaining to the Quayle Council's work on behalf of the FDA procedures. The FDA refused to provide certain documents that concerned "deliberative communications within the Council or otherwise reveal its deliberations."[67] On November 13, the subcommittee voted to subpoena the withheld documents and informed the FDA commissioner, David Kessler, that only the president could claim executive privilege over those materials. The subcommittee informed Kessler that he would be voted in contempt of Congress on November 22 if he did not deliver the disputed documents.

The subcommittee negotiated with the White House Counsel and the FDA for several days before the White House decided against asserting executive privilege and agreed to release all of the disputed documents. The Bush administration gave in to the pressure from the subcommittee just one day before Kessler was to be held in contempt of Congress.

Unlike the Rocky Flats controversy (discussed hereafter), in this case the Bush administration, after weighing the relative risks associated with full disclosure and with nondisclosure, chose not to assert executive privilege. Congress succeeded again in forcing the issue of executive privilege from the cabinet level to the White House.

The Rocky Flats Nuclear Weapons Plant Investigation, 1992

In September, 1992, the Subcommittee on Investigations and Oversight of the House Committee on Science, Space, and Technology began seeking testimony from individuals with knowledge of a five-year-long Federal Bureau of Investigation (FBI) probe of environmental crimes committed by Rockwell International at its Rocky Flats nuclear weapons plant in Golden, Colorado.[68] Although ten criminal violations of environmental law had been acknowledged in Rockwell's plea bargain with the government, no individual culpability had been assigned. The subcommittee, chaired by Rep. Howard Wolpe (D-Michigan), subsequently became interested in examining the plea bargain.

The Justice Department instructed certain individuals who had been called to testify before the Wolpe Committee not to divulge various kinds of information pertaining to the Rocky Flats government investigations. For example, Justice gave an FBI agent who investigated Rocky Flats instructions on what information to withhold. A lawyer from Justice accompanied the man during a congressional inquiry to be sure that privileged information would not be compromised. Justice officials similarly instructed the U.S. district attorney for Colorado, who consequently refused to cooperate with the congressional inquiry.

Wolpe responded by sending a letter to President Bush requesting that the president either personally assert executive privilege or direct the witnesses to the events to testify.[69] The president never responded to the request and there was no presidential approval of the use of executive privilege in the case. White House Counsel C. Boyden Gray wrote to Wolpe to make clear that the White House had no intention of claiming executive privilege and that the Justice Department and the investigating committee should work out their differences.[70]

Without presidential support for a claim of executive privilege, the Justice Department could not withstand further pressure from Congress for candid testimony. The Wolpe Committee threatened to hold the U.S. district attorney for Colorado in contempt of Congress unless certain conditions were met—most importantly, rescinding Justice's "gag rule" over witnesses.[71] The Justice Department agreed to all of the Wolpe Committee's demands and waived all claims of privileged information.[72]

What is noteworthy about this case is that the Justice Department made privilege claims on behalf of the administration—without White House approval—and then backed down when the president would not support those claims. Congress used its powers to full effect in this case—that is, the powers of inquiry and subpoena—in order to get the information that it needed to carry out its investigative functions. Unlike the navy's A-12 aircraft case, the president did not become personally involved, making it easier for Congress to prevail.

EXECUTIVE PRIVILEGE: CONCLUSION

The Bush administration demonstrated that it might be easier to withhold information in the post-Watergate environment by avoiding executive privilege. Bush found a variety of justifications for withholding information from the coordinate branches and the public. He also achieved remarkable success at protecting information that his administration deemed secretive.

Bush did not, however, avoid executive privilege altogether. He personally instructed the use of executive privilege in one information dispute with Congress (the navy's A-12 aircraft controversy) and reluctantly claimed executive privilege to protect his predecessor's diaries from a court subpoena.

On a number of occasions, when lower-level officials claimed executive privilege, Bush chose not to personally approve the use of that power and instead accommodated Congress's demands (for example, the Persian Gulf War document request, the Quayle Council controversy, the Rocky Flats dispute, and, as described later, the overseas arrests memorandum controversy and the INSLAW investigation).

In general, during the Bush years, Congress achieved at least a partial victory—and sometimes a complete victory—when it challenged the administration's exercise of secrecy policies. But Congress did not—and could not—challenge every such incident. As the following shows, although Congress achieved its goal of having the controversial overseas arrests memorandum made public, it was able to do so only after having learned unexpectedly of the existence of such a policy memorandum. The Bush administration Justice Department's "secret opinions policy" shielded vast amounts of information from congressional and public scrutiny. Consequently, the administration lost some information battles with Congress, but it won the information "war" by employing innovative and far-reaching secrecy devices.

The Secret Opinions Policy

One of the most innovative secrecy devices of the Bush administration was the Justice Department's "secret opinions policy," also known as "the Executive Branch policy on the confidentiality of Department of Justice legal advice." Under that policy, Justice could refuse to show Congress legal memorandum opinions from its Office of Legal Counsel.

The secret opinions policy itself was very controversial because Congress traditionally has not been denied access to OLC decision memoranda. Therefore, in addition to the more accepted practice of keeping confidential certain agency discussions, the policy shielded from Congress such vitally important legal memoranda opinions as those pertaining to National Security Decision Directives (NSDDs; Bush changed the title to National Security Directives [NSDs]).

Attorney General Richard Thornburgh created a stir in Congress when he refused all requests for access to secret opinions memoranda, even when the media had reported their existence and Congress held hearings. He refused as well congressional requests for mere lists of the names and dates of opinions. In response to a congressional request for a list of opinions relating to NSDDs, Thornburgh replied: "There are no published or publicly available Office of Legal Counsel legal opinions or analyses on this issue, and *under the Executive Branch policy on the confidentiality of Department of Justice legal advice, we cannot disclose whether the Office of Legal Counsel has provided legal advice concerning the issue.*"[73]

The controversy regarding the secret opinions policy can be illustrated with congressional responses to administration refusals to release NSDD opinions.[74] In the Reagan administration, for example, the president used a secret legal opinion of an NSDD to justify the implementation of actions directly counter to an act of Congress. In 1986, Congress enacted the Comprehensive Anti-Apartheid Act over Reagan's veto. The president issued a classified NSDD calling for "good faith but *non-vindictive* implementation" of the law. The NSDD also committed to the implementation of actions to eliminate state and local antiapartheid laws, contradicting Congress's intent.

To members of Congress, this was the extreme danger of being shielded from executive branch actions: that the administration could purposefully override the will of Congress or conceal important presidential actions by resorting to secret directives. It was one thing to shield confidential deliberations but quite another to use secrecy to thwart the legislative will.

This issue arose a number of times during the Bush years. One such case was congressional requests for information on pre–Gulf War administration actions toward Iraq. Even after various news media reported the existence of an October, 1989, NSD (number 26) regarding the handling of trade restrictions against Iraq, the attorney general refused to make the document available or even confirm its existence.

The secrecy controversy struck many as doubly absurd when the attorney general, in response to congressional requests for information on a specific Justice Department opinion on the legality of secrecy policies, said that the opinion itself was secret. The general counsel to the clerk of the House replied that the logic of this position was "that the Justice Department first may determine that secrecy from Congress is legal, set forth that secret opinion, then refuse to disclose even the existence of that secret opinion, citing further grounds of secrecy."[75]

What concerned many members of Congress was that in addition to shielding vital information, the secret opinions policy gave enormous and, they believed, unconstitutional discretion to the executive to make policy without being held accountable. Two major controversies during the Bush years highlighted the nature of this interbranch dispute.

THE OVERSEAS ARRESTS CONTROVERSY, 1989–92

In 1989, the OLC issued an opinion entitled, "Authority of the FBI to Override Customary or Other International Law in the Course of Extraterritorial Law Enforcement Activities." In brief, the memorandum—which overruled a 1980 Carter administration Justice Department opinion—determined that the FBI could apprehend fugitives abroad without the host country's permission. News of the memorandum resulted in congressional questions regarding the possible lack of statutory authority for such a policy and conflicts with international law. Furthermore, Congress insisted that it could not properly fulfill its oversight function if the recently overruled 1980 opinion was its only available reference point.[76]

The administration made no claim of executive privilege when it refused to divulge the memorandum to Congress. It relied on the newly created "secret opinions policy," a position that Congress refused to accept as legitimate. Nonetheless, the last action taken by Congress was a Judiciary Committee vote to subpoena the memorandum. The issue had become more sensitive because of the January, 1990, arrest of former Panamanian leader Manuel Antonio Noriega and the Justice Department claim that disclosure of the memorandum could harm the government's case against the former dictator. The Justice Department also maintained that the attorney-client privilege would be violated by release of the memorandum because federal agencies in the future would become hesitant to rely on Justice for confidential legal advice.

In the end, both sides "won." A Supreme Court decision upheld the practice of apprehending fugitive criminals in foreign territories. Furthermore, Justice and the House Judiciary Committee agreed to an arrangement whereby committee members could review, but not copy, department documents pertaining to the memorandum as well as the memorandum itself. The committee declared itself victorious and the Bush administration, no longer able to keep the information from Congress, leaked the full memorandum to the *Washington Post.*

THE INSLAW DOCUMENTS CONTROVERSY, 1991–92

One government secrecy controversy that remains unresolved concerns a congressional investigation into allegations that Reagan administration Justice Department officials conspired to force the INSLAW computer company into bankruptcy and then have INSLAW's leading software product bought by another company.[77] When a subcommittee of the House Judiciary Committee sought documents regarding the INSLAW controversy, the Bush administration initially refused to release them, citing the "attorney-client privilege." The Bush White House never formally asserted executive privilege over these documents, although it did consider that option.[78] Instead, after a subcommittee subpoena of the disputed documents and a vote of the full committee to do the same, Justice chose to partially comply with the congressional demands. The department turned over the vast majority of requested materials, yet refused to turn over every document relevant to the congressional inquiry.

The Justice Department position has been that, in ongoing proceedings in which members of the department itself are involved, certain materials must be protected by the traditional attorney-client relationship. Therefore, even though Congress has the power of inquiry, the prerogative of the attorney-client relationship during ongoing proceedings must override that power. Furthermore, Congress's power of inquiry is more compelling when a dispute involves legislation than when a dispute concerns the ongoing operations of another branch of government.

There has been no formal resolution to this interbranch dispute. In addition to never fully complying with the congressional subpoenas, the Bush administration declared that numerous requested documents were "missing." Consequently, the administration partially succeeded in withholding information from Congress without any presidential assertion of executive privilege and Congress partially succeeded in gaining access to disputed executive branch documents. More recently, the Clinton administration Justice Department has been reviewing INSLAW documents in order to edit and remove materials pertaining to national security.

National Security Directives

National Security Directives are an outgrowth of the Cold War era. The National Security Council (NSC) traditionally has issued NSDs in those areas considered too sensitive for open debate and deliberations. What NSDs offer is the opportunity to take secret action precluding the usual checks and balances built into the constitutional scheme. Consequently, from the Truman to the Carter administrations, NSDs were issued sparingly.

The Reagan White House broke precedent and issued more than three hundred NSDDs. As the vice president, George Bush served on the NSC staff and had direct experience with the use of those directives.

As Charles Tiefer, the former House general counsel, reports, the Reagan White House "did not manifest the extremes of secretiveness about directives shown later by its successor administration. At least during the Reagan administration Congress obtained a fair number of whole or partial

NSDDs, and it could track the numbering of NSDDs."[79] Neither the revelations of the Iran-Contra scandal nor the end of the Cold War discouraged Bush from relying on secret directives as a means to further his objectives. Indeed, Bush went well beyond the practices of his predecessors to shield his actions through the use of NSDs.[80]

The Bush administration issued seventy-nine NSDs dealing with such issues as narcotics trafficking, intelligence assistance, intelligence capabilities, covert action, and authorizing the use of force against Iraq. At this writing, there is limited available information on these directives because most of them are still classified. Nonetheless, there is enough available information to explain how Bush protected secret directives.

Although NSDs are directly under the authority of the National Security Council, the national security adviser is not authorized to make them available to members of Congress or the public unless he has the president's consent. Bush's policy was to review congressional requests for access on a case-by-case basis, balancing secrecy needs with those of the legislative branch. Critics of the practice have branded these directives "fugitive laws" because the usual balances built into the separation of powers cannot be employed against unseen laws.

Former representative Lee Hamilton (D-Indiana) laments the growth of NSDs from working position papers to instruments of secretive policy making. These directives, he argues, thwart congressional investigative and oversight duties. "The widespread use of these directives can alter the tenuous balance of power between the Congress and the President," observed Hamilton. "The secrecy and uncertain legality of NSDDs give the president extraordinary power to formulate or alter policy without the knowledge of Congress. The president can amend current NSDDs at will. If Congress cedes to the president the right to withhold information from it, the balance of decisionmaking power shifts dramatically toward the president."[81]

In some cases, Bush's NSDs were statements directing new initiatives in response to emerging technology challenges. As an example, Bush's NSD 42, issued in July, 1990, set forth plans to protect the security of national telecommunications and information systems. The directive identified the problem of technology advances creating substantial challenges for the future of national security and offered a comprehensive plan of protection. It established committees to develop new security procedures and directed the heads of executive departments and agencies to maintain "secure national security systems within their departments or agencies."[82]

Other directives more clearly reflected the concerns that Representative Hamilton raised. Although not intended for public dissemination, Bush's NSD 26, issued in October, 1989, caused a stir when some of its details were reported by the *Washington Post.*[83] The directive was controversial because it established a policy of expanded economic and military ties with Iraq, despite that nation's poor human rights record. In light of the U.S.-assisted Iraqi military buildup that preceded the Persian Gulf War, the revelation of some of the directive's details was especially embarrassing to the Bush administration.

According to the directive, the goal was to provide "economic and political incentives for Iraq to moderate its behavior and to increase our influence with Iraq."[84] The United States committed about $1 billion in loan guarantees to Iraq, much of which was used to finance a massive military buildup. Former Secretary of State James A. Baker III maintains that the administration's efforts to aid Iraq were in keeping with Congress's desire to support U.S. agricultural interests. Iraq was one of the leading purchasers of U.S. agricultural products and had, in Baker's estimation, a "spotless" repayment record. Furthermore, he maintained that NSD 26 gave the administration the flexibility to curtail support for Iraq should its leadership use biological or chemical weapons.[85]

It is difficult to sustain these claims. Iraq had earlier defaulted on loans from the United States, and in 1989, Congress prohibited export-import credits for Iraq. Congress's actions also evidenced a strong desire to curb Iraq's human rights abuses. Consequently, congressional action prior to the invasion of Kuwait displayed a tough stance against Iraq whereas the administration undermined these efforts through secret channels.[86]

After the *Post* broke the story of the directive, members of Congress requested access to it in order to investigate whether Bush's prewar policies actually had precipitated or contributed substantially to Iraq's invasion of Kuwait. National Security Adviser Brent Scowcroft replied that such requests "raise important issues of executive privilege." In this instance, Scowcroft said that the administration's policy generally was to provide access to "relevant directives" to members of congressional committees with jurisdiction and, in certain cases, the staff director and minority staff director. He also noted that the administration would follow that procedure, but provide access only to "relevant portions of the directive." Those reviewing the relevant portions could take notes that would be marked for classification, but could not retain copies.[87]

What happened next illustrates the process of accommodation in some of these types of inquiries. Representative John Dingell, chairman of the Subcommittee on Oversight and Investigations of the Committee on Energy and Commerce, requested that three other staffers be permitted to review the directive.[88] Scowcroft initially refused the request, iterating the administration's policy to limit access only to certain approved individuals.[89] Unsatisfied with that response, Dingell pursued the issue until ultimately the administration agreed, "in the spirit of comity and cooperation," to allow the additional staffers to review portions of the directive.[90]

Adding further controversy to the administration's prewar actions was the revelation that the Atlanta branch of a foreign bank, the Banco Nazionale de Lavoro (BNL), had secured $4 billion in unauthorized loans to Iraq. When Congress tried to investigate the controversy, it met strong administration resistance. In September and October, 1990, the House Committee on Banking, Finance, and Urban Affairs (the "Gonzales Committee") held hearings on the BNL case and voted to subpoena documents.

Upon learning of Congress's investigation, the Bush administration had taken the extraordinary step of trying to persuade the Gonzales Committee not to hold the hearings. Attorney General Thornburgh implored committee chair Rep. Henry Gonzales to cancel the hearings and conveyed strong disappointment when the chairman refused.[91] William Sessions, the FBI director, followed with an appeal that any congressional hearing could compromise the department's "ongoing criminal investigation into these matters."[92] Again the committee proceeded as planned, still unconvinced that the administration was being candid about its reasons for imploring that no hearings be held.

In response to Gonzales's request for White House documents pertaining to the BNL investigation and prewar policy toward Iraq, Attorney General William P. Barr responded more generally: "public disclosure of classified information harms the national security." Barr maintained, but did not support, that Gonzales had previously disclosed classified information and threatened to withhold further documents without an assurance that none would be divulged publicly.[93]

Gonzales continued to demand access to Bush White House documents.[94] His committee made requests for information not only from the White House but also the CIA; National Security Agency; the Departments of Treasury, Defense, Commerce, State, and Justice; and the U.S. Customs Service. The administration directed all agencies to refuse to comply with the requests.[95] The White House also refused the committee's requests for open appearances by the White House or NSC counsel.

Other committees investigating aspects of the BNL controversy and Bush's prewar policies experienced similar difficulties gaining access to executive branch information.[96] In a particularly extreme case, Commerce Department staffers deleted and altered information from relevant documents.

Ultimately, the committees investigating the administration's actions succeeded in getting access to many internal documents, although long after policies had been implemented and changes could be made. The Bush administration succeeded in shielding vast amounts of information that had an enormous bearing on policy development and public perceptions of the wisdom of administration strategies. As Charles Tiefer concluded: "the NSC system gave the president a major advantage" in any disputes with Congress. Moreover:

> Whereas Congress held its debate with full administration participation, the administration, by keeping its NSD-26 and its NSC Committee meetings secret, avoided Congress and the public knowing fully the administration policy and its implementation. The NSC system prevented the possibility that Congress would confront the White House meaningfully on Iraq. . . .
>
> President Bush had conducted foreign policy toward Iraq as he liked, based on his personal hopes of a positive relationship with an unpopular foreign leader without regard to the contrary view of the public and Congress. He had done so not as his predecessor might have through appeals to the country to support his policy, but through the White House staff mechanism left over from the Cold War.[97]

The administration's secret directives also provide insight into high-level perceptions of how policy should reflect changing international circumstances. National Security Review (NSR) 29, issued by CIA director Robert Gates, called for a study of intelligence capabilities through the year 2005. The purpose was to develop a long-range plan to deal with dramatic changes taking place in the world. Among the emphases was that the CIA needed to move beyond the Cold War era mind-set and begin giving greater credence to "many new, non-Soviet issues . . . such as terrorism, narcotics, proliferation, economic intelligence, technology transfer, and others." The many changes in the international environment, therefore, "urgently require a top to bottom examination of the mission, role and priorities of the intelligence community."[98] Hence, although the administration employed Cold War machinery to conduct secret policy, it also moved to update intelligence capabilities in response to dramatic changes in the world.

Secrecy in the Bush Presidency

The Bush administration placed enormous value on protecting governmental secrecy and information control. The president's background was uniquely suited to governing secretly, especially given his extensive experience in intelligence policy, diplomacy, and his service in Congress—no small assets in understanding how to maneuver around the legislature.

To be sure, all administrations take steps to ensure the privacy of internal deliberations and to protect diplomatic negotiations and ongoing investigations. What makes the Bush administration unusual is the extent to which it made policy outside of the normal processes of the separation of powers. Charles Tiefer has aptly referred to Bush's administration as a "semi-sovereign presidency." That is, the president tried to govern "without Congress" whenever possible.[99]

Bush's approach enabled him to work his will through the bureaucracy and avoid public scrutiny and debate of many of his most important actions. Consequently, he achieved a greater lasting impact than credited by observers who have commented on the more visible side of his leadership.

The Bush strategy in part was an accommodation of the realities of divided government. Because his domestic initiatives often met defeat in the Democratic Congress, he focused much more on those areas in which he could act unilaterally to influence policy. In that sense, the public perception of Bush as a foreign policy president was accurate. He had, and had exercised, much greater discretion under the Constitution in the international realm than at home. Yet Bush also created opportunities for unilateral action by aggressively broadening the powers of secrecy.

Scholar Richard Rose described Bush as a "guardian president"; that is, one who "wants to limit the scope of presidential intervention, favoring less, rather than more, government." In this apt description, Rose explained that the guardian president may be passive at home while active abroad.[100] To maintain the status quo required little action at home, but in the international arena it required presidential action in response to events that threatened the order of things. Bush found that he could better achieve his objectives abroad through quiet diplomacy and secret action, even if it meant working around the usual constraints of separated governmental powers. This approach suited Bush's desire for low-key leadership in which the chief executive manages change in a cautious, "go-slow" fashion.

CHAPTER 5

Prudence as Public Policy

Evaluating the Bush Presidency

THE PREVAILING INTERPRETATION of George H. W. Bush's presidency holds that his approach to the office was as a caretaker whose obsession with prudence usually led to inaction. According to this view, he was a president with almost no domestic agenda and a bifurcated record in foreign affairs. One of the most lasting impressions of Bush remaining from his tenure is not even of the president himself, but of comedian Dana Carvey's frequent impersonations on television's *Saturday Night Live.* Carvey's exaggerated—and funny—parodies of George Bush's shorthand syntax and frequent repetition of the phrase "wouldn't be prudent," played to a generalized impression that the president feared doing anything, lest he risk making a mistake.

Bush sought the presidency as Ronald Reagan's political heir and promised continuity with the president whose tenure had marked "a new direction in American politics." Rather than proclaiming his own course for the nation, Bush offered voters a "kinder, gentler" form of Reaganism: that is, a continuation of "the great communicator's" policies, but with Bush's own personal style.

Bush did indeed approach policy with an eye toward prudence, but this approach favored incrementalism rather than inaction. In foreign affairs, he exhibited a commitment to core principles and methods that in some instances led to caution and in others more aggressive action. In domestic affairs, Bush emphasized a political strategy that he believed would lead to modest but substantive policy accomplishments. Underlying both sides of policy was Bush's understanding of *prudence* according to the word's original meaning: not timidity, but a realistic assessment of possibilities.

Foreign Policy

When he assumed the presidency in 1989, George Bush brought to the office the widest experience in foreign policy of any American chief executive since Eisenhower. When he left office after losing the 1992 election, he carried a reputation for both aggressive diplomatic and military leadership in the world (largely because of the Persian Gulf War) and yet timidity in promoting democracy (because of the way he responded to the fall of communism). Could such a Jekyll-and-Hyde characterization accurately describe his foreign policy?

The short answer to this question is no. The George Bush who won the Gulf War is the same man who counseled patience as the Soviet Empire dissolved. As much as it may have appeared that he was too hot in one area and too cool in another, there was a consistency to Bush's approach to world affairs that was not always apparent to his critics. Although his foreign policy was mostly that of an incrementalist, the president at times took leaps rather than small steps to advance his goals. George Bush's foreign policy was grounded in a worldview, a method, and a style that he brought with him to the Oval Office when he succeeded Ronald Reagan.

GEORGE BUSH'S WORLDVIEW

President Bush's worldview was founded in his resume. Like Dwight Eisenhower before him, Bush belied an observation that historian Robert Divine once made regarding American chief executives: "A curious pattern runs through the history of the twentieth century American presidency. In a period when international affairs have loomed large in national life, we have tended to choose Presidents experienced and skilled only in domestic politics. Rarely do we consider ambassadors or secretaries of state as likely candidates for the White House; instead we turn to governors or senators, men whose credentials are frequently based solely on their handling of problems at home. Yet once in office, we expect these executives to deal with complex foreign situations and to exhibit great skill in diplomacy."[1]

Unlike most of his predecessors, Bush shared with Eisenhower the credentials to claim status as a foreign policy professional. Not only did this background give him the air of being "presidential" (that undefined quality sought in candidates for the office), it also gave him a view of foreign policy that pervaded his conduct once in office.

The Diplomat as President

George Bush's pre-presidential career involved dealing with foreign governments, intelligence, and the substantive issues of international affairs as much as it did negotiating in the bare-knuckles world of domestic politics. While Bush had held leadership positions in the Texas and national Republican Party organizations, he clearly preferred dealing with issues of world affairs. When Jimmy Carter was elected president in 1976, Bush—then serving as CIA director—reportedly offered to forswear future partisan politics if the president-elect would keep him on as the national intelligence chief. Carter refused and Bush returned to partisan politics, but he retained the outlook of the diplomat-politician.

George Bush acquired this outlook over the course of his political career. His early ventures into politics revealed no special expertise or ability in international affairs. He had served as a navy pilot in the Pacific during World War II, but many other politicians of his generation had similar military experiences and none claimed any special expertise because of it. He began as chair of the Harris County, Texas (Houston), Republican organization (1961–63) and was later elected to a seat in the U.S. House of Representatives (1967–71). After losing a Senate race in 1970, for which he was forced to give up his House seat, Bush might have faced an early end to his political career. But President Nixon rescued him from political oblivion by appointing Bush to be the U.S. ambassador to the United Nations. That appointment was the turning point of Bush's career: from that point on he became a foreign policy professional.

Bush's appointment sparked some controversy, which perhaps was the impetus for him to develop an expertise in world affairs. The Nixon administration and Bush's supporters touted his intelligence and political skills, but detractors regarded him as unqualified for the UN post. As Bush recounted in his autobiography, critics dismissed him as "a lame-duck Congressman with little experience in foreign affairs and less in diplomacy."[2] Upon winning approval from the Senate, Bush made it his business to prove his critics wrong.

Although the rest of his career was not limited exclusively to foreign policy (he was chairman of the Republican National Committee in 1973–74), he worked hard to gain experience and develop a reputation for expertise in international affairs. He acquired the outlook of the Cold War professionals who managed American foreign policy during this period, for he became one of them. At the United Nations (1971–73), as head of the American liaison office in the People's Republic of China (1974–75), and as the CIA director (1975–76), George Bush schooled himself in the intricacies of international diplomacy and the outlook of its practitioners.

He came to identify with the foreign policy professionals with whom he worked. Even as president, he identified more with foreign affairs managers than domestic political operatives. In his first days as president, Bush met with the State Department's career officers at the department's headquarters in Foggy Bottom. His message was one of appreciation and support for the role that professionals play in the conduct of American foreign policy. During Bush's first foreign trip while in office—to Europe in 1989—he had several opportunities to address American Foreign Service personnel and their families. These talks were unpublicized at the time, so they are especially revealing of how the nation's top politician identified with career officers. In remarks made at the American School in Brussels, where many U.S. government personnel send their children, he said: "Let me say, I have great respect for those of you in the Foreign Service. And you're talking to one who was supported so strongly when I first went up to the United Nations as Ambassador. . . . And it made a profound impression on me. And then I saw it again when I was in China. . . . I have respect for those of you who are attached to the embassies, be it as career people, from Commerce, and certainly our military, USIA [U.S. Information Agency], and many other organizations."[3]

Later, addressing the employees of the American Embassy in Bonn, Germany, he displayed his knowledge of the work and worries of the Foreign Service: "I was on the receiving end of some of these visits when I lived halfway around the world in China, and I know that they can be a pluperfect pain. And so, I would only thank . . . everybody . . . in the political and the economic and every section—communications—every section of this tremendous and effective Embassy that has been involved in this visit."[4]

Bush's identification with foreign policy professionals manifests itself as more than just sympathy for the Foreign Service, however. It left him with a coherent set of entrenched values that governed his outlook on how international relations ought to be conducted. These values placed great emphasis on the need for order and stability in world affairs, good personal relations among national leaders, and sensitivity to the interests and views of other countries.

Bush's Conservative Internationalism

Whatever views about diplomacy he may have had before his years in the foreign policy establishment, by the time he became president George Bush had developed an overall attitude toward world affairs that can be characterized as a conservative internationalism.[5] This approach is shaped by a desire to promote the classical and universal values associated with the American system—including liberty, democracy, and republicanism—but to do so through means that seek to ensure security and stability in the international arena.

Two dimensions of Bush's conservative internationalism can be seen in major world developments during his presidency. In one dimension, there was Bush's cautious reaction to the breakup of the Soviet Union's Eastern European empire and to the fall of the Soviet regime itself. As pleased as any American president would have been to hold office during such momentous events as the fall of the Berlin Wall and the "Velvet Revolution" in Czechoslovakia, George Bush hesitated to claim victory for the West in the rapidly ending Cold War. Nor did he wish to gloat in the face of the Kremlin's problems holding together its empire, despite the obvious fact that it was exactly such developments that had been a central goal of American policy since the articulation of the Truman Doctrine.

The best example of this view—and the most telling statement of it by Bush himself—came in the president's public comments about the fast-moving events of 1990, when the Cold War division of Europe was evaporating and pressure for German reunification was building. As the United States and its European allies worked to manage the winding down of the Cold War, Bush met frequently with British prime minister Margaret Thatcher, French president François Mitterand, and West German chancellor Helmut Kohl. Following one meeting with Kohl, the American president revealed to reporters the concerns that underlay his incrementalism: "The enemy is unpredictability, the enemy is instability."[6] While Germans were eager to embrace the possibilities for reunification made possible by the tremendous changes in 1989, George Bush counseled incremental steps to keep events from swirling out of control. He preached—and practiced—a foreign policy aimed at promoting international stability.

Bush's caution regarding these developments prompted some critics to complain that the president and his foreign policy team were nostalgic for the Cold War's predictability. Yet the president's caution arose from his concern that unpredictability and instability were bigger threats to international peace than Soviet imperialism or the defunct Brezhnev

Doctrine (a Western term for Soviet premier Leonid Brezhnev's principle justifying the brutal crackdown during the "Prague Spring" of 1968: no country would be allowed to withdraw from the Soviet Empire). Bush wanted to promote democracy, but not at the risk of war. His strategy was to move cautiously.

The other dimension of Bush's type of internationalism can be seen in his reaction to Iraq's invasion of Kuwait in 1990. Bush saw the occupation as a violation of international law and the principle of national sovereignty, but his initial response was to be careful in both words and deeds. He resisted making any blunt statements demanding that Iraq withdraw from Kuwait, but when Arab attempts to deal with the crisis failed, Bush turned to international sanctions and ultimately a ferocious war machine to drive Iraqi forces from Baghdad's small neighbor.

These two dimensions highlight the conservatism and the internationalism of George Bush's worldview. On one hand, Bush was committed to an active American role in the world. At the same time, however, he saw the United States as a force for stability and order as it pursued its goals of liberty and democracy. In both of these ideas, Bush reflected the views of the professionals he emulated. Similar to them, he also employed a method that emphasized strong personal relations among national leaders in world affairs.

THE BUSH METHOD OF DIPLOMACY

Commenting on Bush's conduct of American foreign policy from the perspective of his political retirement, Richard Nixon observed: "Bush believes, far more than I, in the effectiveness of personal diplomacy. He believes that if you have a good personal relationship, it helps on substance."[7] Although Nixon added that he disagreed with Bush's confidence in this regard, this observation was accurate nevertheless.

Bush's preferred method for dealing with all issues was through personal interactions. As one chronicle of the Bush presidency put it, "Bush had always preferred the personal touch to the grand gesture."[8] This same narrative described the president as "the master of the one-on-one meeting."[9] White House political director Ron Kaufman echoed this assessment when he discussed the contrast between Bush the weak public persuader and Bush the man of nearly unmatched one-on-one persuasion skills. Kaufman explained that Bush was a great politician in the old school sense: terrific when dealing with individuals outside of the public view. Bush knew every important and even not-so-important political player and could recall almost every detail about that person's family, background, and political views or aspirations.[10] This method of action was clearly on display in foreign affairs, where Bush practiced what more than one observer called "Rolodex diplomacy." Bush's skills therefore were specially suited to the needs of international leadership, where a president can accomplish much through personal interactions with world leaders and not necessarily have to rely on public persuasion.

The Personal Touch

As if to confirm Nixon's statement about personal diplomacy, President Bush made no effort to conceal his belief in personal relations early in his memoir of the end of the Cold War. The first pages of *A World Transformed* (written with Brent Scowcroft) describe a December, 1988, meeting in New York between outgoing President Ronald Reagan, Vice-President and President-elect Bush, and Soviet leader Mikhail Gorbachev.[11] After setting the scene, Bush turns quickly to the subject of his reliance on personal relations among leaders: "I first met Gorbachev on March 13, 1985, when I was in Moscow representing President Reagan . . . at the funeral of his predecessor as Soviet general secretary, Konstantin Chernenko. . . . State funerals allow world leaders to hold brief talks. In addition, these occasions gave us the chance to eye the new man in charge. With the high mortality rate in the top position at the Kremlin during that period, we had little *first-hand knowledge of the personalities of the Soviet leaders*."[12]

Another personal relationship important to President Bush was the one he had with Margaret Thatcher. In comments reminiscent of his introduction of Gorbachev, Bush introduces Thatcher in his memoir by focusing on the length and quality of their personal interactions: "I first met her in Houston back in 1977, when I was asked to introduce her at an English Speaking Union event. She was not yet prime minister, and I was not in public office at the time. I was greatly impressed with her speaking ability. Later, as vice-president, I saw a great deal of her when I traveled to London and on each of her visits to the United Nations. Margaret and I became good friends. I regret that we never were quite as close as she had been to Ronald Reagan."[13]

Bush's attachment to the idea of personal relationships was reinforced by his service among foreign policy professionals, but it is part of a larger pattern in his political style. Bush placed great value on personal relationships in choosing most of his administration's senior officials. His secretary of state, James Baker, was a longtime personal friend and political associate who had served as chairman of Bush's failed Senate campaign in Texas in 1970 and unsuccessful bid for the Republican presidential nomination in 1980. Bush had also worked closely with his assistant for national security affairs, Brent Scowcroft, in the Ford administration, when Bush was CIA director. Indeed, at the news conference introducing Scowcroft as his choice for security assistant, Bush phrased their relationship as one in which he had previously worked *for* Brent Scowcroft in the Ford administration (thus indicating the central role of the national security adviser in presidential conduct of foreign policy). Likewise, Bush's secretary of defense, Dick Cheney, was another veteran of the Ford administration, having served as White House chief of staff. Finally, the president's choice of Gen. Colin Powell to serve as chairman of the Joint Chiefs of Staff had its roots in the Reagan White House, where Vice-President Bush had worked with Powell when the general was Reagan's national security adviser.

President Bush had prior experience with most of his cabinet and senior Executive Office staff. This preference on Bush's part, especially with regard to cabinet appointments, stands in marked contrast to the appointments of nearly all modern presidents. The typical cabinet officer in a new administration may know the president-elect slightly (or not at all), but has been appointed on the basis of experience, reputation, political connections, or a variety of demographic considerations (ethnicity, religion, home state, and so forth). Washington insiders noted that the Bush administration was a "government of friends" rather than strangers (in a twist on Hugh Heclo's characterization of the federal executive branch's upper echelons). Bush valued competence, but he relied on personal relationships in his appointments; it is no surprise that he valued it in his interactions with his international peers.

"Rolodex Diplomacy"

Although he did not always achieve success in cultivating warm personal relationships with foreign leaders, Bush worked assiduously to develop a good working relationship with most of his major international counterparts. He was close to Canadian prime minister Brian Mulroney, Egyptian president Hosni Mubarak, German chancellor Kohl, and even Soviet president Mikhail Gorbachev. With others, his relations were more distant, although Bush never quite gave up trying to do more; this was true of France's Mitterand, South African president F. W. De Klerk (with whom Bush maintained a quiet correspondence), and Israeli prime minister Yitzhak Shamir. Frustrated by his inability to connect with Shamir, Bush asked his aides "How can I get through to this guy?" and tried to learn all he could about the prime minister's hobbies and interests.[14]

The point of this "Rolodex diplomacy" was to cut through the distance of official relationships and facilitate greater cooperation. As Bush related in his memoir: "I believed that personal contact would be an important part of our approach to both diplomacy and leadership of the alliance and elsewhere. . . . I suppose there is a danger that one can be naively lulled into complacency if one expects friendships will cause the other party to do things your way, but I thought that danger was remote. For me, personal diplomacy and leadership went hand in hand."[15]

However, Bush also believed that personal diplomacy helped to serve his goal of stability: "There are actually commonsense reasons for an American president to build relationships with his opposites. If a foreign leader knows the character and heartbeat of the president (and vice versa), there is apt to be far less miscalculation on either side. Personal relationships may not overcome tough issues dividing two sides, but they can provide enough goodwill to avoid some misunderstandings. . . . It can make the difference between suspicion and giving each other the benefit of the doubt."[16]

In a world in which international events might spiral into armed conflict and perhaps even nuclear destruction, the diplomat as president placed a premium on personal relations for preventing instability and unpredictability. Bush's method thus conformed to his worldview.

PRUDENCE AS POLICY: THE BUSH STYLE OF FOREIGN POLICY

George Bush's foreign policy style was initially deceptive. With the generally cautious manner of the professional diplomat and Cold War manager, Bush appeared to be reflexively opposed to strong and decisive action. Nonetheless, his presidency was also marked by actions that belied this overall image of the man who feared doing what "wouldn't be prudent," including sending American military forces to Panama in 1989 and the Desert Shield/Desert Storm operations of 1990–91. How could these apparent differences be explained?

The answer is that the superficial divergence between the cautious Bush and the aggressive Bush conceal an underlying consistency to his style of foreign policy. The two faces of his conduct were united by his worldview and method, as two key issues during his administration illustrate: German unification and the invasion of Kuwait.

German Unification

George Bush's first two years in the White House were times of tremendous change in world politics. During that period, popular uprisings against Soviet-dominated governments in Eastern Europe led to the collapse of the Soviet Empire in that region, an end to the divisions of the Cold War, and the eventual reunification of Germany. When German unification became a reality in October, 1990, Chancellor Helmut Kohl addressed his nation in celebration of the event and made a special effort to "thank the United States of America and above all President Bush" for helping to advance the cause of German unity.[17] What was intriguing about Kohl's remarks was that his tribute to the United States, and specifically to George Bush, stood in contrast to the judgment of many commentators who had characterized the president as more of a bystander than a mover in the great changes that made reunification possible.[18]

What was George Bush's role in German unification? He played a limited but nevertheless important part in bringing about a united and democratic Germany that remained in NATO. Bush saw the push for Germany's reunification as part of a larger process of change sweeping the continent. Indeed, the word "process" is relevant here because this diplomat as president believed in the value of incremental processes for addressing difficult issues in a careful but constructive way.

During the first two years of his presidency, Bush's foreign policy was unified by his desire to build on an overall improvement in U.S.-Soviet relations that had begun during Ronald Reagan's second term (1985–89). In May, 1989, the new president spoke publicly on the need to move "beyond containment" by recognizing the "full scope of change taking place in the Soviet Union itself" and stated, "We seek the integration of the Soviet Union into the community of nations."[19]

Much of this moving "beyond containment" was atmospheric in nature. Consistent with Bush's preferred method, it included cultivating a personal relationship with Soviet president Mikhail Gorbachev. In December, 1989, the two men met in a "summit at sea" held on a ship off the coast of Malta. Although the event had almost no agenda or substantive content, Bush used the occasion to make modest proposals in the areas of arms control and international trade. The meeting's primary point, however, was symbolic: it initiated a personal contact between Bush and Gorbachev that became increasingly important. At the same time, Bush was working to develop personal relations with Kohl and other NATO leaders. The overall point of Bush's efforts was to use "Rolodex diplomacy" to avoid the outbreak of conflict as events in Europe seemed to accelerate the pace of international change.

The first test of Bush's idea of moving "beyond containment" occurred in April, 1989, when Chancellor Kohl issued a public call for negotiations on reducing the number of short-range nuclear weapons in Europe. Kohl was responding to domestic political pressure in his country, whereas Bush and other NATO leaders (especially Margaret Thatcher) feared the undermining of NATO's defensive credibility in the face of a potential attack on Western Europe by Warsaw Pact forces.

Bush's immediate reaction was a characteristic one: he invited Kohl "to come to Camp David or to Washington for an informal talk, just to sort out the issues."[20] Kohl replied that domestic political problems required his attention, but sent his foreign policy adviser instead. Over the next several weeks, Bush met with Kohl's aide, NATO secretary general Manfred Wörner (a former German defense minister and political ally of Kohl's), British foreign secretary Geoffrey Howe, France's Mitterand, and other allied leaders to develop a counterproposal. The resulting plan called for reductions in NATO and Warsaw Pact conventional forces (thus reducing the risk of an invasion that might trigger the use of nuclear weapons). Faced with a united NATO leadership, Margaret Thatcher withdrew her resistance and endorsed the plan. Kohl was able to claim success and endorsed Bush's plan effusively, calling it "bold" and saying that it "once more impressively affirms the United States's leadership."[21] The outcome unified the NATO leaders as events continued to shake the foundations of Europe's postwar balance.

Meanwhile, Bush came under increasing pressure to move "beyond containment." By the early weeks of 1990, the Berlin Wall had been opened and was coming down, a Solidarity-led government ruled Poland, Vaclev Havel was president of Czechoslovakia, Nicolai Ceaucescu had been deposed in Romania, and free elections were scheduled or promised across most of Eastern Europe. Trying to keep up with the rapid pace of events and maintain stability, in February Bush used the occasion of the State of the Union Address to call for further reduction of American and Soviet conventional forces in Europe. Drawing upon his personal relationship with Gorbachev, Bush had already cleared the plan with the Soviet leader and was able to win quick approval for it in the United States.

That summer, Bush continued with his incremental policies aimed at managing change in Europe. Working with Helmut Kohl, he developed a plan to further reduce NATO forces, increase diplomatic initiatives to the

Soviet Union, and negotiate a nonagression treaty with the Warsaw Pact. That proposal, adopted by NATO leaders at a summit in London in July, 1990, ratcheted up the West's response to changes in Europe.

Throughout this period of change, the issue that seemed most threatening to peaceful change was the question of German unification. Germany's division since the end of World War II led to the creation of the central symbol of the Cold War: the Berlin Wall. For Germans, unification was crucial to national identity. But to Germany's traditional adversaries, France and Russia, a reunited Germany represented the potential for war. George Bush's response was to support the concept of German unification but counsel against destabilizing peace in Europe because of excessive enthusiasm for unity.

To that end, Bush stressed the need for stability, process, and incremental advances toward the ultimate (that is, long-term) goal of German unity. He described reunification as a choice the Germans must make themselves, but he never expressed more than cautious optimism about its prospects. He feared an overreaction from the still-formidable Soviet forces. As Bush put it in his memoir, "On the day the [Berlin] Wall opened [November 9, 1989], Gorbachev sent messages to Kohl warning him to stop talking of reunification, and cabled me urging that I not overreact."[22] In response to Gorbachev's message, Bush told the Soviet leader that he "shared his concern that public safety and order be maintained" and "emphasizing the importance of a deliberate step-by-step approach to change in the GDR [German Democratic Republic] and the need to avoid destabilizing the situation in Europe."[23]

Bush saw the pressure for unity as potentially disastrous. He feared that the Germans might accept neutralization in order to diminish Soviet resistance to unity; that a united Germany might revive old questions about the Polish border (which had played a part in the origins of World War II); or that the Soviet Union, fearing the loss of its ally East Germany (the GDR), might use force to prevent unification. He therefore concentrated on the mechanics of unification. The Bush administration played a large role in the creation of the "two-plus-four" process for resolving issues raised by unification: the two Germanys were joined by the four World War II Allied powers (the United States, Britain, France, and the Soviet Union) who still held rights in the Germanys as a result of the settlement of the war. In February, 1990, the two-plus-four framework received formal approval and set the stage for a peaceful resolution of the unification issue.

While emphasizing process, Bush held two substantive positions that ultimately shaped the eventual consequences of the fall of the Berlin Wall. First, he insisted that a reunited Germany accept the Oder–Neisse line that had been drawn after World War II. This was an issue on which Chancellor Kohl wanted to equivocate because of domestic pressures, but Bush emphasized that a united Germany would not be possible if it threatened to reopen an issue as volatile as that one. Second, Bush insisted that the United States would accept reunification only if a united Germany remained in NATO. By June, 1990, he had persuaded Gorbachev to accept this condition, clearing the way for the reunion of the two Germanys.

The Invasion of Kuwait

The second half of George Bush's presidency was dominated by the invasion of Kuwait and the Persian Gulf War that resulted from it. Much has been written and said about the war and its conduct, as well as on the contrast between Bush's decisive role in assembling the coalition against Iraq and his apparent irresolution in response to the American recession of 1991 and 1992. What most analyses of the case overlook, however, is how the president's actions and decisions moved him cautiously toward the overwhelming use of force, and how the end of the war reflects Bush's emphasis on prudence in policy making. The following discussion thus focuses on those aspects of the case.

When Iraq invaded Kuwait in August, 1990, President Bush was on his way to Aspen, Colorado, to address a conference at the Aspen Institute. Prime Minister Margaret Thatcher was already in Aspen when she learned of the invasion, and Bush was due to arrive the next day. Shortly after his arrival, Bush met with Thatcher, who hit him with the full force of her argument for a forceful response to the invasion. As Thatcher later described their meeting, "George Bush just said to me, 'Now Margaret, what do you think?' straight away." Her response was direct: "aggression must be stopped. That is the lesson of this century. And if an aggressor gets away with it, others will want to get away with it too, so he must be stopped, and turned back. You cannot gain from aggression."[24]

Bush agreed with Thatcher on the principle involved in this situation, but he was determined to take a more cautious approach than what the prime minister wanted. As he relates their meeting in his memoir, "Margaret and I saw the situation in remarkably similar ways, which I think was mutually reassuring." Thatcher, however, wanted Bush to respond forcefully to Iraq's aggression. When he confronted the first situation in which force might have to be employed against an Iraqi vessel (in late August, 1990), she said: "look George, this is no time to go wobbly."[25] For his part, Bush did not regard caution as "wobbliness."

Bush's response to the invasion moved through several phases. The first took place in the days immediately following Kuwait's occupation. Speaking to the press in Aspen, Bush and Thatcher jointly condemned the attack. Soon after that, the president returned to Washington and convened a meeting of the National Security Council to discuss options. They initially focused on diplomatic pressures to force Iraq to withdraw, as well as economic sanctions and other peaceful means of action. Meanwhile, Bush was communicating with his counterparts in the Middle East and NATO. At the United Nations, American diplomats successfully made the case for condemning the invasion and were rewarded by the Security Council with resolutions imposing economic sanctions on Iraq. Bush then dispatched Defense Secretary Richard Cheney to Saudi Arabia to seek permission to move American troops onto Saudi soil (an unprecedented action), which was granted by the king. A small force was assigned the task, primarily as a warning to Iraq not to move against Saudi Arabia.

As the fall of 1990 wore on, a second phase took shape. During this period, Bush and his administration engaged in extensive diplomatic efforts to assemble a coalition against Iraq, while also building domestic political support for opposition to the occupation. He enlarged the American military presence in Saudi Arabia, but insisted that although the buildup was intended to make possible an offensive option, it did not preclude a peaceful resolution to the problem. In his memoir, Bush referred to his efforts as "a delicate balance" because he was trying to "avoid force until we had the domestic and international support to follow through with it to the end."[26] To that end, he and his team made efforts along several fronts: frequent direct contacts with international leaders, especially Thatcher, Pres. Hosni Mubarak of Egypt, Prince Bandar (ambassador to the United States) and King Fahd of Saudi Arabia, and Gorbachev; meetings with congressional leaders; negotiations at the United Nations; and a public relations campaign to promote and solidify popular support for the administration's response to the situation.[27] To emphasize that he wanted to avoid conflict, the president told congressional leaders at one meeting, "I have not crossed any Rubicon."[28]

On October 30, 1990, President Bush participated in two key meetings that opened a third phase of the operation. The first meeting was with a bipartisan delegation of congressional leaders. While some of the members of Congress in attendance favored the use of force that seemed to be on the horizon, the leaders of Congress's Democratic majority made it clear to the president that they had deep reservations about a military offensive. Later that day, Bush met with his key foreign policy and security advisers. After an extensive review of options, the president decided to continue with the military buildup to keep open the option of using force. However, the announcement of this decision was not released until after the congressional elections held on November 6.[29]

The focus of attention next shifted to whether or not President Bush would decide to launch an offensive to drive Iraqi forces out of Kuwait. Bush continued with his public and private efforts to build support for a firm response, hoping to encourage Iraq's Saddam Hussein to back down. While he was moving more aggressively than congressional Democrats liked, he also moved more cautiously than allies such as Thatcher wanted. For example, Thatcher saw no need to rely on the United Nations, because "it suggested that sovereign states lacked the moral authority to act on their own behalf."[30] In contrast, Bush regarded a UN-sponsored approach as essential to bringing Arab states into the anti-Iraq coalition and to keeping the Soviet Union from openly opposing the mounting pressure against its former client.[31]

The Bush administration's international lobbying efforts intensified during this third phase, resulting in the passage of UN Security Council Resolution 678 on November 29, 1990. The resolution set a deadline of January 15, 1991, for the withdrawal of Iraqi troops from Kuwait, or else the anti-Iraq coalition of UN member states would be authorized to use "all necessary means" to "restore peace and security to the area."[32] Firm as it was, the deadline reflected a compromise between the original American proposal of January 1 and Gorbachev's desire to move the date back to the end of January. Bush was willing to compromise with the Soviet leader in order to hold his coalition together.

A fourth phase began as the focus of attention shifted to the question of whether Iraq could be induced to withdraw before force was employed. Bush tried more than one diplomatic measure to prevent conflict, including a proposal for meetings in Washington and Baghdad to seek a peaceful solution. The president's public announcement of this idea is interesting for what it demonstrates about Bush's attempts to avoid conflict. One journalistic account of how Saudi ambassador Prince Bandar received the news reveals that what the president thought would be a gesture to promote peace might inadvertently have made war more likely:

> Bush appeared [on television] and went through a 20-paragraph statement about his Gulf policy, listing all the steps he had taken. "However, to go the extra mile for peace," he said, he would receive Iraqi Foreign Minister Tariq Aziz in Washington. "In addition, I'm asking Secretary Jim Baker to go to Baghdad to see Saddam Hussein . . . at a mutually convenient time between December 15th and January 15th of next year."
>
> Bandar nearly shot out of his chair in disbelief and surprise. How stupid, he thought. Americans would never understand Arabs. A peace offering 24 hours after the United States and the coalition had scored the United Nations victory [Security Council Resolution 678] would send precisely the wrong message to Saddam: a message of weakness.[33]

A visit by Aziz was initially scheduled, but eventually canceled by Saddam, who also refused to meet with Baker. Bush made several entreaties to Baghdad to try to hold a meeting before the January 15 deadline, in hopes of arriving at a peaceful solution, but the Iraqi leader eventually agreed to only a single meeting between Aziz and Baker in Geneva on January 9. That meeting was fruitless, however, and the deadline for withdrawal soon passed.

Operation Desert Storm began in the Middle East early in the morning on January 17, 1991 (late evening of January 16 in Washington). It consisted of aerial bombing, naval shelling, and cruise missile attacks. This air campaign went on for a month. Meanwhile, Bush and the coalition laid down another deadline for the withdrawal of Iraqi forces to prevent the beginning of a ground war. On February 22, the president issued a declaration on behalf of the coalition calling on Iraq to begin withdrawing its forces by noon the next day or face a full-scale attack. Hussein tried a last-minute gesture to buy time, but a few hours after the final deadline passed the ground campaign was launched.

The conclusion of the Persian Gulf War was both remarkable and controversial. It was remarkable for the speed with which it occurred and the relatively small loss of life by coalition forces that accompanied it. Barely a hundred hours after it had begun, the ground offensive was halted and President Bush declared victory. This abrupt closure made the war's conclusion controversial, for Bush was criticized then and later for not going all the way to Baghdad and completing the destruction of Saddam

Hussein's dictatorial regime. Bush, however, maintained that he was acting only to the extent of his UN mandate and the political realities of the international coalition. Many of the states that had supported the offensive or acquiesced to it, such as the Soviet Union, would not support carrying the war that far. In short, Bush believed he was being prudent in drawing the war to a close as soon as its objective of rooting Iraqi forces out of Kuwait had been achieved.

The Policy of Prudence

William Bennett, who served President Bush as both federal "drug czar" and partisan supporter, once said that the key to understanding George Bush was to see him as part of the generation of American leaders whose adult lives were dedicated to managing and winning the Cold War.[34] This insight is important, because the Cold War surrounded the American presidency and the U.S. government's entire national security establishment with a mystique that gave foreign policy management the air of an almost sacred art. Critical events of the Cold War—the Berlin blockade (1948), the U-2 incident (1960), the Bay of Pigs invasion (1961), the Cuban missile crisis (1962), Nixon's visits to Moscow and China (1972), and Reagan's summits (1980s)—cloaked the chief executive in a mantle of awesome responsibility.

This mystique was magnified by Cold War thrillers—movies such as *Fail-Safe*, *Seven Days in May*, and even *Dr. Strangelove*—that celebrated the careful management of crises and the avoidance of nuclear war as the highest achievements of statecraft. In this vein, Gore Vidal's *The Best Man* offers a testament to Cold War crisis management: the central character, a secretary of state running for president, tells a colleague that he is the best candidate for the Oval Office because he knows what to do if the Soviet Union or China were to precipitate a crisis, whereas his competitor for the nomination was likely to do something rash and start a war.

George Bush, the diplomat as president, shared much of this outlook. In the introduction to his memoir, he points directly to the president's role as custodian of national security and chief executive of the Cold War: "The Bush Administration reached a national goal sought since the early 1950s . . . freedom for Eastern Europe and the end to a mortal threat to the United States."[35] He was the last Cold War president, and his tenure in office was marked by the end and aftermath of that struggle.

Bush thus addressed foreign policy as one who believed that prudence, personal diplomacy, and incrementalism were the best means to protect international stability and prevent disaster. In the case of German unification, he was neither a bystander nor the architect of a reunited Germany. Rather, he was a kind of facilitator—something like the professional diplomat which he considered himself to be—who helped construct a process for achieving unity, set certain conditions for the shape of that unity, and helped move the interested parties incrementally toward a successful outcome. In the case of the invasion of Kuwait, he also moved cautiously, but with different results. Since he defined the problem as the maintenance of the basic structure of international relations—sovereignty, resistance of aggression, international law—he was led to a much more assertive course than he took in response to the events of 1989. Nevertheless, he always saw himself as acting prudently, despite temptations and pressures to do otherwise.

Domestic Policy

George Bush approached domestic policy with a decided political strategy. As with foreign policy, he wanted to proceed cautiously. He employed an incremental approach to domestic policy that was built around his assessment of the circumstances of his tenure in office, a particular notion of what constituted a successful presidency, and his own ideas about the issues facing the United States in the late 1980s.

Criticism of Bush has always been harshest regarding his domestic policy stewardship. In part, the criticism reflected a preference for greater policy activism than Bush was willing to offer. In part it also reflected the fact that, as Boyden Gray observed, when Bush *did* achieve domestic successes he "did not receive a lot of credit because he didn't do it in a way that broke china."[36] Bush himself has said that his greatest leadership disappointment was the failure to communicate better to the public in 1992 that he had control of the domestic economy and that the nation was moving toward prosperity under his helm.[37] While he was in office, it was not Bush's style to trumpet big plans or to brag about his accomplishments.

BUSH'S ASSESSMENT OF THE PRESIDENTIAL CONTEXT

No president comes to office in a vacuum; nor is any chief executive given a blank check to make policy. As a man whose approach to policy stressed prudence—a realistic assessment of possibilities—George Bush viewed his tenure in the White House as being marked by very specific circumstances relevant to shaping domestic policy. He was Ronald Reagan's successor and he inherited a prosperous nation that had experienced considerable policy change and faced large budget deficits. His administration's domestic policies were constructed in that context. Furthermore, he inherited a politically challenging situation. As Deputy Chief of Staff Andrew Card reminded, "we have a tendency today to forget what the political context was like in 1989, 1990. The Democrats had the votes in Congress. President Bush had to work with both the Democratic majority and the very frustrated congressional Republicans."[38]

The Second Martin Van Buren

During the 1988 presidential election campaign, George Bush liked to remind voters of Martin Van Buren, the vice president who won the presidency in 1836 as Andrew Jackson's successor. Van Buren had won because he was loyal to Jackson. Bush achieved similar success after being Ronald Reagan's loyal second. In his speech accepting the Republican Party's nomination that year, Bush told convention delegates that he saw his life in terms of missions, and that his mission as president would be to continue the Reagan legacy.

As the second Van Buren, Bush tried to make clear that he was in no hurry to initiate changes. For example, he rejected the traditional idea that the first hundred days of a presidency presented the best window of opportunity for introducing new policy initiatives. In an interview with members of the White House press corps in April, 1989, just he reached the milestone of one hundred days in office, Bush made it clear that he did not adhere to this conventional measure of presidential achievement.

> Q. We're coming up to the 100-day mark on your Presidency, which—if you'll look over the past 50 years, every other President, or almost every other President, has come into office at times of crisis, and crisis has been the stage on which we watch Presidents perform. How would you assess your first 100 days so far?
>
> *The President.* About the same as Martin Van Buren's.
>
> Q. Uh-oh.
>
> Q. Can you elaborate on that? [Laughter.]

The President. Martin came in; he was not radically trying to change things. But then, that's about where the parallel ends, because I don't know what he did in the first 100 days. . . . And I don't even think in terms of 100 days because we aren't radically shifting things; this is the Martin Van Buren analogy. We didn't come here throwing the rascals out to try to do something—correct all the ills of the world in 100 days. Now, there's some ills of the world; there's some unsolved problems. And I'm methodically, I think, pragmatically moving forward on these. So, I really don't measure it in terms of 100 days.

Q. I guess we are the ones who measure the 100 days.

The President. You are.[39]

As this exchange reveals, the most salient consequence of Bush's analogy between himself and Van Buren was that he saw his position as Reagan's heir reinforcing his inherent incrementalism.[40] As one elected to continue with existing policies, Bush came to the presidency with a perspective unusual for an American chief executive: he did not feel a compelling sense of urgency to put his mark on policy through decisive victories in his early months in office. As his public liaison director Bobbie Kilberg nicely expressed it: "Bush's overriding philosophy was that if it's not broke, don't fix it. He was not inclined to pursue the big-ticket agenda item just to make some impression."[41]

More typical for an American president, in contrast, is the view once expressed by Lyndon Johnson: that a president should reach for as much change as possible in his first year in office, because never again will the chief executive have the same opportunity to put a stamp on public policy.[42] But George Bush dissented from this view by inclination and by his assessment of what would be prudent for a president in his situation. That is not to suggest that Bush never offered a "big-ticket agenda item." As Kilberg put it, Bush's normal mode of operation was cautious, status quo leadership. But if the president believed that a large-scale federal initiative was merited in a particular case, "the Clean Air Act and the ADA, just to name two examples, he was willing to put himself on the line."[43]

Bush was in a position to win the presidency because the Twenty-second Amendment had forced Ronald Reagan into retirement. Although Reagan was ready to retire in 1988, he remained popular and a number of his most ardent supporters spoke wistfully about a (constitutionally impossible) third term. Bush, who had opposed Reagan in 1980 for the Republican nomination, fended off several Republican challengers by embracing the Reagan legacy in 1988. He promised continuity rather than change, only with a "kinder, gentler" face.

What did it mean for Bush to have embraced the Reagan legacy and promised continuity? Two competing interpretations of that position divided the Bush administration. On one side were those who wanted it to mean another presidential term marked by an aggressive campaign to promote conservative ideas and policies over the objections of Democrats and moderates. Among Republicans in Congress, this led to the rise of Newt Gingrich, who as House Republican Whip organized opposition to the 1990 budget deal in which George Bush broke his "no new taxes" campaign promise. Outside of Congress, conservative activists such as Pat Buchanan were bitter about the fact that Bush—whom they regarded as too moderate—had seized Reagan's mantle. They attacked the president for his shortcomings as a conservative warrior, and Buchanan ultimately opposed Bush for the Republican nomination in 1992. Inside the White House, conservatives such as Charles Kolb (in the Office of Policy Development), Secretary of Housing and Urban Development (HUD) Jack Kemp, and James Pinkerton (also on the domestic policy staff) regarded the entire Bush presidency as a lost opportunity to continue waging war against big government and liberal elites.[44]

On the other side were those who shared Bush's preference for gradualism and caution. These incrementalists were derided as passive or petrified by their conservative adversaries, but their thinking coincided with the president's and they generally held the upper hand in the administration. In domestic affairs, this group included Richard Darman, director of the Office of Management and Budget, Treasury Secretary Nicholas Brady, Assistant to the President for Domestic and Economic Affairs Roger Porter, and White House Chief of Staff John Sununu.[45] Public Liaison Director Kilberg was among a number of key aides who did not deal exclusively in domestic politics but who also fit into this group.

The split between the incrementalists and the warriors affected internal administration policy debates, but in the end it was the president who decided on and adhered to a gradualist approach to domestic policy. Bush not only saw no need to hurry with policy initiatives, but feared that he would do more damage if he rushed ahead to change policy in a time of rapidly changing international events and a domestic situation marked by prosperity and deficits. The result was that he and his advisers developed a political strategy for incremental change and caution in building a record, which would reach a crescendo just in time for Bush's reelection campaign in 1992.[46]

More Will Than Wallet

The second circumstance of Bush's presidency was the economic and budgetary context in which he held office. When Bush became president in 1989, the annual federal budget deficit stood at approximately $155 billion—about twice what it had been eight years before. Although there had been a short-term drop in the stock market in 1987, the economy was strong as the new president entered office. This combination of general prosperity and budget deficits reinforced Bush's inclination to proceed with caution in shaping policy.

The president summarized this situation himself in his inaugural address, wherein he characterized that context as a "peaceful, prosperous time." He noted that while the nation still faced many problems—homelessness, drugs, crime—their solutions did not and could not lie in large and expensive government programs: "The old solution, the old way, was to think that public money alone could end these problems. But we have learned that it is not so. And in any case, our funds are low. We have a deficit to bring down. We have more will than wallet; but will is what we need. We will make the hard choices, looking at what we have and perhaps allocating it differently, making our decisions based on honest need and prudent safety. And then we will do the wisest thing of all: We will turn to the only resource we have that in times of need always grows—the goodness and courage of the American people."[47]

Language such as this did not promise bold initiatives. Rather, employing once again Bush's favorite idea—prudence, this time as "prudent safety"—the new president suggested that Americans must look to themselves rather than to him for action.

As for himself, Bush expressed skepticism about the idea that leadership consists in calling for bold and dramatic changes. Near the end of his address, the president declared: "Some see leadership as high drama, and the sounds of trumpets calling, and sometimes it is that. But I see history as a book with many pages, and each day we fill a page with acts of hopefulness and meaning."[48] Even Bush's metaphors were incremental—history as the slow accumulation of turning pages—so caution and incrementalism were the order of the day.

AN INCREMENTALIST STRATEGY

Incrementalism was more than just a personal inclination for George Bush. It was also the heart of his administration's political strategy. This strategy prescribed that the president conduct himself in a restrained fashion, build what his advisers called a "successful presidency," and employ a minimalist approach to policy change.

Presidential Restraint

As part of his efforts to lower public expectations of what the president could achieve, since the nation had "more will than wallet," George Bush looked for ways to avoid overexposure and exaggerated credit claiming. Of course, this idea of restraint fit well with the president's personality, which was sometimes jokingly referred to as classically WASPish: self-effacing, modest, and stable (almost the antithesis of the style exhibited by Bush's successor, Bill Clinton). Yet, despite the joking references to Bush's upbringing, many of those closest to him saw more than a grain of truth to such a characterization. White House counsel Boyden Gray noted that because of the president's upbringing—"'stop talking about yourself George' is what his mother would say to him"—Bush detested bragging and even avoided credit claiming in cases where credit clearly was earned.[49]

Even before assuming office, Bush consulted his press secretary, Marlin Fitzwater, on how to play to his own strengths while avoiding excessive media exposure. Fitzwater responded with a lengthy memorandum that counseled frequent midday news conferences—to avoid monopolizing television during prime evening time—and that the chief executive not make statements during the many daily photo opportunities for the press. Bush followed his aide's advice, and more: he banned television coverage of many meetings he had with various constituency groups and often succeeded in traveling around the Washington, D.C., area without an escort of journalists.[50] Unlike most presidents in the age of television, Bush actively avoided gaining too much media attention.

At the same time, Bush took other steps to exercise restraint and lower public expectations of the presidency. Rather than have the White House serve as the source of all administration news, responsibility for release of many official announcements was delegated to executive departments and agencies. Indeed, as Fitzwater told the National Press Club in March, 1989: "There are not enough stories out of the White House to keep one honest person doing an honest day's work. . . . An exaggerated preoccupation with the White House has forced stories to come from the president that should be coming from the secretary of state, the secretary of defense, or any one of the other cabinet officials."[51]

Presidential restraint would wean reporters, and ultimately the public, from their habit of expecting the White House to be the engine for all national action. Not only would it draw attention to the rest of the government, but also from the government to the private sector and American civil society. Once the nation grew accustomed to not looking to the president for dramatic solutions to national needs, then Bush's incremental approach to policy could be seen for the steady and prudent course he believed it to be.

Building a "Successful Presidency"

Presidential restraint did not mean inaction or stasis, but the careful building of what Bush's advisers came to call a "successful presidency." White House Chief of Staff John Sununu outlined this project in a crucial senior staff meeting on March 6, 1989, when he identified the achievement of a "successful presidency" as the central goal of the White House for the next four years.[52]

Of what would this "successful presidency" consist? Journalists Michael Duffy and Dan Goodgame, who reported on the staff meeting in their book on the Bush presidency, summarized Sununu's definition in this way: "By putting together a solid record of accomplishment on which to campaign in 1992; a checklist of bills passed that major constituencies would applaud, of bills vetoed that other constituencies—particularly conservatives—had despised; and a tally of presidential actions taken, crises handled, opportunities seized,"[53] the president would win reelection in 1992. That was the meaning of a successful presidency: a modest record leading to Bush's reelection.

Sununu used this definition to identify the task that lay before the president's staff: He told them to think of the sort of record that Bush ought to run on in 1992 and then work backward from that idea. Central to building that record was to compromise with congressional Democrats in order to make incremental progress on a wide range of issues: curbing the use of illegal drugs, stabilizing the banking and credit industry, and reducing the federal budget deficit. The president was eager to make modest progress on many fronts and to share credit with anyone in Congress who would help him do so.

When the president found that he could not work with Congress, he was willing to use his constitutional powers to check or work around the legislative branch. Bush had a strong record of sustaining vetoes and the implied threat of using the veto helped him to shape many legislative initiatives more to his liking. Furthermore, the president shaped policy implementation through the use of signing statements. This little-known device enables a president to attach to his signature on a bill a statement that clarifies his understanding of the meaning of the law. In some cases, Bush used signing statements to provide administrative agencies specific guidance on how to implement policies. The use of signing statements is controversial when presidents attempt to shape the meaning of laws in ways Congress never intended. Bush used the technique a number of times, once again giving him real policy influence through the use of a device outside of the public view.[54]

The Practice of Prudence in Domestic Policy

If prudence was the watchword of the Bush presidency, how was that idea to be translated into domestic policy? Building a successful presidency meant a patient, long-term approach to policy and issues, rather than a major offensive in the short run. Significantly, Sununu did not outline this strategy to the staff until March, 1989, several weeks into the Bush presidency. If Bush was going to take Washington by storm, as had Ronald Reagan, then a strategy session such as Sununu held on March 6 would have been conducted shortly after the election. Instead, well into the president's first hundred days in office, the chief of staff was now discussing the administration's battle plans with senior aides. Those plans would not involve two or three major offensives, but many small (that is, incremental) ones. As Sununu explained to the staff, "If it looks like the president and the government are juggling thirty small balls, that's because they are."[55]

Nor would the goal of building a successful presidency be hurried; it had to unfold incrementally over time. The president often told his aides, "You don't get extra credit for doing things early."[56] Bush offered few policy initiatives to Congress, save his plan to cut the income tax on capital gains. Instead, he concentrated on softening some of the Reagan administration's harder edges by offering additional funding for some programs that Reagan had proposed to eliminate; dropping some of Reagan's more confrontational rhetoric on issues of racism, AIDS, the role of government, and so on; and appointing moderates to many positions where Reagan had installed conservative lightning rods (for example, at the Environmental Protection Agency).[57] Two examples illustrate Bush's incrementalist strategy: drug control policy and education.[58]

DRUG CONTROL POLICY

In his inaugural address, George Bush promised to reinvigorate the federal government's war on illegal drugs, calling their use a "national scourge." He selected William Bennett, Reagan's education secretary, to head the Office of National Drug Control Policy; this appointment and the president's rhetoric indicated that he would make drug control policy a high priority.

Bush's approach to drug control policy reflected his unhurried, incrementalist approach. It was not until September, 1989, that the president made a major speech on the issue of controlling illegal drugs. This address was followed by a document from Bennett's office outlining the administration's plans for drug control. Bush and his team adopted a two-pronged approach to drug control: promoting identification of drug users through workplace testing, and punishment of drug dealers with long prison sentences. The Customs Service, Coast Guard, and Border Patrol all increased their efforts to prevent the smuggling of illegal drugs into the United States, and the U.S. government provided foreign assistance to Latin American and Asian nations to help change the economies of those countries where drug sources were important income producers.

All of these efforts were constructed to be gradual improvements on Reagan administration policies. In the policy blueprint it issued following the president's September, 1989, speech, the Office of Drug Control Policy set incremental goals: it proposed to achieve a 10 percent reduction in the amount of illegal drugs entering the country by 1991, and a 50 percent cut by 1999; it also sought a 10 percent reduction in the number of illegal drug users by 1991, and a 50 percent drop by 1999. Another indicator of incrementalism was funding: in fiscal 1991–92, the Bush administration proposed spending $7.9 billion on drug control, of which only about $717 million was new spending. Funds were shifted from other programs or kept in existing programs and redefined as drug-control efforts.[59] In short, the administration was taking a gradualist approach to its war on drugs.

EDUCATION POLICY

While campaigning in 1988, George Bush proclaimed that he wanted to be known as the "education president." In contrast to most other issues, he approached education with some sense of urgency: in his first State of the Union Address (January 31, 1989), he made fairly specific proposals for reforms in American public education. He called for a $500 million program to reward "merit schools," announced creation of presidential awards for the best teachers in every state, called for a new program of National Science Scholars, and proposed a new initiative to encourage "alternative certification" to increase the supply of teachers for the nation's classrooms.[60] Later that year, the president convened an "education summit" of the nation's governors to discuss education reform.

Overall, however, Bush employed an incremental approach in education policy as in everything else. Federal funding for education programs, for example, would be limited and states were not to look to Washington for a Great Society–style big government initiative: in Bush's first budget, the president proposed spending $440 million on education programs, about $200 million less than had been proposed in Ronald Reagan's last budget.[61] Indeed, as one analysis of his education policy summarized Bush's initiatives: "The federal role would not be one of dramatically increased funding for new education programs. Instead, the administration would concentrate on demonstration projects and changing organizational structures (partially through the use of the introduction of market forces into public education)."[62]

Later Bush proposals built on the earlier initiatives. In 1990, the president called on states to adopt voluntary national standards and student testing, accompanied by parental choice regarding where their children attend school. The administration proposed giving limited financial incentives to states and local school districts to allow parental choice, and assisted in the creation of a private enterprise to help develop nontraditional schools.[63] The administration's overall approach was a familiar one: the slow accumulation of limited proposals and initiatives.

Education reform and drug control policy reflect the incrementalist strategy that Bush preferred and that Sununu outlined to senior staff members. For the president, these proposals were prudent; for critics, they indicated the absence of a domestic policy agenda.[64]

A number of Bush's aides commented in interviews that the president's critics erred when they equated cautious policy development with indifference to the domestic agenda. Boyden Gray said that Bush's "domestic vision" was "to let individuals and free markets to do their thing." To suggest that a market approach meant that Bush did not care about the domestic sphere was a "bum rap," according to Gray. Indeed, Gray perceives the enactment of the North American Free Trade Agreement (NAFTA), the General Agreement on Trade and Tariffs (GATT), welfare reform, and some other policies of the Clinton years as well as the economic recovery as a vindication of Bush's approach.[65]

A major difficulty for Bush, though, was the fact that leading presidential observers equated only big-government programs with having a "domestic vision." Many Bush staffers interviewed for this study objected strongly to the pro-big-government bias inferred from such an outlook. As Public Liaison Director Kilberg perhaps best put it: "If the standard of leadership is how many federal initiatives you champion, that is a Democratic—with a big D—definition of successful leadership. . . . You have to know what the president's philosophy and goals are before you determine what method of leadership works."[66] Although Gray's and Kilberg's assessments accurately reflect the perspective of most Bush staffers interviewed for this book, not everyone in the administration shared their view of Bush's pragmatic wisdom.

Further fueling Bush's problem was the fact that the activist view of presidential leadership permeated some of the hallways of his own White House. The pragmatists who most closely represented Bush's own outlook were content to defend the president's go-slow policy approach. Yet, as in any White House, appointments in the Bush administration reflected an effort to incorporate different elements of the party's competing factions. The conservative Reaganites in the Bush White House were not content with incremental politics and some of them fueled outside criticism of the administration's goals and strategies from within.

For Bush's critics, what also lent credibility to the charges against his administration were efforts within the White House to rebut outside criticism by showing just how activist Bush actually was. Numerous White House documents available even at this early stage show that much effort was directed at rebutting charges of a lack of commitment to the domestic agenda by demonstrating that Bush had actually either proposed or had committed extraordinarily large sums of federal money to education, the environment, crime fighting, drug-abuse prevention, and other priorities.[67] Ultimately, the message from the White House was confusing: Was Bush truly committed to a go-slow approach, or was he actually a big government proponent with a grand governing vision? It is quite clear the former more accurately describes Bush, whereas the latter grew out of White House attempts to rebut common criticisms. Yet, in so doing, the Bush White House ultimately failed to convey a clear sense of its own defensible strategy of policy development.

POLICY ISSUES AND THE DIPLOMAT AS PRESIDENT

Reflecting on the differences between national security affairs and domestic policy, Richard Nixon once told his aides that the nation absolutely needed intense presidential involvement in the life-or-death issue of world politics, but that the country could run itself in the domestic realm. The remark summarizes Nixon's own interest in and preference for the grand issues of Cold War geopolitics, as well as his moderately conservative positions on many domestic questions. Nixon's remark could be attributed with almost equal accuracy to George Bush, the diplomat as president.

Bush's assessment of the issues confronting the United States during his presidency go a long way toward explaining the much greater emphasis he placed on foreign affairs than domestic policy. He made it clear in his inaugural address that the most pressing issues before the nation were those of international change: "We live in a peaceful, prosperous time . . . a world refreshed by freedom seems reborn." Moreover, he proclaimed, the message of the events of the late twentieth century was that freedom, not state power, is the answer to humanity's problems: "We know what works: Freedom works. We know what's right: Freedom is right. We know how to secure a more just and prosperous life for man on Earth: through free markets, free speech, free elections, and the exercise of free will unhampered by the state."[68]

Not only did this reflect the president's view of issues at the outset of his administration, it also reflected his thinking well after his defeat in 1992. Six years after losing to Bill Clinton, George Bush (and Brent Scowcroft) published a memoir of his presidency that broke with the traditional encyclopedic apologia we have come to expect of ex-presidents. Unlike Truman, Eisenhower, Johnson, Nixon, Ford, Carter, and Reagan—each of whom published memoirs that attempted to cover all aspects of their terms in office (especially Truman and Eisenhower, who both wrote two-volume works)—Bush wrote a lengthy and detailed reflection that focused only on foreign policy during his time in office. Even at that, Bush focused on what he regarded as the key issues and events of foreign affairs during that time: the collapse of communism, the unification of Germany, upheavals in China, and the Persian Gulf War.[69] With time to reflect on his administration and the successes and failures of his presidency, Bush held to his conviction that foreign policy was a higher priority than the domestic realm.

In fairness to President Bush, we must state clearly that he did not ignore domestic issues or regard problems within the United States as unimportant. Nonetheless, the overriding point is that Bush's consistent assessment of the most pressing issues facing the country, and his own assessment of the circumstances of his presidency, reinforced his own inclination to focus on international problems and adopt a policy of caution and gradualism in domestic policy. A number of Bush's top staffers reflected that, despite the public's ultimately harsh judgment of the president's leadership by 1992, he was still the right man for the times. Phil Brady observed that successfully managing the end of the Cold War alone was no small feat. Considering the changes taking place internationally at that time, Bush's long career involvement in foreign policy and intelligence issues, and his vast network of diplomatic relationships, the country ultimately benefited from this favorable convergence of Bush's background and circumstances internationally.[70]

The practice of prudence in domestic policy meant that the Bush administration would not be associated with many major initiatives, but that it would be marked by an accumulation of modest proposals, incremental changes in policy, and compromises struck with Congress. For Bush, the incrementalist approach suited his view of the government's proper role and it suited the times. However much his critics or the voters of 1992 might disagree, the president saw himself as acting reasonably under the circumstances.

Evaluating Leadership in the Bush Presidency

How should George Bush's presidency be evaluated? Should it be seen as period of passivity and lost opportunities, or as one of effective, steady incrementalism? These questions have been asked since the early months of George H. W. Bush's tenure in the White House, and have drawn renewed attention as his son assumed the same office in 2001. The answers to these questions are more than merely academic, for they speak directly to the issue of what we expect of our presidents and how their leadership ought to be judged by voters, pundits, and scholars. Such judgments in turn affect how presidents behave in office and what kind of advice they receive. The result is that they influence governance in the United States.

The argument of this book has been that the Bush presidency has not been properly understood. The conventional view has been that Bush was too aggressive on some issues—such as the Persian Gulf War—and too passive on others—especially in domestic policy. Our position has been that there was an underlying consistency to George Bush's presidency: Bush was an incrementalist and conducted his administration as such.

What does Bush's incrementalism mean for the way in which his presidency is evaluated? That is the subject to which we shall now turn. To that end, we will review how presidents are and ought to be evaluated, the record of the Bush presidency, and how an understanding of Bush's incrementalism affects the ways in which scholars assess chief executives.

EVALUATING PRESIDENTIAL LEADERSHIP

As a number of analysts have pointed out, there is a mythology that surrounds the American presidency. Presidents are seen as the center of the government, the sole source of ideas, actions, and movement within the system. This view is reflected not only in the general public's tendency to attribute the state of the economy to whomever is residing in the White House, but it is also reflected in the way scholars evaluate chief executives and what they do in office.

Conventional Expectations of Presidents

Americans have a mythology about the power of the presidency. As political scientist Thomas Mann observed: "We imagine that he leads the government, that he sets the agenda and drives the agenda for legislation affecting the domestic affairs of this country. And it just isn't so."[71] This view is associated with what George Bush called leadership as "the sound of trumpets calling." It holds up a set of expectations about what a president can and ought to do in office: provide visionary leadership that involves significant, far-reaching, and important policy changes, enacted at the behest of a confident and supercompetent figure who articulates ambitious national goals in an eloquent and inspiring way.

This conventional view is held by the public at the behest of prevailing theories in political science. Years ago, Thomas Cronin pointed out that the American government textbooks, such as are used in high school civics classes and introductory college courses, present the presidency in terms that he could summarize only with the label of "Superman."[72] The kernel of this superhuman idea of the presidency is the notion of president-centered government in which White House activism is the only motive force in the political system. According to this idea, the president must provide aggressive, visionary leadership or the nation will stagnate.

In the twentieth century, presidents such as Franklin Roosevelt and Ronald Reagan often conducted themselves in ways that suggested they fit this ideal. However, as Mann pointed out, for most presidents, "it just isn't so." Nonetheless, many presidential observers have come to expect the exception to be the rule. Presidents who do not conform to the ideal simply are not "big enough" for the job.

Such an outlook is a mistake. It compels many observers to hold presidents up to impossible standards of success and encourages some presidents to conform their behavior to suit unrealistic expectations. Then there are presidents such as George Bush, who consciously reject the conventional view and try to lead in their own way. Predictably, many presidential observers have been unkind to Bush for resisting the expectations of those who demand bold, activist leadership. Yet we find that Bush's approach, though imperfect and ultimately politically very costly for him, more closely suits the realities of governing than does the conventional view of leadership.

White House Reality

In contrast to this conventional view, the reality of American governance is that ours is not a presidential government, but a separated system in which the presidency is constrained by a complex institutional and political context. Not only must the president work with Congress, the bureaucracy, the party system, interest groups, and public opinion to advance administration goals, but to be realistic those goals must be framed in recognition of the president's position as "just one player among many."[73]

Of course, recognizing this reality does not mean that the presidency is incapable of bold leadership and "the sound of trumpets calling." It does, however, mean that not every president will be able to accomplish grand and dramatic changes in the direction of public policy. Indeed, if we examine key elements of presidential reality, we can see broad outlines of the potential and the limits of what a chief executive can accomplish.

CONSTITUTIONAL AND INSTITUTIONAL CONTEXT

The most basic fact of presidential reality is that the U.S. Constitution establishes a separated system of power in which power is divided among three branches and two levels of government. Executive power in this system is significant, but limited. Moreover, presidential power is uneven: as Aaron Wildavsky noted decades ago, we have one president but two presidencies. The president is more powerful in foreign affairs than in domestic matters.[74] Congress has far greater interest in domestic issues and far greater control over them than does the president. This fact, along with America's role as a superpower since World War II, helps to explain why all postwar presidents have tended to devote considerable time to foreign policy, even when their own interests are inclined toward domestic matters.[75]

THE POST–WORLD WAR II INTERNATIONAL CONTEXT

In the decades since World War II, the United States has been a superpower with large responsibilities in world affairs. During the period of the Cold War, Washington was the capital of the noncommunist world and the president bore the title "Leader of the Free World." The president was (and remains) NATO's de facto leader, and even in the years since the Cold War ended the president has retained an enormous international role as the chief executive of the world's only superpower.

American foreign policy has been dominated by the structure of this context. For half a century, the overarching goal of presidential policy was containment of the Soviet Union specifically and communism generally. The policy of containment came to a successful conclusion precisely during the period of the first Bush presidency as the Berlin Wall fell, the Soviet Empire and then the Soviet system itself collapsed, and the basic alignments of world politics shifted. The period since the end of the Cold War has been marked by continued American engagement in the world, but with less clarity of purpose than in the previous era.

CYCLES OF DOMESTIC POLICY MAKING

Even a cursory examination of the history of American public policy reveals that there has not been a constant stream of major policy changes adopted by the institutions of the federal government. Instead, there is a kind of ebb and flow in the policy record. Erwin Hargrove and Michael Nelson have discerned a cyclical pattern that has marked the succession of presidents since the time of Theodore Roosevelt. Domestic policy, they argue, "can be understood in terms of recurring cycles of electoral political competition and public policy making within the bounds of American political culture. The focus of these cycles has been the presidency."

They further contend that the heart of these cycles has been a "presidency of achievement . . . in which great bursts of creative legislative activity occurred that altered the role of government in society in the service of some combination of purpose values of liberty and equality and process values of higher law and popular sovereignty." These cycles included parts of the administrations of Wilson, Franklin Roosevelt, Johnson, and Reagan.

Presidencies of achievement are bracketed by two other kinds of administrations. Before achievement, there is the "presidency of preparation" (perhaps more than one), in which the groundwork for change is laid but the incumbent lacks the political base that enables him to see it to fruition (Teddy Roosevelt and Kennedy, for example). After achievement, there is one or more "presidency of consolidation" in which "reform [is] not rejected but rationalized, slowed down, and in effect legitimized" for previous opponents (Harding, Coolidge, Eisenhower, and Nixon).[76] The cycle is occasionally punctuated by the "presidency of stalemate," in which the president's agenda bears little relation to what the public expects and is willing to accept.

Hargrove and Nelson do not see this cycle as deterministic of White House behavior or accomplishment, but the cycles do suggest that executive leadership is heavily influenced by the cyclical context in which an incumbent operates. Presidents who attempt to act "out of turn," such as Truman's push for the Fair Deal when the country wanted consolidation after World War II, tend to fail. Others who have an appealing agenda but lack the political support to win its passage (for example, Kennedy and Carter) serve as presidents of preparation but cannot claim achievement.

POLITICAL CONTEXT

The political circumstances surrounding a president's coming to office can significantly influence what that chief executive is able to accomplish. It mattered tremendously that Franklin Roosevelt won by a landslide in 1932 and that a sense of crisis pervaded the nation. Lyndon Johnson fully exploited a landslide victory, strong partisan majorities in Congress, and the national sympathy for the Kennedys to promote a big domestic agenda in 1965. Ronald Reagan benefited considerably in 1980 from his large margin of victory over incumbent Jimmy Carter, which was accompanied by a shift in partisan control over the Senate to the Republicans.

The conventional view of presidential accession is to see electoral victory as a mandate to implement a distinctive policy agenda. As Charles Jones has demonstrated convincingly, however, this assumption that victory means a mandate for change is one of the big myths of American politics. Some presidents might be seen as having such a mandate, but other chief executives can lay claim only to a mandate for the status quo (for example, reelection in 1956, 1972, 1984), a mixed or *non*mandate (1960,

1968, 1976, 1992), or even an *un*mandate (when there is a setback for the president's party, as in the 1994 midterm elections).[77] The upshot of Jones's analysis and evidence is that most presidents do not hold office under political circumstances that favor making major policy changes.

The reality of the presidency can be summarized in Mann's comment on the mythology of trumpets calling: "it just isn't so." Conventional expectations of the presidency are inconsistent with governance as it is experienced in the White House.

THE FIRST BUSH PRESIDENCY

American intellectuals have a peculiar fascination with schemes for rating presidents by assigning them such epithets as "great," "near-great," "average," and "failed." Indeed, the idea of presidential "greatness" continues to attract scholarly attention, although it is as difficult to define the concept as it is to identify the quality of being "presidential" that pundits and politicians seek in candidates for America's highest office. But just how useful are these exercises?

We submit that these labels tell us little about the presidency and what Americans can and ought to expect from their chief executives. Like any other president, George Bush ought to be assessed in terms of the realities of the White House and in part by the incumbent's own goals for his tenure. Specifically, how did Bush's incremental approach to the presidency fare as a strategy for executing his duties?

The Logic and Risks of Incrementalism

Considering the circumstances surrounding George Bush's presidency, there is a good case to be made that incrementalism was a reasonable approach to presidential leadership. Bush won the Oval Office by a clear majority over Massachusetts governor Michael Dukakis, but his victory did not alter the Democrats' long-standing majority in both houses of Congress. Given the nature of Bush's 1988 campaign, which emphasized themes of patriotism and continuity with the Reagan legacy, the new president came to office with what Jones calls a non- or mixed mandate. To that extent, it would be difficult to argue that George Bush could make any kind of claim for implementing a bold new policy agenda (if he were inclined to do so). Rather, he was expected to be the custodian of continuity while serving as chief executive. As far as Reagan partisans were concerned, Bush was elected to serve, in effect, the constitutionally prohibited third Reagan term.

Indeed, Bush defined himself as the political heir of Ronald Reagan, whose tenure marked what Hargrove and Nelson have termed a "presidency of achievement." Therefore, the most logical place for Bush to occupy in the cycles of domestic policy was that of a "presidency of consolidation," even though Reagan partisans had been hoping for four more years of big achievement. He occupied the same political space as Eisenhower and Nixon. So did Harry Truman, who tried to ignore the need for consolidation following World War II and called for the Fair Deal. Truman was frustrated by an opposition-dominated Congress and won reelection in 1948 only because his opponent ran such a poor campaign. It would have been politically foolish for George Bush to embark on a vigorous campaign for some nonincremental changes in policy. Contrary to what some of his conservative critics thought, there was not sufficient political momentum in the country—and certainly not in Congress—to carry on the "Reagan Revolution." Reagan himself had achieved most of the policy changes he sought during his first term. It would have been essentially pointless to seek drama and trumpet calls in what arguably could be described as a third Reagan term.

At the same time, while consolidation made sense on the domestic side of the policy ledger, historic events were unfolding in the international realm. It would take a rabid isolationist to argue that the end of the Cold War ought not to assume the president's attention. The goal that had shaped American foreign policy for half a century was being achieved during the Bush presidency. The implications of these changes for the United States and international security are difficult to underestimate.

George Bush's response to these momentous changes was consistent with what America's most sagacious foreign policy experts had counseled throughout the Cold War era. When the president told reporters, in reference to the rapidly evolving events of German unification, that the enemy was "instability," he reflected the consensus of professional diplomats, political elders, and security scholars that instability in geopolitics was most threatening to the carefully balanced peace of the Cold War. The "lessons" of the Cold War, repeated in endless analyses, books, articles, and testimonies, was that peace and security in the nuclear age rest on a precarious foundation: if stability could be maintained, war might be avoided; if instability led one side or the other in the great conflict to feel its interests at risk, devastating consequences might follow. When George Bush said that instability was the enemy, he was firmly within the consensus of the foreign policy professionals with whom he identified.

Their insistence on stability may have frustrated those observers who wanted the United States to more eagerly embrace change—at one point, HUD Secretary Jack Kemp and Secretary of State James Baker nearly came to blows during an argument about the administration's caution in foreign affairs—but Bush's policy of caution was consistent with the prescriptions of world-affairs experts.

However much George Bush may have seemed nostalgic for the clarity of the Cold War, his incremental approach to foreign policy helped facilitate the tricky maneuver of creating a reunited Germany that remained a member of NATO. Germans were so eager for unification that the United States feared Bonn might be willing to accept neutralization in order to achieve it, which the administration thought would be a devastating blow to the NATO alliance. The Soviet Union had insisted on German neutrality as the price of accepting unification, but Bush worked hard and successfully to pave the way for unification within NATO. In the years since the breakup of the Soviet Union, Moscow's military forces have become far less formidable, making it easy to forget just how threatening the Soviet forces in Eastern Europe appeared to be throughout the Cold War. In 1968, Soviet troops rolled into Czechoslovakia to crush the "Prague Spring," and Soviet forces waged a bloody and protracted war in Afghanistan in the late 1970s and 1980s. At a time when Moscow's threats and security concerns could not be dismissed lightly, Bush's cautious approach to the end of the Cold War probably helped prevent another round of military suppression.

Bush's incrementalism thus made sense for his time in office, but it was certainly an approach that carried risks. One of these risks was that incrementalism requires patience, which in turn requires that the leader teach patience to his followers. President Bush often counseled patience and the need for caution in public policy, but the contrast between himself and his predecessor meant that he often seemed timid rather than confident and patient. In contrast, Dwight Eisenhower employed an incremental approach during an earlier period of consolidation, but he was able to do so with far more public support than Bush enjoyed. It certainly helped that Ike had been the supreme commander on D-Day and afterward, but that alone does not explain Eisenhower's ability to project steadiness. When critics disparaged him as the "bland leading the bland," average Americans remained unshaken in their trust of the president. Bush, on the other hand, was less effective at explaining and winning trust in his measured approach.

The other chief risk of an incremental approach is that of moving too slowly when more aggressive action is required. To some extent, that is the story of Bush's response to the recession in 1991–92. The president might even have employed incremental steps to addressing the downturn in the economy before ratcheting up the government's response if smaller measures failed, but Bush avoided doing much at all until his State of the Union Address early in 1992. By that point, however, the small measures the president had embraced seemed to be too little, too late. He thus opened himself up to a damaging election challenge from Bill Clinton and Ross Perot. In this instance, Bush's failure was more political than policy based. The strong economic recovery soon after the 1992 election appears to vindicate Bush's caution. Yet, by his own admission, Bush failed to effectively communicate the wisdom of his go-slow approach to handling the recession. It is no mere coincidence that the Bush policy advisers interviewed for this study embraced the president's caution as the right action for its time and the political operatives and communications advisers mostly expressed frustration at the president's approach. As is often the case, good policy was bad politics. Bush insisted on good policy in this case—ultimately to his electoral undoing and subsequent lost opportunity to achieve other goals about which he cared.[78]

An Almost Successful Presidency

In March, 1989, John Sununu told the senior White House staff that the organizing principle of the Bush administration would be to build a successful presidency, which he defined as one with a sufficiently strong record of modest achievements that voters would reward George Bush with reelection in 1992. Although Bush lost that election to Bill Clinton, he came close to reaching that goal.

Any time an incumbent president is defeated in his bid for reelection, he is seen as a loser. By a kind of *post hoc, ergo propter hoc* logic, that incumbent's defeat is rationalized by commentators as almost inevitable given the various weaknesses displayed by the politician in question. Nevertheless, the twentieth century presidents defeated seeking reelection were all redeemed in one way or another as time and circumstance led to reassessments of their presidencies. William Howard Taft came in third in the 1912 election, but made a triumphant return to public life as chief justice of the Supreme Court. Herbert Hoover successfully headed two commissions on federal government organization that made substantial contributions to bureaucratic reform. Gerald Ford saw his reputation restored as time and events magnified the value of his integrity, and as recently as the postelection turmoil of 2000 he was suggested as an elder statesman who ought to help untangle the electoral mess and/or preside over changes in the nation's election laws. In 2001, Ford received the prestigious "profile in courage" award as a belated honor for his once very unpopular pardon of Richard Nixon. Jimmy Carter built a successful postpresidential career as an author, diplomat, and international elections monitor. Scholarly assessments of his presidency have been much kinder to Carter than were his contemporaries. Time also has helped provide some perspective on the presidency of George Bush who, particularly in light of the embarrassments and scandals of the Clinton years, is widely appreciated for having conducted a dignified presidency.

In the administration's own terms, Bush had built an almost successful presidency. He achieved recognition as an international leader and, although there were complaints on the domestic side, for most of his presidency Bush did not appear to face any serious threats to being reelected. Bush experienced setbacks during his tenure in office, such as the 1990 budget deal that divided his party, but by the end of the Persian Gulf War his approval ratings had reached an all-time high of 91 percent. As unrest over the recession came to dominate the news after the war, Bush seemed able to fend off challenges from within and outside his party. Within Republican ranks, conservative pundit Pat Buchanan revealed a level of dissatisfaction with the president, but Buchanan never got more than "thirty-something" percent of the vote in a primary (thus leading him to be tagged the "thirty-something candidate"). Until the middle of 1992, Bush's greatest challenge came from Texas billionaire Ross Perot, who was actually more threatening to the Democrats. For a time, until he temporarily withdrew from the race in June, Perot was ahead of the presumptive Democratic nominee, Bill Clinton. Bush's one-time immense popularity had the effect of relegating the Democratic Party nomination process to a competition among second-level players. The more formidable-seeming Democrats such as former New York governor Mario Cuomo chose to sit out the 1992 campaign rather than take on what seemed like an impossible race.

Bush nonetheless was defeated, but some observers ultimately came to recognize that his incremental leadership style was steadier and more reliable than Bill Clinton's high-stakes, win-big-lose-big style. After watching Clinton in office, several observers found virtue in Bush's more measured approach. A cover story in the *New Republic* in 2000 declared Bush "our greatest modern president," and much of the analysis drew contrasts between Bush's steady-hand leadership and Clinton's go-for-broke style.[79] Also, Leslie Gelb, a former Johnson administration official and an eminence in the foreign policy establishment, described Clinton's handling of foreign affairs as inferior to Bush's. In contrast to the new president, Gelb commented that Bush "was careful about squandering precious American credibility. Overall, he promised less, and delivered it. . . . Style, confidence, and a sense of command had much to do with the favorable perception of the Bush national security team. Bush and his top advisers conveyed a sense of realism and hard-headedness."[80] Political scientist Charles Jones maintains that Clinton's high-stakes political style made less sense in the contemporary presidency than a more restrained approach. Given the modern limitations on the presidency, a powerful Congress resistant to executive leadership, and the absence of a crisis to galvanize support for major change, Jones argues that a president such as Clinton should have taken a much more modest approach to governing than he did: "Much of the Clinton story through his many years of service as a state and national chief executive can be summarized as repeating cycles of risk, restoration, and reelection. . . . Perhaps even he will agree that fostering stability is preferable to risk taking and recuperation."[81]

In the area of personal behavior, Gary Orren of Kennedy School of Government at Harvard observed that "The difficulties that Bill Clinton has had have only amplified the contrasts: in retrospect [Bush] looks even more virtuous. . . Indeed, many people, particularly Republicans, said that after the Clinton scandals they have a new appreciation for Mr. Bush's personal rectitude."[82]

Finally, a detailed analysis of presidential agenda setting by Paul Light found that Clinton's policy proposals actually quite similar to Bush's in many important ways. Light notes that Bush's policy agenda consisted mostly of small-scale proposals and that "His agenda is best described as a collection of fine tunings in the general support of already established ideas."[83] But Light concluded: "Clinton was hardly different. Although he had a much higher proportion of large-scale proposals than Bush, he was only slightly more likely to challenge the prevailing wisdom." While Clinton's rhetoric was often grandiose in its claims, "much as Clinton liked to compare himself to Kennedy, his first-term agenda actually turned out to look much more like the one presented by Gerald Ford."[84]

What then distinguishes Bush from Clinton? Bush practiced a politics of prudence, whereas Clinton practiced what Henry Fairlie once called "the politics of expectation."[85] This style of politics focuses on raising public expectations of what leaders—and indeed government itself—can achieve. Jones corroborates that Clinton practiced this style, noting the "extravagant expectations" of presidential achievement that Clinton led his supporters to hold out when he won the 1992 election.[86] As Gelb observed, Bush "promised less and delivered it," while Clinton promised much and delivered less.

Even for all his political gifts and some policy accomplishments (including NAFTA, which was part of the Bush legacy), Clinton's two terms described a presidency of preparation more than one of achievement. In retrospect, Bush's presidency of consolidation was appropriate for the time and circumstances in which he held office. His incremental approach was not flawless, but it represents an authentic alternative to leadership as "the sound of trumpets calling."

The conventional approach to understanding presidential leadership furthermore fails to capture leadership strategies that tend to occur outside the public arena. As the earlier chapters demonstrate, Bush had substantial success at working his will through such devices as the active use of national security directives, secrecy policies, signing statements, and regulatory actions, among others. Too many studies equate presidential leadership success with big bills enacted or high percentages of positive congressional roll-call votes. Yet these measures tell only a portion of the story of what presidents do to direct governmental action in a desired fashion. Bush was enormously effective at employing powers that allowed him to govern without congressional approval or participation. Although some of his actions were controversial, he deserves credit for success at promoting his governing preferences in ways much different than presidents who achieved big legislative victories. The conventional view of leadership clearly favors the more visible side of presidential action even though equally, and sometimes more important work takes place outside the public limelight.

RETHINKING LEADERSHIP AND PRESIDENTIAL EVALUATION

The mythology that surrounds the American presidency looks for bold and dramatic leadership, and two generations of political scientists since the publication of Richard Neustadt's *Presidential Power* have taught students and scholars that activism is the hallmark of presidential leadership. There is, however, an alternative approach to leadership that has just as much validity for the office, especially when the context of a presidency does not lend itself to major policy changes.

Dwight Eisenhower, Gerald Ford, and George Bush exhibited this restrained and incremental type of leadership. The first of these chief executives underwent a significant reputation revision in the 1980s as scholars such as Robert Divine, Stephen Ambrose, Phil Henderson, and Fred Greenstein broke with previous interpretations of Ike as a passive president and presented him as a shrewd practitioner of "hidden-hand" leadership.[87] Since that time there has been a much wider appreciation of Eisenhower's restrained leadership style.

It is not our claim that George Bush was another Eisenhower, but his incremental style of leadership deserves better treatment than it has received from scholars and pundits who see Franklin D. Roosevelt as the very model of a modern president. If every president tried to be another Franklin Roosevelt, then most presidencies would be disastrous failures, for only a few chief executives are positioned to make the kinds of major policy changes that FDR achieved. Moreover, very few presidents enjoyed the kind of political base that made FDR's achievements possible: large majorities for his party in both houses of Congress, a public desperate to follow the lead of a president, and a supportive news media. Even Roosevelt encountered serious problems and setbacks, as histories of his presidency have demonstrated. Nonetheless, idealized recollections of FDR's "greatness" persist and all presidents since have been held up to an impossible standard of success.

George Bush employed a leadership style that suited him and that was plausible for its time. It was not perfect by any means, nor was Bush a flawless practitioner of it. Nevertheless, his approach to the presidency made more sense than an attempt to be boldly visionary and implement dramatic changes. In a time of divided government, when policy consolidation was in order at home and international events required presidential attention, a strategy of gradualism was more appropriate than a campaign to enact new large-scale programs. Nor did Bush want to create large new government programs, which addresses a final problem with the trumpets-calling, activist-president leadership model.

Many commentators who see presidential activism as the hallmark of leadership undergird their analyses with an ideological bias toward bigger government. There was confusion among these analysts early in the Reagan presidency, when they could not quite understand how presidential activism could be put in the service of limiting government (despite the historical precedent of Andrew Jackson). Using Franklin Roosevelt as a model president is not only a matter of style, but one of policy: Roosevelt represents positive government. As Willmoore Kendall pointed out decades ago, there is a bias in models of American government that center the entire political system on activist presidential leadership; the demand that the president "do something" about a host of problems is a demand that the government do more.[88]

But a leadership model that is tied to a policy agenda, however attractive to some, is inappropriate for the American presidency. Indeed, as Thomas Cronin pointed out, it was the identification of the presidency with the "liberal agenda" (an expansive federal government) that led to the textbook view that only Superman could be president: "With the New Deal presidency in mind, these textbooks portrayed the president instructing the nation as a national teacher and guiding the nation as national preacher. Presidents, they said, should expand the role of the federal government to cope with the increasing nationwide demands for social justice and a prosperous economy."[89]

To tie the presidency to a particular policy agenda conflates a governmental institution with a political party and risks undermining the institution's effectiveness and authority. Moreover, it risks having the same institution tied to a different agenda. For example, Terry Eastland's *Energy in the Executive* tried to make the intellectual case for associating the presidency with a conservative agenda.[90] Were Eastland's view to prevail, partisans of an always-activist presidency might find their heroes—FDR, JFK, LBJ—being ranked well behind Reagan and other conservatives.

Instead of an ideologically driven method of assessing leadership, or a monochromatic view of leadership, what we need is a sense of how a president's conduct in office interacts with the context in which the president operates. Not every president can lead with trumpets calling, nor should we expect every chief executive to do so. What we should expect is presidential leadership that is appropriate to the circumstances and tasks facing the incumbent in question. To evaluate leadership, especially leadership in the White House, we need a realistic assessment of the challenges and possibilities that confront the leader in question. This task requires a virtue that George Bush would understand: prudence.

Notes

Chapter 1: Incrementalism in Theory and Practice

1. See George Edwards, "The Bush Presidency and Public Opinion" (paper presented at the Hofstra University "Bush Presidency" conference, Hempstead, N.Y., Apr. 17–19, 1997).
2. V. O. Key, *The Responsible Electorate* (New York: Vintage Boks, 1996), 61.
3. In that sense, the thesis of this volume differs significantly from that of David Mervin's fine study, *George Bush and the Guardianship Presidency* (New York: St. Martin's, 1996). Mervin writes that "presidents are entitled to be judged on their own terms," a statement that suggests that a president whose goals are completely out of sync with the real needs of the nation could be judged a success for failing to address those needs (ibid., 226).
4. This characterization of effective leadership is very pervasive in press commentary on the presidency. See Mark J. Rozell, *The Press and the Bush Presidency* (Westport, Conn.: Praeger, 1996).
5. Charles O. Jones, *The Presidency in a Separated System* (Washington, D.C.: Brookings, 1994).
6. William Leucthenburg, *In the Shadow of FDR: From Harry Truman to Ronald Reagan* (Ithaca, N.Y.: Cornell University Press, 1983).
7. David Braybrooke and Charles E. Lindblom, *A Strategy of Decision: Policy Evaluation as a Social Science* (New York: Free Press, 1970).
8. A somewhat extreme statement of this view is Edward Banfield's provocative essay "Policy Science as Metaphysical Madness" in *Public Policy in the Eighties,* ed. Robert A. Golden (Washington, D.C.: American Enterprise Institute, 1980). Banfield draws a dichotomy between the practical man of affairs and the social scientist: the former is guided by common sense, experience, and wisdom, whereas the latter is guided by abstract principles with little use in the real world.
9. Braybrooke and Lindblom, *Strategy of Decision,* 71.
10. See journalistic commentary generally in Rozell, *Press and Bush,* and the discussion of "the two George Bushes" in chapter 2 of this volume.
11. See Jones, *Presidency in a Separated System,* generally on this point.
12. Braybrooke and Lindblom, *Strategy of Decision,* 24.
13. To be sure, some of Bush's people said he had no recourse but to run such a campaign in order to win. Fearing that a high-minded issues seminar would have consigned him to the history books as just another failed nominee, they pointed to early campaign polls showing that the public did not have strong affection for the vice president and advised him that the only way to win was to drive up Democratic nominee Michael Dukakis's negatives. The Bush campaign did that most effectively indeed.
14. See Braybrooke and Lindblom, *Strategy of Decision,* generally.

15. See Richard Fenno, *Learning to Govern: An Institutional View of the 104th Congress* (Washington, D.C.: Brookings, 1995).
16. Forrest McDonald, *The American Presidency: An Intellectual History* (Lawrence: University Press of Kansas, 1994), 456.
17. The exceptions would be the obligatory appointments to please the conservative wing of the GOP: for example, William Bennett and Jack Kemp. Dan Quayle's selection for vice president surely pleased conservatives, but Bush chose him for other reasons as well.

Chapter 2: Incremental Leadership in the Bush Presidency

1. Mervin, *George Bush,* 16.
2. Ibid., 17.
3. Gerald R. Ford, *A Time to Heal* (Norwalk, Conn.: Easton Press, 1987), 337–38.
4. Marlin Fitzwater, interview by author, July 9, 1994, Washington, D.C.
5. George F. Will, "George Bush: The Sound of a Lapdog," *Washington Post,* Jan. 30, 1986, A25.
6. Jones, *Presidency in a Separated System,* 41.
7. Walter Shapiro, "The Differences That Really Matter," *Time,* Nov. 7, 1988, 24.
8. Jonathon Alter and Mickey Kaus, "The Big Questions," *Newsweek,* Nov. 7, 1988, 55.
9. Kenneth T. Walsh, "The Passive Mandate," *U.S. News & World Report,* Oct. 31, 1988, 20.
10. Rowland Evans and Robert Novak, "Coasting, Bush Style," *Washington Post,* Nov. 7, 1988, A23.
11. George F. Will, "A Case for George Bush," *Washington Post,* Nov. 6, 1988, C7.
12. Quoted in Mervin, *George Bush,* 33.
13. Quoted in ibid., 34.
14. Although Bush denied any interest at all in the 100-days standard, White House staff members were conscious of the inevitable comparisons observers would draw between the president and his predecessors at that stage of the administration. At Chief of Staff Sununu's request, the staff prepared a lengthy analysis of the first standard. The report discussed the origins of the 100-days standard, detailed FDR's first 100 days' accomplishments, and also analyzed the first 100 days of Bush's predecessors going back to Kennedy (Untitled packet on 100-days standard, n.d., folder, "Transition—Miscellaneous (1989)," OA/ID 01806, John Sununu Files, White House Office of Chief of Staff, Bush Presidential Records, George Bush Presidential Library, College Station, Tex. [Hereafter GBPL]).
15. Roscoe Starek, interview by author, July 1, 1996, Charlottesville, Va.
16. Ibid.
17. Chase Untermeyer, presentation at the University of Virginia, Feb. 15, 1994.
18. Bush White House staff, interviews by author.
19. The president's staff nonetheless thought that the heavy criticism for a slow transition was unfair. The press office responded by producing a weekly update comparing Bush's appointments record to Reagan's at the same stage of their administrations (folder, "Bush Appointments," OA 6553, White House Press Office

Subject File, Marlin Fitzwater Papers, Bush Presidential Records, GBPL [hereafter Fitzwater Papers]).

20. Starek interview.
21. Richard J. Ellis, *Presidential Lightning Rods: The Politics of Blame Avoidance* (Lawrence: University Press of Kansas, 1994).
22. Ibid., 48–52.
23. James Pfiffner, *The Modern Presidency* (New York: St. Martin's, 1994), 80.
24. Kenneth T. Walsh, "Bush's Veto Strategy," *U.S. News & World Report,* July 2, 1990, 20.
25. Quoted in Pamela Fessler, "Bush's Sway with Congress Hits Record Low in 1992," *Congressional Quarterly Weekly Report,* Oct. 17, 1992, 3249.
26. Nancy Schwerzler, "Bush Keeps Veto Win Streak Going, But May Face Future Trouble," *Baltimore Sun,* Oct. 28, 1990, E4.
27. Janet Hook, "Avalanche of Veto Threats Divides Bush, Congress," *Congressional Quarterly Weekly Report,* Sept. 22, 1990, 2991.
28. Veto data compiled by authors. See also Robert J. Spitzer, "The Veto King: The Dr. No Presidency of George Bush" (paper presented at the Hofstra University "Bush Presidency" conference, Hempstead, N.Y., Apr. 17–19, 1997).
29. President Bush, televised address before joint session of Congress, Feb. 9, 1989.
30. David S. Broder, "A 'Willie Horton' Budget," *Washington Post,* Feb. 15, 1989, A25.
31. Walter Shapiro, "Reaganomics With a Human Face," *Time,* Feb. 20, 1989, 32–33. See also Stanley W. Cloud, "The Can't Do Government," *Time,* Oct. 23, 1989, 32.
32. George F. Will, "An Unserious Presidency," *Washington Post,* Oct. 12, 1989, A23.
33. See "A War on the Cheap," *Newsweek,* Sept. 18, 1989, 24; Cloud, "Can't Do Government," 32; Robert M. Morgenthau, "A Drug War, with Little Ammunition," *New York Times,* Sept. 27, 1989, A29; Tom Morganthau, "Now It's Bush's War," *Newsweek,* Sept. 18, 1989, 22–24.
34. "The President Whispers 'Charge!'" *New York Times,* Sept. 7, 1989, A26.
35. See, for example, "The Air Around the President," *New York Times,* June 2, 1989, A30; "Mr. Bush Clears the Air," *New York Times,* June 14, 1989, A26; "Perfection vs. Cleaner Air," *New York Times,* Aug. 22, 1989, A22; "The President's Clean Air Plan," *Washington Post,* June 13, 1989, A26.
36. Quoted in Cloud, "Can't Do Government," 31.
37. R. W. Apple Jr., "The Capital," *New York Times,* May 24, 1989, B6. See also Hugh Sidey, "Is Bush Bold Enough?" *Time,* Oct. 16, 1989, 28; Louis Lief, "A Shrinking American Role in the World," *U.S. News & World Report,* Nov. 13, 1989, 22, 24, 26.
38. Lou Cannon, "Reagan Is Concerned About Bush's Indecision," *Washington Post,* May 6, 1989, A21; George J. Church, "Do Nothing Detente," *Time,* May 15, 1989, 22–23; Richard Cohen, "The 'Nyet' Spirit in Washington," *Washington Post,* May 19, 1989, A27; Steven V. Roberts, "Counterpunching Gorbachev," *U.S. News & World Report,* May 29, 1989, 16–17; Stephen S. Rosenfeld, "Is Bush Being Too Careful?" *Washington Post,* Apr. 14, 1989, A27; Henry Trewhitt, "The Naysayer and New Detent," *U.S. News & World Report,* May 22, 1989, 18–19.
39. See Richard Cohen, "Crazy Legs Bush," *Washington Post,* June 1, 1989, A25; Leslie H. Gelb, "Mr. Bush's Leap Toward Leadership," *New York Times,* June 4, 1989, sec. 4, 30;

Dan Goodgame, "A NATO Balancing Act," *Time,* June 5, 1989, 39; Stephen S. Rosenfeld, "Bush: A Big Hit," *Washington Post,* June 2, 1989, A25; Tom Wicker, "Now for the Hard Part," *New York Times,* June 2, 1989, A31.

40. David S. Broder, "Who Says George Bush Is Boring?" *Washington Post,* Nov. 8, 1989, A23. See also Strobe Talbott, "The Road to Malta," *Time,* Dec. 4, 1989, 32; Kenneth T. Walsh, "Gentlemen Prefer Bland," *U.S. News & World Report,* Dec. 4, 1989, A23.
41. John Barry, "A Design After All," *Newsweek,* Dec. 11, 1989, 33; Thomas M. DeFrank and Ann McDaniel, "Designing 'A New Era,'" *Newsweek,* Dec. 18, 1989, 22; Michael Duffy, "Easier Said Than Done," *Time,* Dec. 18, 1989, 36; Richard Lacayo, "Turning Visions Into Reality," *Time,* Dec. 11, 1989, 39; Hugh Sidey, "A Game of One-On-One," *Time,* Dec. 18, 1989, 38.
42. "Will Mr. Bush *Kowtow*?" *Washington Post,* Nov. 30, 1989, C6. See also "On China: A *Kowtow,*" *Washington Post,* Dec. 3, 1989, C6; Mary McGrory, "Patting the Dragon," *Washington Post,* Dec. 12, 1989, A2.
43. Richard Cohen, "What Went Wrong? Almost Everything," *Washington Post,* Oct. 10, 1989, C1; Brian Duffy, "The Gang That Wouldn't Shoot," *U.S. News & World Report,* Oct. 16, 1989, 26–27; C. S. Manegold, "Amateur Hour," *Newsweek,* Oct. 16, 1989, 30; "On Panama: Luck and Incompetence," *New York Times,* Oct. 8, 1989, sec. 4, 20.
44. William Safire, "The Man With No Plan," *New York Times,* Oct. 9, 1989, A17.
45. David S. Broder, "Being a Good Manager Isn't Enough," *Washington Post,* Dec. 6, 1989, A29.
46. Gloria Borger, "The Year of Living Timorously," *U.S. News & World Report,* Nov. 13, 1989, 26–27.
47. "A Second Chance for Vision," *New York Times,* Dec. 17, 1989, E20.
48. "The Points of Light Initiative Foundation, January 4, 1990," folder, "Thursday, January 4, 1990," OA 4910, White House Press Office Daily Guidance File, Fitzwater Papers.
49. Jim Hoagland, "President Bush Needs a Prime Minister," *Washington Post,* Oct. 23, 1990, A21.
50. George J. Church, "A Tale of Two Bushes," *Time,* Jan. 7, 1991, 18.
51. Among Bush's critics were Rowland Evans and Robert Novak, ". . . A Hunting License for Gorbachev," *Washington Post,* Mar. 30, 1990, A25; idem., "My Pal, Mikhail," *Washington Post,* June 4, 1990, A15; idem., "Soft on the Baltics," *Washington Post,* Feb. 19, 1990, A19; "The Lithuanian Case," *Washington Post,* Apr. 25, 1990, A26. Those who praised his restraint included "Cautious Courage About Lithuania," *New York Times,* Mar. 28, 1990, A28; Michael Kramer, "Anger, Bluff—and Cooperation," *Time,* June 4, 1990, 38; Andrew M. Rosenthal, "Bush Yields to an Impulse to Stay Cautious About the Soviets," *New York Times,* Feb. 11, 1990, sec. 4, 2; Margaret Gerrard Warner, "Defying the Politicians and the Pundits," *Newsweek,* Apr. 16, 1990, 32–33.
52. "A Good Pep Rally," *New York Times,* Sept. 13, 1990, A26. See also R. W. Apple Jr., "Bush's Two Audiences," *New York Times,* Sept. 12, 1990, A1; Bruce W. Nelan, "Call to Arms," *Time,* Sept. 24, 1990, 32; Russell Watson, "The Price of Success," *Newsweek,* Oct. 1, 1990, 20; Mortimer B. Zuckerman, "Are We Willing to Act Alone?" *U.S. News & World Report,* Sept. 24, 1990, 100.

53. Paul A. Gigot, "Two Faced Bush—Tough Abroad, Squishy at Home," *Wall Street Journal*, Sept. 14, 1990, A14.
54. "Desert Sword: Time for Answers," *New York Times*, Nov. 14, 1990, A28. See also "Incoherent Mideast Policy," *Washington Post*, Nov. 6, 1990, A2; Otto Friedrich, "Time for Doubt," *Time*, Nov. 26, 1990, 30; Charles Krauthammer, "The Case for Destroying Saddam," *Washington Post*, Nov. 25, 1990, C7; Carla Anne Robbins, "Lonely at the Top," *U.S. News & World Report*, Nov. 26, 1990, 26; George F. Will, "Did You Ever See a Policy Go This Way and That?" *Washington Post*, Nov. 7, 1990, A23.
55. Michael B. Kagay, "Approval of Bush Soars," *New York Times*, Jan. 19, 1991, A9.
56. "The President's Popularity," *New York Times*, Mar. 5, 1991, A20.
57. Andrew M. Rosenthal, "The First Battle," *New York Times*, Jan. 18, 1991, A31. See also Stanley W. Cloud, "Exorcising an Old Demon," *Time*, Mar. 11, 1991, 52–53; Robin Toner, "Bush's War Success Confers and Aura if Invincibility in '92," *New York Times*, Feb. 27, 1991, A1; Tom Wicker, "Victims of War," *New York Times*, Mar. 2, 1991, A23; "Digging Out from the Gulf War Rubble," *U.S. News & World Report*, Mar. 25, 1991, 26–28.
58. Cecil V. Crabb Jr. and Kevin V. Mulcahy, "The Elitist Presidency: George Bush and the Management of Operation Desert Storm," in *The Presidency Reconsidered*, ed. Richard W. Waterman (New York: Peacock, 1993), 280, 292–97.
59. See "Breathtaking Progress on Arms," *New York Times*, Oct. 7, 1991, A16; Tom Morganthau, "Will Bush's Plan Work?" *Newsweek*, Oct. 7, 1991, 26; Strobe Talbott, "Toward a Safer World," *Time*, Oct. 7, 1991, 18–20; Tom Wicker, "Courage and Vision," *New York Times*, Oct. 3, 1991, A25.
60. Mary McGrory, "Passivity and Crisis," *Washington Post*, Dec. 12, 1991, A2.
61. See, for example, "Help Russia; Push Russia," *New York Times*, Nov. 26, 1991, A20; "Hesitating on Moscow," *Washington Post*, Dec. 29, 1991, C6.
62. Charles Krauthammer, "Where's the Rest of Bush?" *Washington Post*, Dec. 27, 1991, A21.
63. Bush White House staff interviews.
64. Cited in George F. Will, "He Moved His Lips and Said Nothing," *Washington Post*, June 29, 1990, A27.
65. Marlin Fitzwater, *Call the Briefing!* (New York: Random House, 1995), 214.
66. "D.C. Disgust: A *Newsweek* Poll," *Newsweek*, Oct. 22, 1990, 23.
67. See "The President's New Pretext," *New York Times*, Aug. 4, 1991, sec. 4, 14; "Quota? No, More Like a Canard," *New York Times*, May 28, 1991, A20; "Tossing Around the 'Quota' Bomb," *New York Times*, Apr. 7, 1991, sec. 4, 18; "More Civil Rights Slogans," *Washington Post*, Aug. 4, 1991, C6; "Stonewalling on Civil Rights," *Washington Post*, Sept. 27, 1991, A28; Richard Cohen, "Exploiting Quotas," *Washington Post*, May 28, 1991, A19; Anthony Lewis, "Nixon and Bush," *New York Times*, June 7, 1991, A35; Tom Wicker, "Justice or Hypocrisy?" *New York Times*, Aug. 15, 1991, A23.
68. "Thumbing His Nose at Congress: Mr. Bush Signs—and Undermines—the Rights Bill," *New York Times*, Nov. 22, 1991, A30.
69. David S. Broder, "Thomas: Dilemma for Democrats," *Washington Post*, July 7, 1991, B7; See also idem., "October Fiasco," *Washington Post*, Oct. 20, 1991, C7.

70. See, for example, Russell Baker, "The Process Baloney," *New York Times,* Oct. 19, 1991, A23; Leslie H. Gelb, "Mr. Bush Packs the Court," *New York Times,* Oct. 13, 1991, sec. 4, 15.
71. Michael Duffy, "Wake-Up Call," *Time,* Nov. 18, 1991, 22–24.
72. "Martin Van Bush," *Wall Street Journal,* Nov. 7, 1991, A14.
73. George Gallup Jr., *The Gallup Poll: Public Opinion 1992* (Wilmington, Del.: Scholarly Resources, 1992), 142.
74. See, for example, Ann McDaniel, "A Case of the Political Flu," *Newsweek,* Jan. 20, 1992, 31.
75. Michael Duffy, "Mission Impossible," *Time,* Jan. 20, 1992, 14.
76. McDaniel, "Case of the Political Flu," 30.
77. Ibid., 31.
78. "Will George Do It?" *Wall Street Journal,* Jan. 30, 1992, A12.
79. "The Tinkerer: Mr. Bush's New War and the Paper Sword," *New York Times,* Jan. 30, 1992, A20.
80. "The State of the Union," *Washington Post,* Jan. 29, 1992, A20.
81. These comments were made by: Mary McGrory, "Bush's Muscular Message," *Washington Post,* Jan. 30, 1992, A2; David S. Broder, "The Costs of Opportunism," *Washington Post,* Feb. 2, 1992, C7; and William Raspberry, "What Is the President Waiting For?" *Washington Post,* Jan. 17, 1992, A21.
82. Andrew M. Rosenthal, "Bush Encounters the Supermarket, Amazed," *New York Times,* Feb. 5, 1992, A1, 19.
83. Jonathan Yardley, "President Bush—Checkout-Challenged," *Washington Post,* Feb. 10, 1992, B2.
84. See, for example, Betty Glad, "How George Bush Lost the Election," in *The Clinton Presidency: Campaigning, Governing, and the Psychology of Leadership,* ed. Stanley Renshon (Boulder, Colo.: Westview Press, 1995), 22.
85. James W. Ceaser and Andrew Busch, *Upside Down and Inside Out: The 1992 Elections and American Politics* (Lanham, Md.: Rowman and Littlefield, 1993), 34.
86. See, for example, Mary McGrory, "Don't Take Us For Granite," *Washington Post,* Feb. 20, 1992, A2; "Now Do Something," *Wall Street Journal,* Feb. 20, 1992, A14.
87. Ann McDaniel, "Is Buchanan Running the Country?" *Newsweek,* Mar. 16, 1992, 29. *New York Times* editorial quoted in ibid.
88. Kenneth T. Walsh, "Face-off: Bush vs. Clinton," *U.S. News & World Report,* Mar. 30, 1992, 36.
89. See, for example, David S. Broder, "Now the 'Character Question' Has Been Written in Fire," *Washington Post,* May 5, 1992, A25; Mary McGrory, "Bush's No-show on Los Angeles," *Washington Post,* May 5, 1992, A2; idem., "Ueberroth, a GOP Role Model," ibid. June 9, 1992, A2.
90. Dan Quayle, *Standing Firm* (New York: Harper-Collins, 1994), 351.
91. Michael Duffy, "The Incredible Shrinking President," *Time,* June 29, 1992, 50–51.
92. See, for example, David S. Broder, "Baker's Move: Good for the Campaign, but What About the Country?" *Washington Post,* Aug. 14, 1992, A23.
93. See Kenneth T. Walsh, "Prisoner of Washington," *U.S. News & World Report,* Aug. 24, 1992, 22–26.

94. See, for example, Howard Fineman and Ann McDaniel, "Bush: What Bounce?" *Newsweek,* Aug. 31, 1992, 28; Molly Ivins, "A Feast of Hate and Fear," *Newsweek,* Aug. 31, 1992, 32; Jonathan Yardley, "Giving Family Values the Freudian Slip," *Washington Post,* Aug. 24, 1992, B2.
95. George F. Will, "This Thick Soup of Values-Blather," *Washington Post,* Aug. 23, 1992, C7.
96. See, for example, Charles Paul Freund, "Bush Comes to Shove," *Washington Post,* Aug. 23, 1992, C5; Ivins, "Feast of Hate and Fear"; Anthony Lewis, "The Price of Lies," *New York Times,* Aug. 24, 1992, A15; Will, "This Thick Soup."
97. "Mr. Bush's Action List," *Washington Post,* Sept. 11, 1992, A22; Kenneth T. Walsh, "The A Team's Sales Drive," *U.S. News & World Report,* Sept. 21, 1992, 30.
98. See, for example, "An Incomplete President," *New York Times,* Nov. 8, 1992, sec. 4, 16; "The Economy Stupid," *Wall Street Journal,* Nov. 6, 1992, A14; David Gergen, "A Farewell to Mr. Bush," *U.S. News & World Report,* Jan. 25, 1993, 80; J. F. O. McAllister, Bruce van Voorst, and Yuri Zarakhovich," *Time,* Jan. 11, 1993, 18, 19; Kenneth T. Walsh, "Caretaker: From Here to Uncertainty," *U.S. News & World Report,* Nov. 16, 1992, 82, 84–85. See esp. Michael Duffy and Dan Goodgame, *Marching in Place: The Status Quo Presidency of George Bush* (New York: Simon and Schuster, 1992).
99. Richard Rose, *The Postmodern President: George Bush Meets the World,* 2d ed. (Chatham, N.J.: Chatham House, 1991), 308.

Chapter 3: The Public Presidency of George H. W. Bush

1. One of the authors (M. R.) conducted interviews for this chapter in Washington, D.C., with the following persons: Phil Brady, assistant to the president and staff secretary (Aug. 20, 1999); Andrew Card, assistant to the president and deputy chief of staff (Sept. 10, 1999); Mary Kate Cary, senior writer for communications and speechwriter (Apr. 19, 1995); David Demarest, director of the White House Office of Communications (July 8, 1994); Marlin Fitzwater, press secretary (July 9, 1994); Andrew Furgeson, speechwriter (Apr. 21, 1995); C. Boyden Gray, counsel to the president (July 26, 1999); Ronald Kaufman, White House political director (July 21, 1999); Bobbie Kilberg, deputy director of public liaison (July 29, 1999); Dan McGroarty, deputy director of speechwriting (Apr. 28, 1995); Curt Smith, speechwriter (Apr. 21, 1995); Tony Snow, director of speechwriting and deputy assistant to the president for media affairs (Apr. 24, 1995). Unless otherwise specified, quotations are from these interviews.
2. Marlin Fitzwater, memorandum, "A Few Observations About 'The Domestic Agenda'," Aug. 22, 1991, folder, "Domestic Agenda [2]," OA 6788, White House Press Office Subject File, Fitzwater Papers.
3. Mark J. Rozell, "The Limits of White House Image Control," *Political Science Quarterly* 108, no. 3 (fall 1993): 453–80.
4. Ron Nessen, telephone interview by author, July 5, 1990.
5. Mark J. Rozell, "President Carter and the Press: Perspectives from White House Communications Advisers," *Political Science Quarterly* 105, no. 3 (fall 1990): 419–34.

6. Mark Hertsgaard, *On Bended Knee: The Press and the Reagan Presidency* (New York: Farrar Straus Giroux, 1988).
7. Bush apparently communicated this preference very clearly as opinion polls showed that about 90 percent of the public was aware of his dislike of broccoli. Reporter Kenneth T. Walsh quipped, "It was one of the few issues on which he had taken a firm stand." (*Feeding the Beast: The White House Versus the Press* [New York: Random House, 1996], 81).
8. See Rozell, *Press and Bush.*
9. "Building a Better America, 1989," OA 6785, White House Press Office Subject File, Fitzwater Papers. See also David Demarest to Opinion Leaders, memorandum, Dec. 15, 1989, ibid.
10. David Demarest to Pres. George Bush, memorandum, Dec. 15, 1989, case no. 09809955, FG001, White House Office of Records Management (WHORM) Subject File, Bush Presidential Records, GBPL. The accomplishments report was an elaborate undertaking as some twenty-four members of the White House staff reviewed and commented on drafts of the report before it was completed and mailed to the media (Drucie Scaling to Terry Good, memorandum, Jan. 25, 1990, case no. 110274, FG001, WHORM Subject File, Bush Presidential Records, GBPL).
11. See Rozell, *Press and Bush,* 54–55.
12. George Bush to Michael Boskin, Dec. 14,1990, case no. 199636, FG001, WHORM Subject File, Bush Presidential Records, GBPL. See also "Bush Accomplishments, 1990," OA 6028, White House Office of Speechwriting, Bush Presidential Records, GBPL.
13. See John Anthony Maltese, *Spin Control: The White House Office of Communications and the Management of Presidential News,* 2d ed. (Chapel Hill: University of North Carolina Press, 1994), 179–214.
14. See, for example, "Today's News Events," folder, "MIPODS—1989 (Today's News Events)," White House Press Office Subject File, Fitzwater Papers.
15. David Ignatius, "Press Corps to Bush: Manipulate Us," *Washington Post,* May 7, 1990, B1, 4.
16. Charles Kolb, *White House Daze* (New York: Free Press, 1994), 5.
17. Robert E. Denton and Gary C. Woodward, *Political Communication in America,* 2d ed. (Westport, Conn.: Praeger, 1990), 235.
18. See James Fallows, "Rhetoric and Presidential Leadership" (paper prepared for Miller Center Research Project, University of Virginia, Mar. 1, 1979).
19. See John Podhoretz, *Hell of a Ride: Backstage at the White House Follies, 1989–1993* (New York: Simon and Schuster, 1993); also Kolb, *White House Daze,* 4. Podhoretz wrote speeches for "drug czar" William Bennett.
20. An examination of the speech files at the Bush Library confirms this complaint among the writers that there often were too many hands in the speechmaking process. To cite just one example, the speech staff prepared a brief, 750-word speech for Bush at Andrews Air Force Base upon his departure for a diplomatic trip to Europe. Nine different staffers vetted the speech, with the office of legal counsel making wording changes, some staff members inserting marginal changes, and National Security Adviser Brent Scowcroft requesting a number of significant

revisions that would cover "more of the substance of the summit" ("Departure for Europe, July 9, 1989," OA 3539, White House Office of Speechwriting, Bush Presidential Records, GBPL.).

21. Peggy Noonan, "Why Bush Failed," *New York Times*, Nov. 5, 1992, A35.
22. James Pinkerton, *What Comes Next?* (New York: Hyperion, 1995), 165.
23. Gray interview.
24. I am grateful to Mary Kate Cary for sharing with me her notes from that meeting.
25. Quoted in John E. Yang, "An Enigmatic President Is a Study in Contrasts," *New York Times*, Feb. 12, 1992, A19.
26. Betty Glad, presentation at the University of Virginia, June 23, 1994.
27. Peggy Noonan, *What I Saw at the Revolution: A Political Life in the Reagan Era* (New York: Random House, 1990), 301.
28. Quayle, *Standing Firm*, 104.
29. Kolb, *White House Daze*, 3.
30. Quayle, *Standing Firm*, 103–104.
31. For example, Tony Snow to Samuel Skinner et al., memorandum, July 21, 1992, folder, "Op-Eds [Proposed Schedule for End of 1992 Campaign]," OA 6548, White House Press Office Subject File, Fitzwater Papers. See also, John Undeland and Floyd Jones to Marlin Fitzwater et al., memorandum, Aug. 13, 1992, folder, "NAFTA," OA 6547, ibid. This memorandum is an example of tracking editorial opinion on a specific issue.
32. For example, Marlin Fitzwater to John Sununu et al., memorandum, Nov. 14, 1989, folder, "Malta Meeting, December 1–3, 1989," OA 7956, White House Press Office Subject File, Fitzwater Papers. This memorandum details a two-month "media plan." It constitutes merely a list of Bush's planned media appearances during that time.
33. For example, "Communications [2]," OA 6787, White House Press Office Subject File, Fitzwater Papers.
34. For example, Edward Goldstein to Roger Porter, memorandum, Nov. 27, 1990, folder, "Public Opinion '91," OA/ID 06681, Ed Goldstein Files, Office of Policy Development, Bush Presidential Records, GBPL. This memorandum is one of many regular public opinion updates that staff presented to Porter to track Bush's standing on domestic issues.
35. For example, "President Bush's 1988 campaign Promises and Measures Taken to Fulfill Them, May 26, 1992," OA 6785, White House Press Office Subject File, Fitzwater Papers.
36. Indeed, Fitzwater's August 22, 1991, memorandum ("A Few Observations About 'The Domestic Agenda'") emphasized the point that Bush lacked an organizing theme for his domestic agenda and that the result was that others outside the White House were defining the president. Fitzwater suggested a number of possible catchphrases similar to the earlier use of "Operation Desert Storm," but the White House did not adopt any of them, or even an alternative. Quayle similarly recalled in his memoirs that there were proposals in the White House for a "Domestic Desert Storm" but "it never amounted to very much" (Quayle, *Standing Firm*, 273).

37. Quayle, *Standing Firm,* 137.
38. Quoted in Yang, "Enigmatic President," A19.
39. A White House document from Fitzwater's files written during the 1992 campaign discussed various media requests that Bush should accept and media outlets that he should avoid. Indeed, Bush had conveyed his stand against participating in interviews with such daytime talk show hosts as Phil Donohue, Oprah Winfrey, and Sally Jesse Raphael, among others. Untitled documents in the same folder express the view that there was a strategy to keep Bush in "presidential" contexts to convey "dignity" and "character." Therefore, not only did Bush believe that the tabloid shows were beneath the dignity of the office, but his staff perceived such a principled looking stand as being good public relations. See "Communications [2]," OA 6787, White House Press Office Subject File, Fitzwater Papers.
40. Kolb, *White House Daze,* 3.
41. Roger B. Porter, the president's economic and domestic policy adviser, offers an alternative view of Bush's domestic agenda. Porter portrays Bush as a visionary on the domestic front who merely was thwarted by a hostile Democratic Congress. See Roger Porter, "George Bush, Father of the 'Contract,'" *Wall Street Journal,* Dec. 13, 1994, A18.
42. Walsh, *Feeding the Beast,* 77.
43. Ibid., 78.
44. The key phrase here is "as he understands them." Many congressionalists disagree that Bush played by the rules of the game when it came to respecting the legislative power. It may be that Bush believed that he respected the legislative power, but construed his own authority—especially in foreign affairs—very broadly.
45. See Kerry Mullins and Aaron Wildavsky, "The Procedural Presidency of George Bush," *Political Science Quarterly* 107, no. 1 (spring 1992): 31–62.
46. See the reports on media coverage of the Bush presidency conducted by the Center for Media and Public Affairs, Washington, D.C. These statistical analyses showed the decline in presidential coverage during the Bush years when contrasted to the coverage of the Reagan presidency.
47. Porter, "George Bush."

Chapter 4: Information Control in the Bush Administration

1. See description of the E-mail controversy in the introduction to Tom Blanton, ed., *White House E-Mail* (New York: New Press, 1995).
2. Bill McAllister, "White House Drops Appeal of Ruling in E-Mail Case," *Washington Post,* Dec. 16, 1995, A14.
3. The most searching critique of the U.S. claims regarding civilian casualties and damage to property was a CBS-TV *60 Minutes* report on September 30, 1991, nine months after the invasion and much too late to have any policy impact.
4. See President Bush's statements on Noriega in "Remarks to the Council of Americas," *Weekly Compilation of Presidential Documents* (Washington, D.C.: GPO, May 2, 1989); and "Address to the Nation Announcing the United States Military Action in Panama," ibid., Dec. 20, 1989.

5. Stephen F. Knott maintains that restrictions on covert actions, in particular those that prohibit the assassination of foreign leaders, may have had the effect of encouraging Bush to achieve through military intervention—at a cost of many lives—what he could have achieved through a U.S.-backed coup against Noriega. See idem., *Secret and Sanctioned: Covert Operations and the American Presidency* (New York: Oxford University Press, 1996), 183–84.
6. Peter Schmeiser, "Shooting Pool," *The New Republic,* Mar. 18, 1991, 21; Sydney H. Schanberg, "A Muzzle for the Press," in *The Gulf War Reader: History, Documents, Opinions,* ed. Micah L. Sifry and Christopher Cerf (New York: Random House, 1991), 370.
7. *New York Times,* May 5, 1991, 20.
8. "Journalists in a War of Strict Press Rules," *Broadcasting,* Jan. 28, 1991, 22.
9. Walter Cronkite, "What Is There to Hide?" in *Gulf War Reader,* ed. Sifry and Cerf, 383.
10. Robert Fisk, "Free to Report What We're Told," in *Gulf War Reader,* ed. Sifry and Cerf, 379.
11. Howard Kurtz, "News Media Ask Freer Hand in Future Conflicts," *Washington Post,* July 1, 1991, A4.
12. Michael Massing, "Debriefings: What We Saw, What We Learned," *Columbia Journalism Review,* May–June, 1991, 23.
13. William Boot, "The Press Stands Alone," *Columbia Journalism Review,* Mar.–Apr., 1991, 23.
14. Quoted in Massing, "Debriefings," 23.
15. Cited in Tom Wicker, "'Marketing' the War," *New York Times,* May 10, 1991, A23.
16. *New York Times,* May 5, 1991, 20.
17. Quoted in *New York Times,* Feb. 15, 1991, A9.
18. Richard Zoglin, "It Was a Public Relations Rout Too," *Time,* Mar. 11, 1991, 56.
19. Schanberg, "Muzzle for the Press," 372.
20. *New York Times,* May 5, 1991, 1.
21. Fisk, "Free to Report," 378.
22. Quoted in Barry Dunnsmore, *The Next War: Live?* (Cambridge, Mass.: Harvard University Shorenstein Center, 1996), 16.
23. Ibid.
24. *New York Times,* May 5, 1991, 5.
25. Cited in Boot, "The Pool," *Columbia Journalism Review,* May–June, 1991, 24.
26. Cited in John Corry, "TV News and the Neutrality Principle," *Commentary,* May, 1991, 24.
27. Cited in Arthur E. Rowse, "The Guns of August," *Columbia Journalism Review,* Mar.–Apr., 1991, 27.
28. "Crisis in the Gulf: TV News Coverage of the Persian Gulf Crisis, Phase I," *Media Monitor* 4, no. 9 (Nov., 1990): 3.
29. Patrick O'Heffernan, "Television and Crisis: Sobering Thoughts on Sound Bites Seen 'Round the World," *Television Quarterly* 25 (1990): 11.
30. Walter Goodman, "Arnett," *Columbia Journalism Review,* May–June, 1991, 30.
31. See Jim Naureckas, "Gulf War Coverage: The Worst Censorship Was at Home," in

The FAIR Reader: An Extra! Review of Press and Politics, ed. Jim Naureckas and Janine Jackson (Boulder, Colo.: Westview Press, 1996), 28–44.

32. See Jarol Mannheim, "Strategic Public Diplomacy: Managing Kuwait's Image During the Gulf Conflict," in *Taken By Storm: The Media, Public Opinion, and U.S. Foreign Policy in the Gulf War,* ed. W. Lance Bennett and David L. Paletz (Chicago: University of Chicago Press, 1994), 131–48.
33. Gladys Engel Lang and Kurt Lang, "The Press as Prologue: Media Coverage of Saddam's Iraq, 1979–1990," in *Taken By Storm,* ed. Bennett and Paletz, 59–60.
34. Duffy and Goodgame, *Marching in Place,* 147.
35. Ibid., 186–87.
36. John Prados, *Keepers of the Keys: A History of the National Security Council from Truman to Bush* (New York: William Morrow, 1991), 554.
37. The strongest argument against executive privilege is Raoul Berger's *Executive Privilege: A Constitutional Myth* (Cambridge, Mass.: Harvard University Press, 1974). The proexecutive privilege view is presented in Mark J. Rozell, *Executive Privilege: The Dilemma of Secrecy and Democratic Accountability* (Baltimore: Johns Hopkins University Press, 1994).
38. The most important case is *U.S. v Nixon* 418 U.S. 683 (1974).
39. Ibid.
40. See Rozell, *Executive Privilege,* chap. 4.
41. See ibid., chap. 5.
42. Jim Lewin, telephone interview by author, Nov. 19, 1992.
43. Douglas M. Kmiec to Oliver B. Revell, memorandum, "Congressional Requests for Information From Inspectors General Concerning Open Criminal Investigations," Mar. 24 1989, 1; reprinted in U.S. Congress, *Department of Justice Authorization for Appropriations For Fiscal Year 1990,* House of Representatives, Committee on the Judiciary, 101st Cong., 1st Sess. (Washington, D.C.: GPO, 1989), 64.
44. Steven R. Ross and Charles Tiefer, memorandum, "Justice Department Memorandum Directing the Withholding from Congress of Inspector General Information," May 2, 1989, 2; reprinted in U.S. Congress, *Department of Justice Authorization . . . 1990,* 78.
45. Kmiec to Revell, 7–8; reprinted in U.S. Congress, *Department of Justice Authorization . . . 1990,* 71–72.
46. Ross and Tiefer, 12; reprinted in U.S. Congress, *Department of Justice Authorization . . . 1990,* 88.
47. Charles Tiefer, telephone interview by author, Nov. 23, 1992.
48. This section is summarized from various news reports in the *New York Times, Washington Post,* and *Wall Street Journal.*
49. David Johnston, "Reagan is Ordered to Provide Diaries in Poindexter Case," *New York Times,* Jan. 31, 1990, A20.
50. Tracy Thompson, "Justice Department Asks Delay On Reagan Diary Ruling," *Washington Post,* Feb. 3, 1990, A3.
51. David Johnston, "Reagan Rejects Poindexter Plea to Yield Diaries," *New York Times,* Feb. 6, 1990, A1.
52. Ibid.

53. Paul M. Barrett and Amy Dockser Marcus, "Reagan's Videotaped Testimony Ordered," *Wall Street Journal,* Feb. 6, 1990, B10. Reagan's attorney had met the February 5 deadline for formally refusing to release the diary entries, but he never used the phrase "executive privilege" in doing so. That led to some confusion over whether Reagan had met Judge Greene's condition of having to assert executive privilege by that date as the basis for refusal. Reagan's attorney, Theodore B. Olson, made it clear on February 7 that Reagan indeed had relied upon executive privilege as the basis for withholding the diaries: "No court has declared that the protection afforded the privilege for confidential presidential communications may be invoked only by reciting the phrase executive privilege. However, if this court intended . . . that the privilege may only be invoked in that fashion, the former president reaffirms that was, indeed [his] intention" (quoted in Joe Pichirallo, "Reagan Attorneys Assert Executive Privilege," *Washington Post,* Feb. 8, 1990, A4).
54. David Johnston, "Reagan to Give Tape Testimony on Iran-Contra," *New York Times,* Feb. 10, 1990, 28.
55. David Johnston, "Poindexter Loses Fight for Reagan Notes," *New York Times,* Mar. 22, 1990, A20. The issue of executive privilege also arose in connection to the Iran-Contra trial of Lt. Col. Oliver North. In this case, North sought to subpoena Reagan's diaries and the testimonies of President Reagan and President-Elect Bush. The three subpoenas were quashed. Because earlier conspiracy charges against North had been dropped, Judge Gerhard A. Gesell determined that the defendant's needs did not overcome the "presumptive privilege" accorded to the president and president-elect. See, Comment, "Legitimacy: The Sacrificial Lamb at the Altar of Executive Privilege," *Kentucky Law Journal* 78 (1990): 822–25; Joe Pichirallo and Ruth Marcus, "Reagan, Bush Subpoenaed By North; White House to Fight Testimony Demand," *Washington Post,* Dec. 31, 1988, A1, 12; Ruth Marcus, "Subpoenaing the President," *Washington Post,* Jan. 11, 1989, A7; Michael Wines, "Key North Counts Dismissed By Court," *New York Times,* Jan. 14, 1989, 1, 7; George Lardner Jr., "North Asks Court to Overturn Convictions," *Washington Post,* Feb. 7, 1990, A3.
56. H.Res. 19, 102d Cong., 1st Sess., Jan. 3, 1991.
57. C. Boyden Gray to Rep. Dante B. Fascell, Jan. 23, 1991, copy in author's collection.
58. Reps. Dante B. Fascell and Les Aspin to Pres. George Bush, Feb. 7, 1991, copy in author's collection.
59. Brent Scowcroft to Rep. Dante B. Fascell, Feb. 20, 1991, copy in author's collection.
60. The following sequence of events is summarized in: Rep. Ted Weiss to Rep. John Conyers Jr., May 21, 1991, and Steven R. Ross and Charles Tiefer to Rep. Ted Weiss, memorandum, June 20, 1991, copies in author's collection; and Kenneth J. Cooper, "Executive Privilege at Education Department," *Washington Post,* May 17, 1991, A23.
61. Edward Stringer to Rep. Ted Weiss, May 7, 1991, copy in author's collection.
62. Edward Stringer to Rep. Ted Weiss, May 13, 1991, copy in author's collection.
63. Ross and Tiefer to Weiss.
64. This section is based on Patricia A. Gilmartin, "Congress Increases C-17 Scrutiny In Wake of Reported Cost Overruns," *Aviation Week & Space Technology,* Sept. 2, 1991, 25–26; personal interviews with: Charles Tiefer, deputy general counsel to the House clerk, Nov. 23, 1992; Eric Thorson, staff member, House Committee on

Government Operations, Nov. 20, 1992; Morton Rosenberg, specialist in American Public Law, American Law Division, Congressional Research Service, Nov. 21, 1992; U.S. Congress, *Oversight Hearing on the A-12 Navy Aircraft,* Hearings Before the Legislation and National Security Subcommittee of the Committee on Government Operations, House of Representatives, 102d Cong., 1st Sess., Apr. 11 and July 24, 1991; U.S. Congress, *A-12 Navy Aircraft: System Review and Recommendations,* Twenty-First Report by the Committee on Government Operations, House of Representatives, 102d Cong., 2d Sess., Aug. 27, 1992.

65. Pres. George Bush to Defense Secretary Richard Cheney, memorandum, "Congressional Subpoena for an Executive Branch Document," Aug. 8, 1991, copy in author's collection.
66. This section is based on U.S. Congress, *The Quayle Council's Plans for Changing FDA's Drug Approval Process: A Prescription for Harm,* Twenty-Sixth Report by the Committee on Government Operations, House of Representatives, 102d Cong., 2d Sess., Oct. 9, 1992; and Dana Priest, "Competitiveness Council Under Scrutiny," *Washington Post,* Nov. 26, 1991, A19.
67. Kay Holcombe, acting associate commissioner for Legislative Affairs, FDA, to Rep. Ted Weiss, Oct. 16, 1991, quoted in *Quayle Council's Plans,* 6.
68. This section is based on author interviews with Charles Tiefer, Morton Rosenberg, and Monica Wrobelewski; and various congressional documents provided by Ms. Wrobelewski, including: Statements of Rep. Howard Wolpe before the Subcommittee on Investigations and Oversight of the House Committee on Science, Space and Technology, Sept. 23 and Oct. 2 and 5, 1992.
69. Rep. Howard Wolpe to President Bush, Sept. 24, 1992, copy in author's collection.
70. C. Boyden Gray to Rep. Howard Wolpe, Oct. 1, 1992, copy in author's collection.
71. Rep. Howard Wolpe to Attorney General William P. Barr III, Oct. 5, 1992, copy in author's collection.
72. Assistant Attorney General W. Lee Rawls to Rep. Howard Wolpe, Oct. 5, 1992, copy in author's collection.
73. U.S. Congress, *Department of Justice Authorization for Appropriations, Fiscal Year 1992,* Hearings before the Committee on the Judiciary, House of Representatives, 102d Cong., 1st Sess., July 11 and 18, 1991, 80.
74. Ibid., 85–91.
75. Ibid., 87.
76. This section is based on Joan Biskupic, "Panel Challenges Thornburgh Over Right to Documents," *Congressional Quarterly Weekly Reports,* July 27, 1991, 2080; David Johnston, "Administration to Fight House Panel's Subpoena," *New York Times,* July 30, 1991, A12; U.S. Congress, *Department of Justice Authorization for Appropriations, Fiscal Year 1992;* and author interviews with Morton Rosenberg, Nov. 21, 1992, and Charles Tiefer, Nov. 23, 1992.
77. This section is based on Biskupic, "Panel Challenges Thornburgh," 2080; U.S. Congress, *The Attorney General's Refusal to Provide Congressional Access to "Privileged" INSLAW Documents,* Hearings Before the Subcommittee on Economic and Commercial Law of the Committee on the Judiciary, House of Representatives, 101st Cong., 2d Sess., Dec. 5, 1990; U.S. Congress, *Department of Justice*

Authorization for Appropriations, Fiscal Year 1992; and "The INSLAW Investigation," *Washington Post,* May 29, 1993, A30.

78. Johnston, "Administration to Fight," A12.
79. Charles Tiefer, *The Semi-Sovereign Presidency: The Bush Administration's Strategy for Governing Without Congress* (Boulder, Colo.: Westview Press, 1994), 91.
80. Ibid., 94–95.
81. Quoted in ibid., 93.
82. National Security Directive 42, "National Policy for the Security of National Security Telecommunications and Information Systems," July 5, 1990, available at http://bushlibrary.tamu.edu/research/nds/NSD/NSD_42/0001.pdf, accessed Jan. 2, 2003.
83. See Don Oberdorfer, "Missed Signals in the Middle East: Why Was the Administration Blindsided by Iraq's Invasion of Kuwait?" *Washington Post Magazine,* Mar. 17, 1991, 19ff.
84. National Security Directive 26, "U.S. Policy Toward the Persian Gulf," Oct. 2, 1989, available at http://bushlibrary.tamu.edu/research/nsd/NSD/NSD_26/0001.pdf, accessed Jan. 2, 2003.
85. James A. Baker III, *The Politics of Diplomacy: Revolution, War and Peace, 1989–1992* (New York: G. P. Putnam's Son's, 1995), 263–64.
86. See Tiefer, *Semi-Sovereign Presidency,* 95–101.
87. Brent Scowcroft to Rep. John D. Dingell, Apr. 17, 1991, copy in author's collection.
88. Rep. John D. Dingell to Brent Scowcroft, May 10, 1991, copy in author's collection.
89. Brent Scowcroft to Rep. John D. Dingell, June 6, 1991, copy in author's collection.
90. William F. Sittmann, executive secretary to the National Security Council, to Rep. John D. Dingell, June 17, 1991, copy in author's collection.
91. See Richard Thornburgh to Rep. Henry Gonzales, Sept. 26, 1990, copy in author's collection.
92. William S. Sessions to Rep. Henry B. Gonzales, Oct. 5, 1990, copy in author's collection.
93. William P. Barr to Rep. Henry B. Gonzales, May 15, 1992.
94. See his responses to Barr in Rep. Henry B. Gonzales to William P. Barr, May 15, 1992; and Rep. Henry B. Gonzales to William P. Barr, June 15, 1992, copy in author's collection.
95. See Rep. Henry B. Gonzales to Pres. Bill Clinton, Jan. 22, 1993, copy in author's collection. The independent counsel appointed by the Bush administration did not find evidence of any purposeful "cover-up" of executive branch activities. See *Report of the Independent Counsel: Frederick B. Lacey on the Preliminary Investigation* (Washington, D.C.: GPO, Dec. 8, 1992), 95–153.
96. See details of such difficulties in Rep. John Dingell to Rep. Henry B. Gonzales, May 28, 1992, copy in author's collection.
97. Tiefer, *Semi-Sovereign Presidency,* 104, 116–17.
98. National Security Review 29, "Intelligence Capabilities, 1992–2005," Nov. 15, 1991, available at http://bushlibrary.tamu.edu/research/nsr/Nsr/nsr_29.pdf, accessed Jan. 2, 2003.
99. See Tiefer, *Semi-Sovereign Presidency.*
100. Rose, *Postmodern President,* 307.

Chapter 5: Prudence as Public Policy

1. Robert A. Divine, *Eisenhower and the Cold War* (New York: Oxford University Press, 1981), vii.
2. Quoted in George Bush, with Victor Gold, *Looking Forward* (New York: Doubleday, 1987), 108.
3. "Remarks at the American School in Brussels," *Public Papers of the Presidents: George Bush, 1989,* vol. 1 (Washington, D.C.: GPO, 1990), 664.
4. "Remarks to the American Embassy Employees and their Families in Bonn, Federal Republic of Germany," *Public Papers: George Bush,* 649.
5. For a corresponding discussion of this subject, see Ryan J. Barilleaux, "George Bush, Germany, and the New World Order," in *Shepherd of Democracy? America and Germany in the Twentieth Century,* ed. Carl Hodge and Cathal J. Nolan (Westview, Conn.: Greenwood, 1992), 161–72.
6. "Upheavel in the East: Excerpts from the News Conference Held by Bush and Kohl," *New York Times,* Feb. 26, 1990, A9.
7. Quoted in Michael R. Beschloss and Strobe Talbott, *At the Highest Levels: The Inside Story of the End of the Cold War* (Boston: Little, Brown, 1993), 166.
8. Duffy and Goodgame, *Marching in Place,* 51.
9. Ibid.
10. Kaufman interview.
11. George Bush and Brent Scowcroft, *A World Transformed* (New York: Alfred A. Knopf, 1998).
12. Ibid., 3–4. Emphasis added.
13. Ibid., 69.
14. Quoted in Duffy and Goodgame, *Marching in Place,* 53.
15. Bush and Scowcroft, *World Transformed,* 60.
16. Ibid.
17. Quoted in Serge Shemann, "Evolution in Europe; Two Germanys Reunite After 45 Years with Jubilation and a Vow of Peace," *New York Times,* Oct. 3, 1990, A9.
18. The following discussion draws heavily upon Barilleaux, "George Bush."
19. George Bush, "Remarks on the Texas A&M University Commencement Ceremony in College Station," May 12, 1989, *Public Papers of the Presidents: George Bush,* available at http://bushlibrary.tamu.edu/papers/1989/89051201.html, accessed Jan. 3, 2003.
20. Bush and Scowcroft, *World Transformed,* 66.
21. Quoted in *Facts on File,* June 2, 1989, 393.
22. Bush and Scowcroft, *World Transformed,* 150.
23. Ibid.
24. "Interview with Margaret Thatcher," oral history interview on the Persian Gulf War, *Frontline* page available at http://www.pbs.org/wgbh/pages/ frontline/gulf/oral/thatcher/1.htm.
25. Bush and Scowcroft, *World Transformed,* 319.
26. Ibid., 357.
27. Ibid., 416.

28. Quoted in Bob Woodward, *The Commanders* (New York: Pocket Books, 1991), 312.
29. Bush and Scowcroft, *World Transformed,* 395.
30. Margaret Thatcher, *The Downing Street Years* (New York: HarperCollins, 1993), 821.
31. Bush and Scowcroft, *World Transformed,* 416.
32. Security Council Resolution 678, quoted in ibid., 414.
33. Woodward, *Commanders,* 322.
34. Conversation between William Bennett and a gathering of faculty and students at Miami University, Oxford, Ohio, Oct. 15, 1992. In contrast, some have attempted to understand Bush—a man of the World War II generation—by casting him in the mold of their critical view of the culture of the 1980s. This effort is somewhat understandable in the case of partisans who have a stake in promoting such a misinterpretation of Bush, but it is inexcusable in the case of an academic study that purports to offer a balanced analysis. Cazenovia College professor John Robert Greene devotes the first chapter of *The Presidency of George Bush* (Lawrence: University Press of Kansas, 2000) to a critique of Reagan and the 1980s culture.
35. Bush and Scowcroft, *World Transformed,* xiii.
36. Gray interview.
37. Broadcast of President Bush's presentation to Yale Distinguished Alumni meeting at New Haven, Conn., on C-SPAN, May 13, 2001. Observed by author.
38. Card interview.
39. "Interview With Members of the White House Press Corps, Apr. 20, 1989," *Public Papers: George Bush,* 583–84.
40. The first hundred days of the Van Buren administration were actually a disaster. The country fell into a deep recession, unemployment soared, the banking system collapsed, and there were public riots in response to the economy. After media reports of these facts, Bush stopped using the Van Buren analogy.
41. Kilberg interview.
42. This view of Johnson's was recounted by his former aide Harry McPherson in *Chief of Staff: Twenty-five Years of Managing the Presidency,* ed. Samuel Kernell and Samuel L. Popkin (Berkeley: University of California Press, 1986), 96–97.
43. Kilberg interview.
44. See Kolb, *White House Daze.*
45. Ibid. See also Duffy and Goodgame, *Marching in Place.*
46. This point will be developed below. See Duffy and Goodgame, *Marching in Place.*
47. George Bush, "Inaugural Address," Jan. 20, 1989, available at htttp://www.bartleby .com/124/pres63.html
48. Ibid.
49. Gray interview.
50. Duffy and Goodgame, *Marching in Place,* 45.
51. Fitzwater, as quoted in ibid., 45–46.
52. Ibid., 59.
53. Ibid., 58.
54. For examples of Bush's signing statements, see folder, "Legislation [Signed by the President]," OA 6547, White House Press Office Subject File, Fitzwater Papers.
55. Quoted in Duffy and Goodgame, *Marching in Place,* 60.

56. Quoted in ibid., 61.
57. See Ryan J. Barilleaux, "George Bush and the Changing Context of Presidential Leadership," in *Leadership and the Bush Presidency: Prudence or Drift in an Era of Change?* ed. Ryan J. Barilleaux and Mary Stuckey (Westport, Conn.: Praeger, 1992), 3–23.
58. The following discussion of drug-control policy and education relies heavily on the work of Robert J. Thompson and Carmine Scavo in "The Home Front: Domestic Policy in the Bush Years," in *Leadership and Bush Presidency,* ed. Barilleaux and Stuckey, 149–64.
59. Ibid., 154.
60. George Bush, "Address Before a Joint Session of Congress," *Weekly Compilation of Presidential Documents,* May 13, 1989, 563–66.
61. "Doing Without Money," *The Economist,* Feb. 25, 1989, 25.
62. Thompson and Scavo, "Home Front," 158.
63. Ibid., 160.
64. See ibid., 149–64.
65. Gray interview.
66. Kilberg interview.
67. See, for example, "The Bush Administration and the Environment: Accomplishments and Initiatives, October 10, 1991," folder, "Environment and NAFTA," OA 6790, White House Press Office Subject File, Fitzwater Papers. Two addenda to this document are most telling. One is a table demonstrating the percentage increases in government spending on environmental initiatives during the Bush years, showing ranges of a 24 percent increase (for Superfund) to a 155 percent increase for land acquisition and reforestation. The table touts an average 97 percent increase in funding on environmental programs overall by Bush. The other is a chart that contrasts large budget increase proposals by Bush for environmental programs with congressional actions significantly cutting the president's spending preferences. The message is that Bush was pushing the big-ticket, major federal initiatives and the Democratic-led Congress was guilty of being cautious about spending. Another example is a press release touting big spending increases proposed for Environmental Protection Agency programs by the president ("The president's commitment to the environment is reflected in the resources he has provided for the EPA to carry out its mission. The budget will contain a $120 million increase. . . . This represents a 54% increase over the FY 1989 level"). See "Highlights of the President's Environmental Budget for Fiscal Year 1993, January 23, 1992," folder, "Environment and NAFTA," OA 6790, White House Press Office Subject File, Fitzwater Papers.

    White House "talking points" papers frequently made the same case to rebut common criticisms that the administration was pushing bigger and bigger spending in this or that program. To present just one example, the talking points regarding the president's policy proposals for the 1990 session of Congress emphasized a "major increase" in a program budget, "full funding" of a program, "the highest [spending] ever proposed" for another program, an "increase substantially" in spending on another program, "comprehensive programs," "major new initiatives," and so forth. Nothing in the memorandum says that the president planned to go slow, rescind spending, reduce the federal commitment, or even merely maintain current spending levels. Everything is couched in big government, big spending terms ("Talking Points: Highlights of President Bush's 1990 Agenda," case no. 108647SS, FG001, WHORM Subject File, Bush Presidential Records, GBPL).

68. Bush, "Inaugural Address."
69. See Bush and Scowcroft, *World Transformed,* esp. xi.
70. Brady interview.
71. Transcript of Hedrick Smith, "The Elected: The Presidency and Congress," *People and the Power Game,* PBS Television, available at http://www.pbs.org/powergame/files/ electedtrans.html.
72. Thomas Cronin, *The State of the Presidency,* 2d ed. (Boston: Little, Brown, 1980), 78.
73. Ibid.
74. Wildavsky's "two presidencies" hypothesis has been widely discussed and is accepted here. For further discussion, see Steven Shull, ed., *The Two Presidencies: A Quarter Century Assessment* (New York: Burnham, 1991).
75. For elaboration on this point, see Ryan J. Barilleaux, *The Post-Modern Presidency* (New York: Praeger, 1988).
76. Erwin Hargrove and Michael Nelson, *Presidents, Politics, and Policy* (New York: Knopf, 1984), 67.
77. For elaboration on these concepts, see Jones, *Presidency in a Separated System,* chap. 5.
78. Bush nonetheless did not hold himself or his administration blameless for the failure to adequately communicate that his economic policies were sound. Twelve days before vacating the White House, Bush penned a note to Michael J. Boskin, chairman of the Council of Economic Advisers, saying: "we faced this ghastly prejudiced national press. They, I know, wanted us to lose. Their reporting on what we did and tried to do was ugly. Some day history will be more kind" (George Bush to Michael J. Boskin, Jan. 8, 1993, BE004, WHORM Subject File, Bush Presidential Records, GBPL).
79. Jonathan Rausch, "Father Superior: Our Greatest Modern President," *New Republic,* May 22, 2000, 22–25.
80. Leslie H. Gelb, "Can Clinton Deal With the World?" *Washington Post,* Mar. 6, 1994, C1.
81. Charles O. Jones, *Clinton and Congress* (Norman: University of Oklahoma Press, 1999), 187–88.
82. Orren quoted in Richard L. Berke, "Two-Way Presidential Coattails," *New York Times,* July 25, 1999, 14.
83. Paul Light, *The President's Agenda,* 3d ed. (Baltimore: Johns Hopkins University Press, 1999), 291.
84. Ibid., 292.
85. Henry Fairlie, *The Kennedy Promise: The Politics of Expectation* (Garden City, N.Y.: Doubleday, 1973).

86. Jones, *Clinton and Congress,* 45.

87. See Fred Greenstein, *The Hidden-Hand Presidency* (New York: Basic Books, 1982); Divine, *Eisenhower and the Cold War;* Philip G. Henderson, *The Managerial Presidency* (Boulder, Colo.: Westview Press, 1988); and Stephen E. Ambrose, *Eisenhower,* 2 vols. (New York: Simon and Schuster, 1983–84).

88. Willmoore Kendall, "The Two Majorities in American Politics," in *The Conservative Affirmation,* ed. Willmoore Kendall (Chicago: Regnery, 1985), 21–49.

89. Cronin, *State of the Presidency,* 78.

90. Terry Eastland, *Energy in the Executive* (New York: Free Press, 1992).

Index

ISBN 1-58544-291-7
90000
9 781585 442911